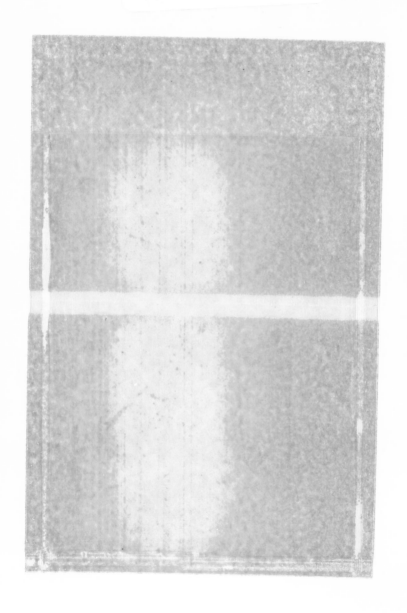

THE POLITICAL TESTAMENT
OF HERMANN GÖRING

AMS PRESS
NEW YORK

THE
POLITICAL TESTAMENT
OF HERMANN GÖRING

A selection of important Speeches and Articles

by

FIELD-MARSHAL HERMANN GÖRING

Arranged and translated by

H. W. BLOOD-RYAN

LONDON

JOHN LONG LONG

LIMITED

1939

Library of Congress Cataloging in Publication Data

Göring, Hermann, 1893-1946.
  The political testament of Hermann Göring.

  Reprint of the 1939 ed.
  1. Germany--Politics and government--1933-1945.
2. National socialism. 3. Hitler, Adolf, 1889-1945.
I. Title.
DD247.G67A3 1972   320.9'43'086   71-180403
ISBN 0-404-56127-6

Reprinted from the edition of 1939, London
First AMS edition published in 1972
Manufactured in the United States of America

AMS PRESS INC.
NEW YORK, N. Y.   10003

PREFACE

THE responsibilities of a translator are great, more particularly so when the translation is from the language of a nation whose political system is different from that of a democracy, so-called, and when the words to be translated are spoken by such an iconoclast as Field-Marshal Göring. I have therefore taken great care with these speeches, and at the risk of appearing stilted in places, have sought not to fall into the same pitfall as did the B.B.C. on the evening of the 28th April, 1939, when reporting, recording, and interpreting the Reichstag speech of Adolf Hitler.

On several occasions inaccurate translations were read out by the announcer, which became more glaringly apparent to those listeners who understood German, since recorded sections in the original German language were played over on records, before each section of the speech was discussed.

A particular instance (and one calculated to inflame any reasonably minded listener without knowledge of the German language) was the reference to that part of Hitler's speech where he announced that the German nation would never again go to the conference table (as the B.B.C. put it) ' without arms '. The key word in this sentence was *wehrlos*, which any standard German-English dictionary translates as ' defenceless '. Without arms in German is *waffenlos*. The inference is obvious, and many slips like this are giving the Germans grounds for attacking us and magnifying such instances in their national Press.

At this fateful time in civilization's history, are we to provoke or worsen ill-feeling, leading perhaps to ultimate bloodshed, through the careless use and misinterpretation of words ? These seemingly small matters (not confined to

5

the case above ; I quote that merely as an instance, which was remarked upon by many listeners) in the treatment of Anglo-German affairs cannot but impress one with the feeling that, aggressive as are the German leaders in the field of foreign affairs, relations are being deliberately worsened, quite apart from the provocation of the Czecho-slovakian affair, by some sinister force in England. Can it be that the passions of the people are intended to be stirred to cover the incompetence of many, who, during the past five years, should have been the protectors of the British people, or have the international financiers made their pile out of central European rearmament and, knowing that their customers are by now pretty well stocked and that further orders might not be paid for, are finding a means for testing their pop-guns at the same time creating, as they think, a further market ? I have not asked the above question thoughtlessly ; in fact some readers may agree with me, in wishing to remove the interrogation mark and to rewrite it as the proposition of an indictment. Why is England so suddenly confronted with a German menace, which, existent to-day, was just as surely existent five years ago ? Leaders of Germany have always voiced their aims for expansion and the literature of Nazi Germany is full of references to the ultimate world success of national socialism. The Germans have divided the world into two rival ideologies —the soviet hammer and sickle, and the swastika. Those who do not agree with national socialism are considered, by the Nazis, to profess communism and, peculiar as it may seem, we of the democracies, by not understanding nazism, are categoried as belonging to the Russian camp. That this is untrue and has no foundation in fact we all know, but the recent approach by Britain to Russia sustains the Germans in that idea, until now every German (who did not believe it a year ago) is convinced, because he has been told so, accompanied by quotations from the British Press to support it, that Britain is out to destroy him and his country. Writing with a knowledge of such things, I can confirm the suspicion voiced by Mr. Winston Churchill during a debate in the House of Commons in April, 1939, when he said that it appeared to him that matters known to the British Intelli-

gence Service were filtered and watered down before they
reached the responsible ministers.

In 1939 there are people who stand aghast at what is
known as ' the might of the German machine '—people
who shudder at the thought of the wrath to come from
across the North Sea and say : " We must stop the expansion of these Germans, before it is too late." Too late for
what ? Both the British and German leaders of political
action are at fault. There has been too much double-
dealing and chicanery on both sides of the North Sea, and
it has not been confined to the last five years. It has gone
on ever since Germany sprouted into a first-class power and
the chief points of misunderstanding between the two
nations are what Bismarck called the imponderables of
politics, in history, and I would say, particularly in the
realm of ideas. I feel sure that British people will never
understand national socialism, which is a twentieth-century
socialism administered in a manner akin to feudalism. It
is mystical, ideal, all-pervading, and ruthless in its application, and it cannot be denied that it has benefited the lower
classes in Germany providing they toe the line in the
national work and interest. National socialism has brought
about the paradox of making rabid nationalists out of
truculent international-socialists and the events of the past
few years have unified Germany into a history- and future-
proud race, which will one day become a force to be
reckoned with.

Looking around at my fellow members of the British
Empire, listening to many of them and reading much of
their work, I have the feeling, rightly or wrongly, that they
have just realized the intentions of the Germans—to secure
for themselves a place in the sun. Have they not always
wanted that, whether led by Emperor, President, or Führer ?
The Germans are no second-class race. They possess
admirable qualities and it is a duty of the British Empire
to see that the industry of the German is turned to world
economic revival and not to its destruction. We must talk
plain language to the Germans, for that is the only language
they understand. They have ever been poor diplomats
and kid glove diplomacy will avail us nothing. If we are

honest with ourselves and with them, we will tell the German government, without any equivocation, that we expect treaties honoured and in that we must see to it that we keep our word also.

It is fallacious to believe that ninety million Germans want to fight—they are just as much afraid of war as we are. Just as many Germans as English fear what may come across the North Sea. But propaganda can make both Englishmen and Germans fight, and at the end of it all there would be still an old Kaspar telling little Peterkin and Wilhelmine that what they fought about he could never make out.

For six years the British people have had served up on their breakfast table, in the folded news sheets before them, tales of atrocities, racial oppression, scandals of the Nazi party, most of which has been true, and Dr. Goebbels' propaganda speeches, and articles quoted from his newspaper *Angriff*, but very little indication has been given of the steady progress made, under cover of the ' gas barrage '. Our sympathies for Catholic and Jew have been enlisted, and an attempt has been made to untie our purse-strings in their aid, through the medium of appeals made by famous Englishmen, while thousands of English men, women, and children are starving and the army of the unemployed and its dependents stands, hungry and without hope of work, looking on in bewilderment.

We have been regaled with everything about Germany which would make us believe that the Nazi system is likely to break down at any moment, but we have only rarely been told of German activities here and there ; of the really great concentration of effort and the implications of the activities and speeches of the German leaders, among them Field-Marshal Göring, who, next to Herr Hitler, is the most dominant figure in the Third Reich.

Since 1933, in public speeches over the network of the German broadcasting system and in articles in the German and foreign press, for all to hear and read, Hitler's right-hand man has virtually warned the nations of Germany's ambitions. Instead of taking heed to these speeches and articles, the people who shape world opinion have gone on steadily recounting scandals when facts should have seen the light of day.

The spoken and written words of Hermann Göring are not lightly to be cast aside as of no moment, they are not words of a professional politician or diplomat, but they come straight from the shoulder. In places of this collection the German Field-Marshal will be found to be floundering just a little—that is because he is on a subject unfamiliar and of not too great an importance to him, because after all, he is first and foremost a soldier. In places he is naïve, but then his naïveté is overshadowed by his sense of humour, at times somewhat grim. His hatred of all the things he cannot understand rises to the surface and his invective is poured upon it, but his appeal to youth and his evident understanding of the young is vividly shown in his speech to the young Air Force officers 25th May, 1936. These speeches must not be considered as just straws fluttering in the wind, willy-nilly. They are portents. They may be flamboyant, but by this very nature they appeal to the average German, to whom words like fatherland, blood and earth, duty, courage, work, sacrifice, national honour, freedom and comradeship are very dear.

In many of his speeches Field-Marshal Göring refers to a doubtful ' they '. Very often he means the ex-allied powers, especially when he is challenging the Treaty of Versailles, but he must, in fairness, acknowledge that the British have been foremost in recognizing that certain German claims were based on justice and common sense and were denied equitable settlement unreasonably. For this reason (and not because we were decadent) British opinion was unwilling to resist the occupation of the Rhineland, the Anschluss with Austria, and the recovery of Sudetenland and Memel. Field-Marshal Göring will also remember that the British army of occupation left Germany voluntarily, long before the time agreed to by the German delegates at the peace conference. British public opinion is guided by the very principles on which the Nazi movement and the new German state has challenged the Treaty of Versailles, and if the Germans really were made aware of this, much discord and fear for the future in both countries would disappear.

While some of the things mentioned in these speeches may seem strange to English people, they are nevertheless a faithful record and translation of what was said. The mixed cases, tenses, and persons indicate that most of the speeches are extempore and, in order not to interfere with the spirit in which the speech was at the time delivered, I have allowed them to remain in the translation. This retention is also a guide to the personality of the speaker.

It will be noticed that the German Air Minister always uses public meetings to state a national grievance or argument, often quite foreign to the body he is addressing. By following these speeches I have found that it becomes possible to forecast, with some measure of accuracy, German policy a few months ahead.

I had intended to write a commentary on each speech, but as this collection will be mainly read by students of contemporary German affairs I have assumed that they will be sufficiently informed as to be able to read the implication or purpose in each speech and from the whole, form some very concrete ideas about the ability and versatility of the German Field-Marshal, who will probably one day succeed to the direction of the lives and activities of nearly one hundred million German-speaking people.

The speeches as a whole indicate the trend of affairs and views in Germany to-day, and the reader is left, without a mentor, to form his conclusions and to pronounce his own judgment.

My grateful thanks are due to my wife, without whose assistance, particularly in the case of obscure German idiom, this translation would not have taken on the accuracy which allows it to present a fair picture of the personality of the speaker.

CONTENTS

TRANSLATOR'S NOTE

VOLKSGENOSSE has been translated throughout as meaning Compatriot. The national socialists created this word out of *Volk*=people, and *genosse*=Companion, hence companion of the people. Before the Third Reich, the communists always referred to their members as *Genosse*.

The word *Weltanschauung* has been retained in many places as being considered a better form. This is one of those words which will find their way into any other language. *Weltanschauung*—a conception of the world. An envisaging of world affairs through the spectacles of a particular party, creed, faith, sect or idea. This again is a built-up word, achieving great popularity in the time of the *Kulturkampf* of Bismarck. Schade's *English-German Dictionary*, Leipzig, 1816, fails to disclose such a word, which is fair evidence of its late introduction into the German language.

Words appearing in the speeches in parentheses are inserted by the translator for the sake of clarity. The parentheses in the articles contain the words of Field-Marshal Göring.

PUBLIC ADDRESS OVER THE GERMAN BROADCASTING NETWORK ANNOUNCING THE BIRTH OF THE THIRD REICH-NIGHT, 30th January, 1933.

MY German compatriots ! While I am standing here at the microphone, there are thousands of Germans crowding outside below the windows of the Reich Chancellory. The atmosphere is only comparable with the enthusiasm which prevailed at that time when Germany had to call its fathers and sons to arms, comparable with that day in August, 1914, when there also rose a nation to defend the most valuable possession of the fatherland—honour and freedom !

The 30th January will go down in history as the day on which the nation found itself again after fourteen years of torture, sorrow, shame and disgrace. At last this long awaited day has come—to-day we see it ! With it we close the darkest chapter of German history and start anew. The headline of this new chapter will be : ' Freedom and honour are fundamental to the coming state.' Filled with thanks we look up to the leader of our organisation. To him all German hearts are flying ! We also thank the aged Field-Marshal von Hindenburg, who has to-day formed a firm union with the young generation. At the side of the venerable Field-Marshal, Germany's leader in the Great War, now stands Adolf Hitler, the young leader of Germany, who created out of nothing a strong, faithful and powerful movement, whose strong arm will now lead once again people and Reich to a new, better and brilliant time ! We look upon it as a lucky omen that to-day, all in Germany who still believe in people and fatherland have been brought together.

We look upon it as a symbol that the Field-Marshal of the

Great War has put his trust in the leader of the young generation. Now all hands will be busy again—confidence will return, and hope will restore the German human being. Now the future will at long last bring us that for which the leader and his faithful followers, hopefully, in spite of disappointments and setbacks, have worked and fought : Bread and work[1] for the German people ; Freedom and honour for the nation !

[1] *Arbeit und Brot* was a Nazi slogan in incessant use from 1923 until Hitler's chancellorship, after which time the promise was redeemed, a fact which accounts for much loyalty, which would perhaps not otherwise be given, from the working and middle classes.

SPEECH TO THE OFFICERS AND N.C.O.s OF THE PRUSSIAN POLICE FORCE, IN BERLIN, 7th February, 1933.

COMRADES ! With special pleasure I greet you as the wearers of the Prussian police uniform. For the most part you and I are united through the field-grey coat of honour of the German front-soldier. Therefore we belong together !

There are two pillars on which the safety of the state rests. The army and the police. The police are the bearers of armed power within the state. It is my firm will to assist the police, not only in their duties, which during the coming months will require one final drive on every front, but in the attainment of their rights. Before the war the Prussian official was the best in the world, just as the Prussian soldier before the war, and more so during the war, was the best in the world.

I am going to strive to retrieve for us once again the best official—and although before the police I must say it—the best soldiers. Therefore it becomes necessary for you all to help me in this task. I demand from the police officer that he shall take notice of the old virtues of the Prussian officer —of his conception of duty and of his comprehension of honour. In future your work will be guided by the principle of throwing one's own person into the breach, wherever it may be necessary. Errors of commission are thought more of by me than errors of omission.

Follow this principle and your actions will be covered to the full by me. About this I want you to be clear. As long as it is possible we will try to get along with simple means, but should the situation require it we will employ every means at our disposal, and, without hesitation, utilize to the full our heaviest weapons.

To the police sergeant-majors I would like to say that I
understand their awkward position to the full. Any point
in doubt to me I will try to master in the shortest possible
time. There are, naturally, some things about which I am
still without knowledge, but I bring to my task two things :
a warm heart and iron nerves. When you have drawn
your arms in the lawful execution of your duty, in the fight
against criminality and the international rabble, you will in
future not be dragged through the mire by the press and
courts of inquiry. Those times, I promise you, are gone.

You shall all see. My chief officer (in your force) shall
not only be your superior under me, but he shall also be
my first comrade ! In this sense we will work together for
the welfare of our German fatherland.

[EDITOR'S NOTE. Göring had just purged the Prussian police of non-Nazi
elements. The new officers were, in the main, tried hands of the Nazi party.
This is treated of fully in *Göring, the iron man of Germany*, p. 185 *et. seq.*, by
H. W. Blood-Ryan. John Long.
  Immediately prior to this speech the *Gummi Knüppel*, or rubber truncheons,
wielded by the police had been withdrawn and revolvers issued in their
stead. Hence the reference to arms above. This action, coupled with the
speech and followed by several others of a like nature, was considered to be an
incitement to the use of arms.]

SPEECH AT A CONVENTION OF THE NATIONAL-SOCIALIST PARTY, Frankfort-on-Main, 3rd March, 1933, in which Göring assumes, on behalf of the Nazi Party, the full responsibility for actions in the Third Reich.

MY dear German compatriots and more especially my dear comrades in the brown shirt! How much time has changed since last I stood before you, when, for the last time, I was able to shake you up with temperamental words in the fight for freedom, for which we all longed. Compatriots! When I stood to-day, just an hour before my departure, on the balcony of the Prussian Ministry of the Interior—the late Severing Palace[1]—and when below in the Unter den Linden, thousands upon thousands in their brown shirts marched past with flying banners and ringing music, there came suddenly to me the realisation of how much God in His mercy has favoured us, how at last all this longing and hoping of the past fourteen years has now become reality.

Fourteen years we have fought—fourteen years we have suffered, so immeasurably as never a people have suffered. For fourteen years we and our movement have been oppressed by terror, for fourteen years they tried to instil into this nation a sense of serfdom, into us, a nation which can look back on a thousand-year-old history of heroism. People strange to our race believed themselves capable of

[1] In Nazi vocabulary the Prussian Ministry of the Interior had become known as the Severing Palace, named after its one-time occupant, Karl Severing, Social Democratic Reichstag deputy, who was at one time Reich Minister of the Interior, and later, in Otto Braun's Cabinet, Prussian Minister of the Interior. He was deprived of his office during the Chancellorship of Franz von Papen on 20th July, 1932, during the famous ' rape ' of Prussia. Because of the building's association with the old regime, Göring would never use it as his official ministry, and since 1933 the work of the Prussian Ministry has been carried on by him from a nineteenth-century building in Leipziger Strasse, next to the Air Ministry.

remoulding this nation, a nation which fifteen years ago had
resisted a world of enemies, this nation which maintained a
heroic fight for four years at the front and at home, the
same nation which for four years protected its soil from
the enemy, the nation whose land the enemy only saw as
a prisoner but never as a conqueror. Such a nation they
tried to make into serfs.

That alone, compatriots, marks the madness and frenzy
which had taken hold upon these 'Celebrities'. They
believed that they could draw their own conclusions from
their own cowardice as example. They believed, because
to them worldly goods counted for all, that the German
people could live without ideals. So thought the so-called
representatives of a people which has proved in a thousand
years of history that it was always ready to sacrifice its
last possession when its honour and freedom were in danger.
Honour and freedom were stolen from us on that cursed
day in November, 1918, when they stabbed the front line
in the back.

They spoke so often about the 'Legend' of the stab
with the dagger, and so often about the 'fairy tale' of
betrayal. No, compatriots, there is nothing to hide. The
betrayal was a fact. To-day we know the fruit that cursed
9th November brought us. We also know the criminals.
We must have our revenge on these betrayers. They shall
not go on poisoning the German people.

Fourteen long years this nation has trodden its path of
suffering. Remember how bitter the suffering was and how
it crept into the meanest and last little room, till no one
knew a way out any longer. At that time people said:
"The peace of Versailles will only hit the rich." But
quickly enough the whole nation felt how it had been
made the pack-mule on to which all burdens were loaded.
For fourteen years, compatriots! I ask you to look back
just once more before you cast your political vote on
Sunday. Look back into those fourteen years for just one
quarter of an hour and remember, in spite of our fast-
moving times, what these years have meant to you, what
Germany has lost and given up, and think how unspeakable
the suffering was, how bitter the sorrow, and you will then

recognise what it meant—to be governed for fourteen years by marxism !

What would have happened if destiny had not turned at last ? If this movement, started by very few people, had not fought hard, in spite of all its setbacks, and had not taken hurdle after hurdle, if this movement—which went through the hardest battles and which was nearly dissolved, which has lost hundreds of dead and thousands of wounded—had not stormed again and again the marxist castle ? Not out of its own inner strength (for that was at the time shattered), but out of the mission it had for the people, it always found new strength again. The movement had the leader, it grew, in spite of demolishing battles, into a steel block, and in one single daring attack which lasted a decade we (in the movement) beat the opponent, boarded the ship ourselves and, getting hold of the rudder, steered, at last, Germany away from the rocks into the straight course towards a clear endeavour.

A decade of tremendous struggle ! Who does not remember the small beginnings ? What was the most difficult ? Not the ridiculous terror of the ' red Hoodlums', not those clownish plays of the ' party minister,' and not in the least the liquid manure that was poured over us. Not the lies and not the prohibitions. All these we pushed aside smilingly. We took it all as it came along, knowing that this was going to make us only the more stronger and greater ! Not even, bitter as it may sound, the ten thousand wounded and not even our dead were in the long run the bitterest things ! For their blood was martyr blood ! Their blood was seed for the harvest and the fruit. Their blood has written our programme, about which we are asked again and again and which was sealed with the blood of the fighters for German freedom.

All this was not the most heaviest thing to bear. The most difficult of all was the fight for the individual compatriot—the fight for the German soul, the fight for the German human being. In the bitter fight, with the ever-present poisoning marxism, to rescue the German, to make him individually once more into a valuable link of the nation, to plant in him, who was tired and stupified by lethargy, once again the spark of resistance—in him, who despised all and who wanted to know nothing any longer of his Germany—to plant in *him* once more the love of his own people—that was the most difficult. That was a tough fight !

We (in the movement) have worked night after night, evening upon evening, and we went from town to town, from county to county and again we whipped you up. Again and again we hammered it into your brains : again and again we planted it in your hearts. And so we grew. Only yesterday we were enemies—outsiders and knew better (in political thought), to-day we fight together. Bigger and bigger the army grew : harder and harder grew the struggle. At last we heaved against the mausoleum of a hollow state and with one push it was opened. Now we form the Germany of the future.

Compatriots ! What we have seen was a ruin. Everything lies about on the ground—destroyed. Everywhere there are bare walls. German life, German economy in all its branches, German culture, wherever you look there lies only the smoking ruin. A battle-field—deserted and rotted, it lies there : nothing blooms and nothing gives promise of bud. Everything has died from the poisonous gas which has rotted and destroyed for fourteen years all living things.

That is the saddest chapter in the marxist rulership. The national economy and wealth, they once said, was to be given to the people. The people themselves were to be the owners of this economy. The people themselves were to be the owners of the goods produced by the national economy, and many other lies culled from the text-book of marxian socialism were put over on the people, all things which the marxists knew to be untrue and impossible of performance. Under this regime capitalism rose to the heights of most shameless exploitation. One trust was founded after another, destroying with it the personal responsibility of the small man. The factories, which had for centuries gone down from father to son, were swallowed up. They deprived business men of personal responsibility, and put the anonymous shareholder in their place, because by this means they could rob and overpower the people more easily. This was also the reason why the false fronts tore apart[1] ; they could not manage a united people.

No ! These economic differences had to be preached. The workman was told : ' There, do you see that factory owner—he is your enemy.' Because he was a factory owner, in spite of his being, perhaps, the best man on earth or the best German, he was declared to be an enemy.

On the other hand the factory owner was told : ' That workman—he is your enemy ! He is against you and you are against him.' So they tore open the fronts. So stood employee against employer—in two fronts, instead of standing together against the Jewish exploiters. The agrarian was given a death blow. Why ? As long as the farmer sits on his land, as long as his feelings remain deeply rooted in the land on which he was born and raised, as long as words like fatherland, blood and earth remain to his ears holy— he was a menace to their system. On him they had to start. He had to be uprooted, made homeless, torn away from the soil on which he was born and had his home—away from his kind. They had to poison his brain, destroy his feelings and his heart, and so they made out of the once proud farmer, however little he owned, an international proletarian, and he cried with them : " Proletarians of all lands ! unite ! " So the farmer was urbanised and weaned from the soil under the pressure of the fight and they pretended that they wished to help him again. They tried to place farmers on fresh lands, on which they could not establish themselves. They developed new farms and allowed the old matured ones to go to ruin instead of rescuing them. To us this seemed to be the first thing requiring attention. Adolf Hitler realised this in one of his first cabinet meetings, when he declared : " First of all the farmer, who is still fighting to eke out his existence, must be saved ; then one can start with the others and work new land."

The marxists also cracked the whip over the middle classes. The middle classes were the broad masses of the people, fitting each into his allotted place and who cherished

[1] A reference to the many parties in Germany and their alliances from time to time—all intent upon destroying the other.

their old inherited estates, however small. So long as they owned estates they could, under certain circumstances, be a prop for good governmental thought, they could—worst of all—still have national feelings in their bosom. So they had to be uprooted and impoverished. And then came the impoverishing ' stunt ', carried out in such a refined manner as no nation has ever seen it done before. The inflation came, which in a few months destroyed all that remained of estates and goods in Germany, and in so doing impoverished the whole nation. And the rest ? Slowly, a few savings were made again, but they were taxed heavily— such mad taxation which had nothing to do with legitimate Government taxes. They were all out and out expropriations. It was a matter of ' Give us what you have left '. And so the proletarianisation of a people went on apace. Old families, landowners for generations, where have they got to to-day ? Here and there there may yet be a family which still clings on to the old house which was once built by its ancestors, but they do not live there as free owners, if they are still there at all. They are there as unpaid porters and housekeepers.

What has become the destiny of these people ?

So they (the previous regime) have broken up everything systematically. Where the little merchant had a shop, which he perhaps had inherited from his father, there now stands a big store—a chain store. The Jew has robbed him of it for himself. So, all over the place, were the rights of ownership destroyed—in just those places where it was responsible and where it was handled with that certain responsibility necessary to the people and the nation.

Thus were thrown more and more people into the great trough of international proletarianism. Thus was the great attempt at uprooting more and more people from their land and from among their kind, in order that they might be ruled easier. We have often been laughed at when we described the German as a ' slave '. But compatriots ! how does one define the word slave ? A man works, and through his own labour he creates something. When this creation remains his own, then he is a free man. When he has to give it away to some stranger, then he has become a slave, for then he does not work for himself any longer.

They were going to make out of one of the most industrious, most work loving and perhaps the most capable of all nations, the most industrious slaves. That was the long view of their plan. Not only was the German to be uprooted from his soil and expropriated, but his thinking and feeling were to be destroyed, culminating in tearing him away from his history—German history. History—from which always, when a nation becomes impoverished, it takes its last strength. From history which generations before us, who have lived through evil times, had made and who yet, in their turn, had strength to climb up again and get their new vigour out of history.

Therefore they said : away with German culture—it would eventually chain the one or the other, through his feelings, to the fatherland. Therefore—away with German art ! Here, too, the ' wirepullers ' are the same again.

Compatriots ! I wish you could look just for once behind the scenes. The mask is different, but the grimace behind it has always remained the same.

In destroying all German feelings and German ways of thinking, they had of course to destroy all conceptions of moral and ethical value which we have inherited from our fathers. Therefore corruption was given a free hand—one sink was next to the other, and out of each there trickled a poison into the German people of different classes. Immorality was lifted up and upheld as morality, and German morals were kicked aside in company with all else which we held holy, and all was smothered in dirt—everything for which we had fought for four years and for which many had lost their lives. They took all the good from us and the substitute they called : ' To live in a state of true beauty, freedom and dignity.' Look at the last years of internal politics. Internal politics of terror against everything which was still national. Internal politics of force against everything that stood up against them—internal politics of corruption and decay—against everything that was still called decency. And do you want to look at their foreign politics ? Only they who are bred by cowardice can treat cowardly !

Consisting of submission[1] and fulfilment for years and years.

In this ruinous field marxism grows its most terrible, most ill-reeking marsh plant. On this ground, which is manured with immorality and traitorousness, grows communism.

When the ' Gentlemanly ' social democrats tell me that they object strongly to be thrown into the same pot with the communists, my answer to them is : " The stinking steams of communism came from your pot. It was your Mr. Severing, the brave one, who declared that the communists were political children. Now you are becoming excited that I see them, not as political children, but as criminals. Compatriots ! I do not want to repeat what I said the day before yesterday, as a member of the Reich Government, in my wireless broadcast speech about the communist movement, about communist designs and about communist crimes. I will repeat only one thing I said then : ' The " gentlemen " must understand one thing. I do not dream of fighting them in the manner of a good citizen— with faint-heartedness and only out of a sense of protection. No ! I give the signal for a fight on the whole front.' "

Compatriots ! my measures will not be vitiated by any legal doubts. My measures will not be weakened by any bureaucracy. Here I have not to exercise righteousness ; here I have only to destroy and to clear. Nothing else. This fight, compatriots, will be a fight against chaos and such a fight I do not lead with ordinary police means. That a ' state of citizens ' may have done. Certainly I will also use the full powers of the state and the police to their utmost measure, my dear communists, in order that you do not draw wrong conclusions, but the fight to the death, in which I will ' put my fist in your necks ', I will lead with those down there, my brownshirts ! I will make it clear to the people that they have to defend themselves. I will make it clear to them that all strength has to be mobilised, and therefore I declare with full purpose : " In future, gentlemen, only those can enter the state who come from the national strength and not those who crowd around and lie."

---

[1] A reference to the policy of fulfilment of the Peace Treaty pursued by Brüning and Stresemann.

I am not disturbed when certain ' critics ' get excited about these measures and cry for more ' justice '. I measure with two measures.[1] I would not be just if I did not send the communists to hell at last. Too long have they lounged about in easy chairs and lived on our money—it is high time they went ! Fourteen years long they have oppressed this national Germany, and for fourteen years not even a porter in a ministry was allowed to be a national socialist. That was ' justice ' for you ! For fourteen years they have suppressed it. No. He who acknowledges the state now, him the state will recognise—but he who tries to destroy the state, him the state will destroy.

Do not dare to come to me, you red and pinkish gentlemen, and say that we (the Nazis) have been enemies of the state once and that we too wanted to overthrow the state—and have done so. No, gentlemen, that is not a true bill, because there was no state, but only a system of bigwigs. Therefore we had to struggle to bring about a state. We are no enemies of the state, but we have become tired of bigwigs and hoodlums. You, my gentlemanly Marxists, at one time overthrew the state by dirty means, but we have thrown out a system of swindlers by fair means.

You said that we were against the Republic ! ' Gentle-men ', if the German Republic had been a republic of freedom—if the German Republic had organised a passionate resistance in 1918 and 1919, we all would have been staunch republicans. You seem to have forgotten how your republic ever came about. You seem to have forgotten that it was begotten in perjury—you seem to have forgotten that you sullied this ' Republic '. When you declare to-day that we have been against the banner of the republic, against the black, yellow and red, we say, yes ! we were against it, gentlemen. If you had at that time (1918) planted this flag as a banner of resistance on the towers of Strassbourg Minster declaring : ' Thus far and no further ! ' we, the old soldiers, would have knelt in homage and ardour beneath this flag. But you had hoisted it above treachery, disgrace

[1] This relates to a statement he made earlier at Dortmund when, *inter alia*, he wound up : " People are prattling of two sorts of law, aye, I know two sorts of law because I know two sorts of men : Those who are with us and those who are against us."

and shame and therefore we thank God that He did not allow the old glorious symbol to flutter in the breeze over your ' new ' Germany during the past fourteen years. We thank destiny that it rolled up the old glorious colours at the right time.

Compatriots ! my first official task as the president of the new Reichstag will be to propose to the Reichstag that the old black-white-red flag, together with the shining swastika, shall from now onwards flutter as the new banner of victory over a new Germany.

We will show you (still speaking for the benefit of the Communist and Social-Democrats), and at last prove to you, that your time is absolutely over and that it will never come back again. We will prove to you that we have built a new foundation, far away from your house which you erected fourteen years ago and on which even the front has toppled in.

This foundation of ours will be cemented together by our own outlook (*Weltanschauung*),[1] by the views which at last bring together Nationalism and Socialism. These two shall no longer stand opposite each other in deadly animosity—misunderstood—and shall no longer cause millions of people to fight each other. The enemy camps shall now be welded together into a whole—therefore shall this *Weltanschauung* (of National Socialist creed) be the foundation of the new Reich. Only to those who have understood the cry of such unity—any, from among whatever profession, class or occupation—shall fall the honour to reconcile where reconciliation is needed. The union of the Reich, compatriots, remains an empty sham when the people are torn apart, therefore only through unity among the people can a unified Reich receive its true form. To bring about this unity is the life's work of Adolf Hitler, and because he wants to form this unity, because he wants to bring the people, from all classes, conditions, professions and occupations together into one faction, which will, in all great questions of (national) destiny think in unison, he has therefore declared the fight to the death with

---

[1] World philosophy (of the person holding it) conception of a particular outlook of a movement, creed or party—world picture, as one wishes it to appear.

Marxism. For where Marxism holds sway, it does so only through the hate of disrupted classes. Therefore it had to sink. Therefore let them burn and murder—let them lie and lie again. We work and rebuild. And when to-day the foreign press, inspired by Marxist and Communist circles, declares that none other than Minister Göring himself started the Reichstag fire, in order to obtain (false) proof against Marxism, then I say, ' gentlemen ', for that I had no need to start a fire in the Reichstag. There is sufficient proof of your crimes to get judgment against you.

Compatriots ! all these things are spotlights thrown over the people like lightning so that it may recognise the danger in which it stands.

Two days hence you will once more be called upon. On the 5th March the call will ring. And the song that you so often sang with us will be heard. For the last time on the 5th March there will be a trumpet call to arms—German destiny makes an appeal ! The German people will have to line up for Germany, for the fatherland is in danger. We men (the leaders) are ready to bear the responsibility before God and the people—that we will do ! God will give us the strength if you will give us your faith. Then we will push aside the night and clouds. Then we will bring back the sun to you.

EDITOR'S NOTE. This was one of the last speeches made before the election of 5th March, 1933, at which the electorate had to confirm the National Socialist regime. It was a confirmation rather than an election, because Adolf Hitler was already Reich chancellor and his ministers were in office.

Result :

National Socialists	17,300,000
Nationalists	3,100,000
Communists	4,900,000
Social Democrats	7,200,000

PRESIDENTIAL SPEECH TO THE REICHSTAG, 21st March, 1933.

LADIES and Gentleman! my comrades! Through a cursed crime we have been forced to move out of the house which was once built for the German people.[1]

Through an outrage the Chamber has been destroyed. You all know what has moved an opposition party to perpertrate this outrage. You all know that this outrage is only the outcome of the instigation against the Reich which has been carried on against the people and the state for a decade. This attempt is intended to be a signal to create chaos and anarchy in Germany at a moment when the first attempts are being shown for a rebuilding of the Reich by the new order.

We are standing in a great time. In a few weeks the holy flame of the national revolution has taken hold of the people. The President of the Reich has asked the German people if it is willing to place itself behind the men of the national concentration in whom he has reposed his faith, and into whose hands he has placed the leadership of the German people. An overwhelming majority has given its assent. A majority the like of which has never been known in the history of the German Parliament. One great flame of national passion, a great flame of hot enthusiasm has taken hold of the German people and has now proved that finis is written to the past, against which we fought for fourteen years. New representatives of the people have arisen for

[1] This is a reference to the fact that the Reichstag was meeting in the Kroll Opera House, not far from the Reichstag building proper, in the Tiergarten. It is significant that the Reichstag in 1939 continues to hold its sessions in the Opera House—although the damage to the Reichstag building has been repaired. It may be taken as a sign that the leaders of the Third Reich do not wish to meet in what was the meeting place of German democracy.

the first time without parliamentary ' cowdealing '[1] (more
properly, huckstering), without party interests and without
all those things that have, up till now, kept the German
parliamentary representative low down in the eyes of the
German people—to work from now on to improve the lot of
the German people. It is perhaps a singular omen, which we
will take as a high and significant one, that the Reichstag is
being opened to-day, on the 21st March. It may not be
known to all of you that once before a German Reichstag
was opened on the 21st March—the first German Reichstag
of 1871, in which, on that day, Prince Bismarck saw for the
first time the united German race represented in the German
Reichstag. We will take this as a good omen for our future
work. At that time the German Reich was founded—at
that time there was granted to the German people the
frame, the chain which linked all the German races together.
But slowly the people within this framework were disturbed
and finally torn apart into tatters. It is now up to us to
replace in this uniting frame the contents of the linked union.
The fact that the Reich alone is standing, but with the
people torn asunder, is meaningless. Unity—close relations
of the people to each other, united thinking and feeling in
all great problems, in all great questions of the fate of the
German nation—must be restored.

We therefore give thanks, here in this place, that there was
a man who, fourteen years ago, undertook the task, in the
midst of chaos, in the middle of downfall and in the depths
of the darkest night, to restore the faith and the hope,
which must not and cannot be lost in Germany as long as a
man of action himself believes in the future. In painful
labour, in a powerful struggle against terror and suppression,
this movement[2] has pressed forward from seven men to
thousands, thence to tens of thousands, until at last millions
were enflamed by the fire of love for the fatherland, and were
carried onward by the hope and faith that Germany could

[1] *Kuhhandel.* This word is often used by Nazi orators as a term of opprobrium, indicating shady methods.
[2] Meaning the Nazi movement. All Göring's speeches are shaped in this
fashion. He treats of individuals and then, without warning, proceeds to discuss
movements, ' gentlemen ' and ' they.' These are usually the members of the
left wing in the old German political structure. In the use of ' they ' he
appears to be contemptuous of going into greater description.

rise once more. Fourteen years of distress, fourteen years of shame, fourteen years without honour lie behind us. Everything that once held a meaning in Germany was trodden on and destroyed. To-day we experience once more the beginning of a new era. When in 1919 people believed that it was necessary to organise Germany on the basis of democracy and parliamentarianism and in the spirit of pacifism, did they introduce the new order symbolically too? They had, in no uncertain fashion, turned away from Potsdam, and the word alone was sin. They thought that they had to get out of the Potsdam spirit and enter into the spirit of Weimar, and even then they did not catch the real spirit of Weimar. To them the spirit of Weimar was the sign of an anonymous majority of democracy and parliamentarianism.

Now Weimar is overcome and to-day too it is symbolical that the new Reichstag, which will once again build up the Reich to its old greatness, its old dignity and its old honour and freedom, has returned to the place from which Prussia and, from Prussia, Germany once sprang. We have gone back to Potsdam because we want to show the world that the spirit of Potsdam shall fill us in future ! Because we want to make known that this spirit, once made fun of, has nothing to do with parade grounds and parade ground manners, but that the spirit of Potsdam stands for duty, discipline, work and cleanliness ; that it was the spirit of Potsdam which once unified a people torn apart and thus created the greater Germany ; that it was the spirit of Potsdam which always, in times of greatest dilemma, shone brightly and could always lead Germany upwards again. That it was the spirit of Potsdam which made it possible for us to face the whole world for four years. That it was the spirit of Potsdam which once guaranteed honour and freedom for Germany. Therefore we went there to-day in humility. We went to Potsdam[1] in thankfulness and were deeply moved. The national revolution is not yet ended—

---

[1] After the 5th March elections, the Third Reich was dedicated in the Garrison Church at Potsdam. President Paul von Hindenburg, during the service, laid a wreath on the tomb of Frederick the Great. Many held at the time that the act of the aged President was symbolical of the passing of junkerdom and its rights as the traditional ruling class of Prussia.

it marches on to end what must be ended in order that our people shall be blessed.

Comrades, gentlemen, you see to-day in the German Reichstag, new emblems. Every people and every nation chooses its own emblems around which it seeks to build up. I do not hesitate to declare that we thank a merciful fate that, in a moment when Germany ceased to be governed by ideas of honour and freedom, but when shame and disgrace were ruling, the old victorious banner was rolled up in mercy and the new emblem (of the republic) was created. But I point out here that it is not we who have sullied the emblem of black-red-gold (the colours of the Weimar republic), it is not we who have destroyed this flag, but they themselves—they who created it. If in 1918, in the moment of dilemma and desperation, they had planted the black-red-gold flag as a standard of resistance, as the signal flag to cling on to Germany's honour and greatness—if they had brought us that flag as the uttermost straining of our strength, then we would have honoured that flag and carried it as our colours.

But they forced that emblem upon us as a badge of slavery, suppression, shame and lost honour.

We therefore had to put that sign away from us in a moment when a new Germany had dawned. And now we have married the old victorious flag, under which two million men died as a sacrifice to Germany's greatness, with that other emblem of victory, which for fourteen years has fluttered in front of us through hardship and through struggle, which has always given us back faith and hope and renewed strength. We have kept the old colours, but in the middle of the shining white we have put the ancient sign of our ancestors and always young, eternally new, the sign of the sun, the sign of purity, honour and a rising nation !

So both flags are now married and I am happy, as the president, to be able to open the Reichstag under this victorious badge—which from now on shall flutter over the whole of Germany. There is still vibrating in us what fate allowed us to experience this morning. I believe that no one who was out at that victorious place will ever in his life

c

forget what he heard, being, as he must have, deeply moved by the association with great happenings. I believe that the most touching incident of all was when the old Field-Marshal stepped forward to the tomb of that great king, who once made out of a broken Prussia a world power and who through example, morals, iron industry and incomparable fulfilment of duty, through courage and strength of character, laid the foundation of our Germany of to-day. In reverence we bow down to this great king and in reverence we remember that we are able to open this Reichstag so near his last resting-place.

With all our heart we also thank our peoples' chancellor (Volkskanzler) that to-day he found words at the place out there (Potsdam) such as perhaps no other German could have found. Words which have penetrated deeply into our soul, words which made it clear to us in what great times we live and the tremendous task in front of us.

Herr Reichskanzler, I thank you in the name of all those millions who on the 5th March were standing behind you, for those words you spoke to us : Germany is going to have its honour restored : we thank you ! For with that you have given us the best that any nation can possess—its own honour and freedom. Those are the pledges on which a nation alone can build itself up. We promise you in this hour that the Reichstag will stand behind you and will help you to carry your responsibility and your tremendously heavy office. Freedom and honour from now on will be fundamental of the new Germany.

AN ADDRESS ON NATIONALISM AND SOCIALISM TO THE N.S.B.O. (NATIONALSOZIALISTISCHE BERUFSORGANISATIONEN), NATIONAL SOCIALISTIC OCCUPATIONAL ORGANISA-TIONS, at a meeting held on 9th April, 1933, at the Sports Palast, Berlin.

GERMAN women and German men ! I have spoken at countless meetings—have offered my views on countless problems, and yet to-day is a very special day for me. A special day because I can stand among Germans who must exclusively live daily in hard work or bitter need, and who, therefore, have learned from their own experience what National Socialism is and the meaning of its victory to every working compatriot.

My dear compatriots ! We are living in a National Socialist Revolution, and in pronouncing it we are putting the accent on the socialist, because there are many who are purposely speaking of a national revolution. That is not only suspicious, but untrue, for it is not only German nationalism that has won through—we are especially happy that also German socialism has proved victorious. There are, I am sorry to say, still people among us to-day who place too strong an accent on the word national (*in the title of the Nazi movement*) and who do not recognise the second word of our *Weltanschauung*—therefore it proves that they have not even understood it. They are people who have no right to call themselves National as long as they continue to be blind to the question of German socialism. For only people who put the accent on German socialism are truly national. People who refuse to think or speak about socialism or who pretend to see in socialism only the game of marxism, people to whom socialism rings awkward—those people have not got the (right) idea about nationalism

35

either. They have not yet understood that one can only be truly national when one realises and appreciates the existence of social problems as well. But again, one can only practise socialism when one also sees the other side—that nationalism must, under all circumstances, predominate in order to secure *Lebensraum* (living space) for the nation externally.

As much as nationalism is a sentinel on the periphery[1] so socialism is the sentinel within the nation. We require that the national strength of our nation shall increase internally and that the people shall be soldered together in one solid block. The individual German must recapture that feeling of security and realise that no matter how mean and humble is his social condition, there is a means of existence for him and a possibility to live. He must see to it that his innermost self is deeply rooted in the people and fulfil his duty to this people with every means at his disposal.

When I am going to give to the individuals living in Germany the possibility to make a living—when we can all get busy again and work—so that each one of us can exist again by our own work—when I do this, I shall have to take care that I also create the foreign opportunities so that this may be achieved. We have not made a national revolution in the sense that it is an empty, antiquated, jingoistic one, but this revolution has become in the truest sense of the word a national socialistic one. Until now these two were strange to each other—both rested, full of hate and animosity, on their own sharply confined fronts, on the one hand the upper and middle classes posing as bearers of nationalism, living in empty jingoism and stifled by pacific cowardice, while on the other hand stood the marxist front, which recognised neither nation, Reich nor people. As much as marxist socialism was degraded to an empty wage and stomach question, so did the middle class party world degrade true nationalism to an empty jingoism. Therefore both these things had to be cleaned up and shown to the people new and as clear as crystal. The national socialism of our *Weltanschauung* came therefore at the right time. Our movement seized hold of the cowardly marxism and took

---

[1] Extravagant use of the word—meaning here, frontiers.

from it the meaning of socialism. It also deprived the cowardly middle class parties of their nationalism and, throwing both into the cauldron of our *Weltanschauung*, there emerged crystal clear the synthesis : German National Socialism ! That was the foundation of the rebuilding of our nation. That is why this revolution was a national socialistic one. The idea grew out of the nation itself— and, because it grew out of the nation, led by the unknown corporal of the Great War, therefore this idea was also chosen to put an end to the dissension among the people and once more to unite them into one unit. The outer frame of the Reich was weak—it was only in existence on paper ; inside there was the people, torn apart and bleeding from a thousand wounds ; inside there was opposition—of all parties, professions, classes, confessions and occupations. Our leader, Adolf Hitler, realised that the Third Reich could only be saved and rebuilt if one could put inside this outer frame a united people. And that was the work of our movement during the past fourteen years—to make out of a people of divergent interests, religions, classes and occupa- tions—a new and united German people.

My German compatriots ! How often have we stood here on this spot, how often in other places in Germany, in one town or another. We hurried from place to place—spoke— and lifted up the people—those who were disinterested and those who were desperate. Again and again we hammered it into the masses—not one hundred times but thousands of times : a German nation must be created ! And so we tore the discord out of all parties, classes and ranks and converted them all into props and pillars of this new Reich. So we worked laboriously, and for years ! To-day, in the day of victory, when one hears only the jubilations, one should, during a quiet hour, think back to that unspeakable fight, back to the terrible disaster, which we often thought we would not be able to master and which yet always spurred us on to new fights—always pushed us forward to try again. The movement had broken up into splinters and yet it rose again up to the light. What terrible immensity of work, of sacrifice and devotion. Therefore, we ought now, when we hold meetings and celebrate the awakening of our people to such a great extent, always think of those who have sacrificed their all that this should come about. Countless ones are no longer alive—others have been made cripples, and others, again, are lonely. They have fought and sacrificed their all and work alone was their watchword.

When the 'reds' on the other side say that we are the hoodlums—my compatriots—we can only say that we did not have *time* to become hoodlums—we had no time because we had too much work and too much fighting—which strengthened us. We only want to be workers for the rebuilding of the German spirit—builders on a German task. We have created by hard work and the utmost output of energy what has now arisen.

The parties lie smashed on the floor. They shiver in cowardice—they are cowardly because they were begotten in cowardice. Cowardly was the system[1] and in cowardly spirit they handed this 'system' over. How miserably have they left—taken away by one officer and two men.[2] Not even twelve were needed. How these leaders have betrayed the workers. I can tell you !

If I had the time and possibility to let the workman have a look into the records of his so-called leaders, to show him all the countless requests by these 'gentlemen' for financial help, even when they were in the highest posts—then he would see how matters stood about his leaders. We could show you the requests made by red bigwigs—who in addition to their (Trade Union) salaries required payment for acting as editors (of Social Democratic papers), and as such betrayed the nation. They were not ashamed to demand pensionable retirement at thirty and forty—their working years, inclusive of military service, starting at eighteen. Such were the red 'gentlemen' ! Therefore, because they swindled the German nation and the German workman, because they thought only of themselves and gave no thought to the lot of those whom they were leading, they lost the leadership of those people. Nobody asked of them that they should live badly, but everyone did ask of them to

---

[1] Reference to the Weimar Republic.
[2] Reference to the dissolution of the Trade Unions and the arrest of the officials.

remember those whose conditions required improving. They were required to work for others, not for themselves. That has always been the spirit of work in the Germany of the past.

Out of these dissensions of the parties we have now started slowly to unite. To-day these parties only play a comic role. When to-day I mention the name of a particular party, in order to say something about it politically, I can't finish my sentence because there is regularly an outbreak of mirth, my audience refusing to take these parties seriously. To-day who knows much about these funny parties and little groups of parties? Everybody only laughs about them. They are single little relics of another age upon which we look as upon prehistoric animals—and about which one wonders, looks and shakes one's head that such things could have been true in the German Reich.

Only after Adolf Hitler had created this union as a basis could he think to use it as a means of strengthening the frame of the nation externally. Union had been the hope and dream in Germany for centuries. He reinstated German unity with one single law—the law of the German *Reichstatthalter*[1]. Where have they got to—the bigwigs of the parties? They who said only a few months ago : South of the Main line[2] Mr. Hitler would soon experience the end of his play.

Through this law we have achieved that for which generations longed. The power of the Reich, the sceptre of the Reich rules in all countries (in the Reich). The manifoldness and peculiarities of the ways of life of the inhabitants of these countries we want to maintain.

Now that the Reich holds all these lands together once more as in an iron vice—now we must unite the German people themselves. And here are you German workmen from the work cells (*Betriebszelle*)—the smithies in which we can remould the German Reich. You must work for it in all your cells, in all your factories. You must again and again woo your compatriot—must teach him and try to

[1] Governor-Viceroy—the chief executive of the Reich in the allotted state or district.
[2] River Main. Implying that disruption in the Southern States would break up the Hitler movement.

make clear to those frozen in hate against us for what we stand. That, compatriots, was for years the subject of our fight—the eternal fight for the German soul. To get every individual German man, to reform him, to free him from all the dirt of the corrupt system and to make him once more into a German fighter and a German human being. This you must now continue in your factories. You must struggle again and again for every single soul. You must shake the indifferent ones out of their lethargy and those filled with hate you must convert and teach.

Of course, we have won a great victory and symptomatic of every victory is the opportunist. We know that there are many who, in their heart of hearts, have no real bond of association with us, who have no real understanding of National Socialism, yet have become overnight the most dashing National Socialists. They have sprung up like mushrooms.

Here great care is necessary, for not the outside coat matters, not the party badge, the wearing of which has caused persecution for a decade, not the greeting of *Heil!*—no— only the heart decides if such a man is a National Socialist. We do not want fighters and National Socialists who are such just because their brains tell them to be. No! It must come from the heart. Then they shall come to us and be of us. Therefore we will try to look sharply, clearly and coldly into the hearts and not into the brains—then we shall see if they have become National Socialists. On the other hand, compatriots, we must also be magnanimous. We should not take our little revenges. We are, after all, the victors. What does it matter to us that the one or the other has said on occasion that we were criminals or that we were brown bandits or many other things? What does it matter what they said years ago? Years have passed and they have come to us out of their inner conviction, after all. We too are not National Socialists by birth. So let us be magnanimous, let us realise that we too thought differently at one time or another and let us be thankful to those who have led us into these wonderful times. And the more we ourselves are National Socialists, the stronger and freer we feel as such, the easier we can find it to be magnanimous and overlook the past and stretch out our hands to make up. On the other hand, where there have been crimes committed against the nation, the revenge must be ruthless. For that is the first supposition for friendship with the others. The big ones must be caught—not the small fry. The little ones we will let go, but the big ones, who have always known how to juggle and slip from side to side, making business here and business there—these must be pursued with inexorable keenness to a just punishment. In this connection now, when everything is cleaned and rebuilt, we have to understand the new official and civil service laws. Compatriots! We must not be mistaken. It is a heavy law. It strikes the individual, where it must (whoever he may be), with terrific blows. It destroys existences if it is wrongly handled. Therefore, because it is so harsh and because it must be so harsh, I have stipulated that no one but the Minister[1] himself can decide the question of dismissal or retention in office of an official.

The law will remain the same and apply equally to the Secretary of State or workman or porter, for it strikes the same blow. Therefore we must be clear about this. The application of the law must not lead to a situation where everyone thinks that he can allow his personal feelings to cry havoc, or to use its clauses for his personal revenge because he has been at daggers drawn with one or the other since they sat at the same school desk. That must not be. The only rule is : Is the person in question for the state or against the people ? That is the only rule which can decide. Only the official with a clear conscience can personally lift up his head. To him, as to others of his kind, not a thing will happen. Insofar as human beings have the power in them to be just, we will do all this in justice. You must be clear about this terrible responsibility, for this responsibility rests not only on us ministers, but on you also.

I know that in these days the denouncers are coming along—they crowd up in heaps—they come along with a case about the one or the other—most actuated by jealousy, competition or perhaps one man wants the other

---

[1] This refers to the purge in governmental employment.

man's job. Perhaps one man (in a position of authority) is awkward.

Compatriots ! the informer stamps himself and marks himself out already for attention by doing so.

He who steps forward openly and says : " I accuse," will be listened to, but he must stand by his accusation. Others, by their backstair methods and dirty anonymous letters, proclaim their guilt in their own lies.

We must keep ourselves, our people and our state clean. Well and good ! Every man has the right to accuse, but if his accusations are false, then he will be punished. When we observe these basic points then I am sure, that in spite of the harshness of this law, we can turn it into a blessing for our people.

Compatriots ! When we spoke just now about the fellow who was quick in taking chances, he whom I called opportunist, believe me in this one thing when I say that not everyone who came to us recently has done so out of opportunity. Believe me, in spite of all their noise, fussiness and *Heils*, the ' opportunity knights ' have been only a very small part. There is another cause bringing thousands upon thousands to us now. Partly, you all know yourselves —pressure has been brought to bear on many in the past so that they could not join us. But that alone is not the decisive cause. No, do not forget, there is something else and of which we can be happy and proud. During the last few years millions have walked about in Germany without having the slightest notion of what National Socialism was. They may have read the ' terror ' stories in the Jewish press about the brown columns which they saw pass—they read how bad the Nazis were. They read of all the things that would crash together if the National Socialists came to power—how everything would become rotten and pass into anarchy and dissolution again. And so they were blinded. They did not know us. Their feelings were blunted too much to take any more notice of the nation. It was not worth it any longer—it was too drab and sad and the desperation was too great. And now, all at once, our movement breaks through—breaks through the clouds and for the first time in many years the sun shines again. Now we see them, hundreds of thousands—yes, millions of them, suddenly awake ! They are blind no longer—they see something wonderful—they see how a movement has been slandered, has been made an enemy—they see how that movement carries the torch in its hands. They are happy that a new spring is coming and that all will be well. New joy and fresh hopes begin again. A faith is being uncovered that has been lost for long. And they are those people who come to us to-day and who say : We did not know ! Accuse us that we have been sluggish—but we have not been bad. We did not know that all of what we dreamt—that which was in our subconscious mind—has become a truth ! Therefore let us join you.

Those, compatriots, let those come to us, for those are the right ones. Those are already fighters in our lines to-morrow. Those you shall further awaken and strengthen in their zeal. They shall form the great army, so that in times to come Germany will think only National Socialist. For them the union of this people will be eternal.

Men and women of the work cells. You shall deal in your cells with social and economic problems. You, most certainly, shall be a social help to those comrades with whom you work—yet that is not the main objective.

The encouragement of ideals is more important than the material side of life. The works organisations are, naturally, specially chosen to make and mould the German worker and official in our *Weltanschauung*, to teach them until they have become German National Socialists. The main point you must make clear to the man who used to be, perhaps, a Marxist or a Communist, is that work is no curse but a blessing.

That is our socialism—we have restored to the individual the right to work. One may do his work better than another—then let the achievement of the better men encourage the other to further effort. Slowly and with hard work we are going to give the German work once more so that he shall earn his own bread. We will sow once more and try to prove that men can live without assistance from (state) allowances. Naturally, the whole of the nation and people is responsible that a man shall not starve because someone has stolen from him his right to work. But we must ask of the nation that every individual puts all his strength at the disposal of the people and the nation.

Compatriots! In the last few weeks many things have happened. In those weeks we have seen many new things. In those weeks Marxism was apparently broken up. By means of laws, prohibitions and many other things it became possible to break Marxism superficially—but only superficially. The Reich, the Government and the executive can only break its outer form, but you shall destroy the marxist idea completely. An idea cannot be destroyed by measures. The power to overcome this idea must come from inside. An idea can only be destroyed when one puts another into its place. That other idea must be clearer, better, be more active and possess more energy, in order to wipe the old one off the face of the earth. Working upon this supposition, the National Socialist movement has destroyed the marxist chimera with its *Weltanschauung*. It now remains for the works organisations to attack marxism in this spirit and this you can all do out of your own experiences. The power to drive you forward comes from trust : Trust in what we are preaching, in what we are doing, in what we wish to do.

Furthermore : Blind faithfulness—faithfulness to the leader who has created all this which we see around us to-day. Your power will grow if you keep to a strict discipline. A superior force, with every known advantage, without iron self-discipline would be beaten straight away— a little force, well disciplined, can always defeat a superior but undisciplined force. Therefore, self-discipline is needed —discipline of the individual which gives strength to the whole of the movement to which he belongs.

There are two further wells of strength from which you must draw and they are most important if you are to bring in your idea and break the old one. The first is the unshakable belief that Germany must live—that Germany will live because we will it—because it is necessary. This belief will give you strength. And secondly, growing out of this belief will come hope. Hope, the longing which always restores mankind when it is down, even when it is desperate. Night may be around us, but as long as the torch of hope is alight, no one will be beaten. Out of these inner wells of strength must come the deed. You must carry these ideas and help them to victory. Faith, belief, discipline, trust and hope—they are the pillars on which our movement must rest, because this movement has become the bearer of a powerful idea.

We have the will to live and that is why we will live. In front of us lies a tremendous waste land. All is broken up, undermined, as it were. We have already commenced to clear away here and there. Already there are indications of firmer ground on which we can build. But still, there is, far and wide, the huge expanse of waste ; it is empty and yields no fruit.

And for you, compatriots, you who are used to work and accustomed to turn your hands to any job—there is for the future only one word—work. Work for the people and for the fatherland, which must be built up once more. Fresh to the work and God bless our labours !

SPEECH AT A MEETING OF THE PRUSSIAN DIET,

18th May, 1933, dealing with the mission of Prussia in the Third Reich.

MEN and women of the Prussian Diet. In collaboration with the state government, the N.S.D.A.P. has put before you on its own initiative a proposal for an authorisation law. The Diet meets to-day, convened by its president, to receive this proposal. This meeting also gives to the government the opportunity of introducing itself to the Diet and to put forward its proposals for the rebuilding and reorganisation of Prussia. The governmental enactment pronounced by the chancellor contains, on broad lines, the principles of the measures which are applicable to all states in the Reich. Broadly, it indicates the aims for rebuilding Germany. The declaration of the Prussian state government must therefore accommodate itself within this framework, and it will only put forward proposals insofar as they fit in with the plans of the chancellor. Months have passed since the Prussian Diet met in its new form and it may seem odd that I can only to-day place the Reich government declaration before you.

In other states of the Reich this declaration has already been approved and passed—to-day it will be passed in Prussia. Months of work lie behind us—months in which slowly but surely the deed of freedom of the 20th July, 1932,[1] has been improved upon and ordered along more constitutional lines.

The most important law introduced by the Reich govern-

---

[1] This refers to von Papen's suspension of the powers of the Prussian government, whereby he became Reich commissioner for Prussia. The enabling act was used by President von Hindenburg to give von Papen this power and thenceforward the Reich commissioner for Prussia ruled by and through decree. The Prussian deputies were still *de facto* but not *de jure*—they received salaries but were ' on holiday ' in so far as their political duties were concerned.

ment is the *Gleichschaltungs*[1] law, which is followed immediately by the appointment of *Statthalter*.[2] This law
marked a century-old development in the spirit of unity
and firmness of the different tribes (peoples) and the German
Reich has been thus achieved.[3]

The discriminating eye of the leader and statesman Adolf
Hitler readily realised the need for this (Law) and has pulled
it through with a firm will. The dualism of Reich and
Prussia, which has existed since that unfortunate day in
1918[4] and which has furthered the weakening and ruin of
the politics of the German Reich, and indeed did the same
to Prussia, has at last and for ever and in everything disappeared. Prussia, following its ancient victorious mission
and tradition, must now become the corner stone of the
Reich. As much as Prussia grew out of the Mark of Brandenburg, so then did Germany grow from Prussia. Not in
opposition, but only in combination with Prussia and the
Reich can great aims bear fruit. How necessary the
co-ordination (*Gleichschaltung*) of Prussia with the Reich is
and how much the co-ordination is really the basis of
development is best shown by the fact that the Reich
chancellor is also *Statthalter* of Prussia.

The brain of our leader and chancellor, Adolf Hitler, has
therefore become the basis for the Prussian government. The
Reich Government, which to-day appears for the first time
before the Diet, has received its appointment from the Reich
chancellor, Adolf Hitler. Through his trust—and to me
that is the greatest honour—I have been appointed the
head of the (Prussian) government as its Minister President
(Prime Minister). Through his trust I am favoured in
being made Minister with the right of a *Reichstatthalter*.
This trust shown in me by my leader and chancellor is the

---

[1] Co-ordination law, whereby all administration in Germany was brought
into line on a common basis. The law of the Reich being the only effective
law in every state of the German confederation. For amplification of this see
Göring, the Iron Man of Germany. John Long.

[2] Governor. Hitherto viceroy of the Emperor.

[3] The German word is *Stämme*, and as Göring always uses this archaic form
to describe various peoples of the German race, it has been retained as ' tribes '
meaning, Bavarians, Würtembergers, Rhinelanders, Pomeranians, Prussians,
Saxons, Thuringians and so on.

[4] Actually, of course, this dualism existed before this time, in the days of
the German Confederation and in Bismarck's Reich.

starting point at which I myself and the whole government will begin our dealings. It shall permeate our thoughts and our feelings.

It is now over a decade since I first stood shoulder to shoulder with my leader—for more than a decade I am proud to say I have been his follower and loyal servant—for more than a decade I have been favoured to learn from this man —who to-day holds the destiny of Germany in his hands. His thoughts are familiar to me, his will is known to me and his will has become my will—and so I take over the government in Prussia, not only as the Prime Minister, not only in my rights as *Reichsstatthalter*, but in all and everything, firstly—as the most faithful paladin of my leader, Adolf Hitler. From now on it follows that Prussia must shape its politics in the strictest co-operation with the Reich and along lines laid down by the leader in which, always though in conformity with the will of the chancellor, the just and important interests of Prussia as the greatest state in Germany will be maintained in full measure.

The chancellor has appointed me guardian over Prussia and has instructed me particularly to keep in good condition the property of the state. Under no circumstances are Prussia's possessions or institutions to be taken from it— except only in the case of need of it for the benefit of the Reich. The daily practical experiences of Prussia shall become the basis on which the Reich shall found its new legislation. The chancellor wishes that the political and administrative system of Prussia shall become for all time the basis of the Reich—so that to Prussia falls the most important mission—the same mission as it had in the last century—the formation of the foundations of the German Reich. As much as the new Prussian government is being trusted by the chancellor, so it was only possible for this new government to be born out of the victory of the national and national socialist revolution. Out of that must grow, in our state leadership, the holy duty to form its politics in the spirit of this national and national socialist revolution. The spirit of this revolution must be shown in success as they (successes) have been achieved in the past and by the task which we have set ourselves for the future. The most

important success of this revolution—and the most decisive
one—was the seizure of power in the political and civil life
in Prussia and in the Reich. The national socialist movement has, as a bearer of this revolution, conquered a most
important place in the Reich, just as it has in Prussia and in
other states. That was the supposition for the rebuilding
of Prussia and of the Reich. That was the supposition
for the unfolding of all the working plans of the National
Socialists.

The Prussian government will know how to use the power
which it finds in its hands! It is equally aware of the
responsibility it is taking on and which is connected with
this power. It will never be slow to assume responsibilities
which are in the interest of the state. The taking over of
power by the government could not have been done without
any harsh handling here and there. The government found
matters in tremendous disorder. Even to-day we have still
to retain sharp measures. We are still surrounded by
nothing but ruins left behind by the marxism and communism of the past system. This epoch, in which one had
to fight one's way through in face of hindrances from within
as well as without, has to a great extent passed. In spite of
hindrances the national revolution goes on, but it now passes
into a new epoch, into an epoch of reconstruction. What has
already been achieved by the government will be recounted
later.

The most important measures of this second epoch seem
to be the following : The most far-reaching spiritual
re-creation of the German human being, the organic rebuilding of the state along new lines and, indeed, of all civil life,
accompanied by a general improvement in the private life
of the German, as far as general welfare necessitates ; and
more especially, the reconstruction and expansion of the
economic life of the citizen as the basis of his material
existence, and of the people as a whole. There are especially
rich possibilities for the activities of the Prussian state
government in these three great territories of planning.

The idea of the government for spiritual re-creation is
very closely related to the old Prussian spirit, which in past
time has proved to be of great value and which made not

D

only Prussia great, but the Reich also. This spirit, which was externally truly national and domestically truly social, will provide for the Prussian government an open door everywhere and—exclusive rulership. It will have the same effect in the family as in the schools—for the university—for science and art and in every other place pervaded by the German spirit. Out of this will emerge the highest standard of re-organisation in all state and public administrations. In order to restore such an administration we have to be thrifty, clean in the extreme and faithful to duty. Once more there must be created the official type who will prove worthy of Prussia's past.

Measures will have to be taken to accommodate every individual citizen to the new form of the state in such fashion as will ultimately prove of benefit to all. The citizen who is state conscious and wishes to prove it must not be hindered in his opportunity for showing it. Just opposite. The free initiative shall be strengthened and promoted, and with that will arise new hopes and the joy of work. The individual person shall create new work, but always on the basis that the welfare of the individual shall not come before the welfare of the state. In the first place stands the authority of the state. The activities of the individual have to be so ordered as to subordinate him to the welfare of the state and the people as a whole. The state government has already expressed its will to maintain respect for the authority of the state by terminating individual control in irresponsible departments. Even the best citizen and the most well-intentioned organisation have no right to so overreach themselves as to usurp the power and functions of the state. This opinion will be rigidly adhered to by the Reich government under all circumstances.

Because we have said that the welfare of the state comes before that of the individual, we do not mean that the initiative of the individual shall be suppressed and replaced by state activities. The free development of every able person shall not be hindered, but the activities of the individual shall have as their frontiers the highest consciousness of responsibility towards the colleague, the (national) economy and to the state. This formula for subordination and ordination is entirely intended for the protection of the national economy and of the state.

Along these great lines the Prussian government has built its main basis for the tackling of problems, and from here it will continue to go about the ordinary business of the state. Our aims will become perfectly clear when single items taken in hand by the government are discussed, and other schemes which are proposed for the future.

Following upon the fundamental thesis that the Prussian government has first of all to re-create the necessary spirit, we have to solve certain questions in the sphere of cultural administration. It has been noticeable in the past that certain persons have isolated themselves from the people, from the land and from the (nation's) spiritual unity. Even this does not comply with the false conceptions of the spirit of the liberal science of enlightenment.[1]

The German revolution,[2] in contrast to the French, is not being made in conformity with this science of liberal enlightenment but against it. Arising out of this fact have come points difficult of comprehension to the liberal-minded German and foreigner. They could not understand why it was that the masses who lived in misery grasped our ideas before they were comprehended by the professors—they could not understand why the younger generation, in spite of, or perhaps because of, their imperfect intellect and education, understood this revolution earlier than the brains of the intellectual. The association of the creative persons with earth and blood, with the long line of generations connected with the soil and ideas of nationalism, with the fate of the countryside which is their home, is not vouchsafed the enlightened scientist, with his definitions, in so high a measure. Therefore, to-day's task of Prussian cultural politics is to stir to consciousness the valuable instinct in the German people which at present is crippled, and to make of it a basis for cultural political measures of the German revolution.

First of all we have taken measures for the unification of

[1] Referring to the national life in Germany under the Weimar Constitution 1919–1933—the steady growth of class hatred and unnatural clashes, alien, as he implies, to German tradition and development.

[2] At this time it was implied that the revolution was still in progress.

Weltanschauung[1] in the Prussian universities. In our view, and according to our plans, it has been taken for granted that only such teachers as are of this nation and who feel themselves tied to it by inner bonds shall lecture in Prussian universities. At the same time we have taken steps to attract more young teachers to our universities and to give them every encouragement. For this purpose we are holding new elections for rectors and senates of the universities at the beginning of the new term. We propose to organise smaller faculties from among the representatives of the more important faculties and to grant to them, as well as to the deans, far greater tasks of leadership and responsibilities of leadership than was usual in the parliamentarian constitution of the universities up to date. At the same time we propose creating a social equalisation within the *Dozent*[2] and student corps by reducing the student subscription and college fees. We propose also to find a way to bring about an equalising of the earnings of *Dozents*, which will operate for the good of the rising academic generation.

The state will in future wield stronger influences in choosing the tutors, and by this means the unity of the spirit of the universities with the spirit of the people will be achieved. Subject selection will also be another means for furthering this unity—by the strongest preference for history, racial science, national science, political education and history and the organic science of national economy supplemented by a study of the laws of the nation.

Through the Prussian student laws the student corps in the universities and in the state have recovered their old status of equality as a member of the whole. Bound together in close association through the principle of leadership and discipline, the student corps inside the universities shall train themselves in obtaining the best that is in German science, as well as in the leading ideas of the national socialist revolution and its outcome and influence in all

---

[1] In this case literally ' World Outlook '.

[2] *Dozent* in this case must be regarded as the equivalent of the tutor in the English university system. *Dozent* in Germany has a great breadth in meaning —professor, lecturer, demonstrator, tutor, teacher—and in some cases (*Privat* understood) *Dozent* can mean a brilliant graduate who undertakes tutorial or coaching work unsalaried. It must be remembered that the German university system differs from our own.

scientific and practical walks of life. Furthermore, they shall, in conjunction with other compatriots, and by means of sport and labour camps, nurse the concept of unity of a greater Germany and thereby help in rebuilding the Third Reich. This work will be also furthered through the abolition of disciplinary punishment laws[1] (until lately) operated by the liberal system and by the active assistance of these students who are members of defence organisations (S.A., S.S., *Stahlhelm* and Labour Service). As opposed to the centralisation and bureaucratic methods of the large towns, the Prussian cultural organisations must point out the possibility of unity in country life and encourage the settling of persons on the land. The universities, too, shall feel that they are tied, spiritually and materially, to the country-side in which they live. That also holds good for the high schools for the education of teachers, in which the Prussian elementary school teacher shall be trained from now on in the place of the old pedagogic[2] academies.

This principle will be introduced immediately in the newly founded teachers' training college near Lauenburg in Pomerania, as well as at the new National Political Education institutions in Potsdam, Plö and Köslin, as a model for the direction of cultural politics for the next few years. The reform of these universities and institutions will convert the individualism of the townsfolk, with their intellectual onesidedness picked up in the liberal period, into an educational idea of unity of the nation and will encourage settlement on the land and develop strength of character.

That reform cannot be without model was readily understood when the ministry restored the poets' academy in Prussia. Here it was not just that there should be a professional organisation or a matter of the representation of ideas, but rather that those things that serve for models of the spiritual life of the nation should be given recognition and kept in the foreground. Therefore we are trying to make good choice from among German poets and writers,

[1] A reference, *inter alia*, to the prohibition of student duelling, which was proclaimed legal and honourable by the Third Reich.
[2] Used in its contemptuous sense.

who hold themselves far apart from that uprooted intellectuality and the representatives of hollow patriotism foreign to us.

In the territory of art during the past year of liberalism, that far-reaching propaganda of Germany's enemies—cultural-bolshevism—took deep root and art grew up as a material thing, flowering under a ' protection ' economy and being part of a scarcely envisageable system of corruption. Art, least of all, cannot be organised and ordered about, for it must grow out of the people and the land. It is the duty of the state, nevertheless, to exercise absolute care and cleanliness in the public places of art. Already during the past few months we have taken decisive steps in this direction. The state government will take care that, especially in the different departments of art, recuperation and progress will take place organically. This development must not be disturbed by clumsy hands, however well meaning they may be ; with due respect laid on real German spirit, it must not be forgotten that this can only be done by artists. I repeat my words of some time ago : That it is possible to make an excellent National Socialist out of an artist, but that it is quite impossible to make an artist out of an untalented National Socialist.

Cultural politics of the national revolution will have reached their goal when the opposition between the educated and the uneducated, the opposition between general and German education has disappeared. When all the people live in one spirit and work with it, when instead of individualism, town isolation and unhealthy intellectualism—health of body and spirit and union of the people with the land become a spiritual truth in Prussia !

Important steps have been taken by the department of the Interior[1] and by the department of Justice towards a national revival in the national life and in the state.

Inside this department of the Interior itself there had to

---

[1] The German title, in the states of the confederation, was *Innere verwaltung*, meaning literally internal administration, but whenever this appears it has been translated to conform with the English conception of the department, namely the equivalent to our Home Office. In the Reich, of course, the department is described as *Innen Ministerium*, but when discussed in English, according to choice, it is described as Home Office or Ministry of the Interior.

be solved important problems in order to make the police a strong instrument ready to strike and to equip it with the power of the state. The main task of the police is to see that a quiet and lawful internal development is being created, and to throttle all movements that are directed against us and which are apt to disturb the proceedings of our powerful work. The opposition in the state shall realise that we will stop them and their destroying deeds with inexorable austerity. To the working and industrious people the police will be friend and protector.

Arrangements in the police force, particularly in the case of the political police, judging from experiences made so far, have proved to be totally inadequate for overcoming obstacles and the normal execution of duty. In this field of administration the sins of the party system have been greater than elsewhere. Since the national revolution, the leaders of those organisations, which have been enemies of the state, have been brought to the fore through their attempts, assisted by enemy circles in foreign countries, to sow their poisonous seed in Germany from outside the country. This asks from now onwards for the creation of a powerful and strict uniformed organisation, the leadership of which must be in my hands—in the hands of the Prussian Prime Minister (Minister President) and Prussian Minister of the Interior. Therefore the Gestapo (State Secret Police), with its headquarters in Berlin, has been created and accorded special authority. As all along, it will be my most noble task to step in with ruthless energy and with all the power of the state behind me, against all activities, whether they come from within or without, which may be directed in any way against the new state and its security. This higher task, which moving times have brought with them, have also required measures of re-organisation in the ordinary police, which will endeavour to make the highest efficiency its aim. In changing heads of departments we have been careful to see that the re-organisation shall proceed according to plan. We will do all in our power, using all our strength, to do justice to the manifold problems that present themselves to the police, both now and in the future.

In this respect we will maintain our present foreign political tie-ups, at the same time creating a keen instrument of state power, which shall serve only and alone for the reconstruction of the fatherland. Therefore I must protest strongly against the assertions made in Geneva, which claim to put the Prussian police on a military basis, as if the Prussian police force is part of the army.

The re-organisation of the civil service is one of the most important undertakings for the security of the state and in securing the rebuilding of a new Prussia. A law, put forward by the Reich government, concerning the civil servant is already in operation. This law will cleanse the official body from those persons who can no longer find a place in the public administration of the national Germany. Having made this law effective, the Prussian civil service will once again possess the full respect and honour proper to an official body beyond reproach. In the interest of the state this cleansing operation has to be done. Apart from this, the Prussian state government has undertaken the task of improving the quality of the official. In a short while, in order to quicken the advancement and basic renewal of the higher official body (of civil servants) of the Prussian Interior administration, there has been re-introduced the system of special education for Government referendaries[1] (registrars), which six years ago was banned for political reasons. The establishment of government referendaries gave single quality to the history of Prussian administration, and, in the past, gave to successive governments of Prussia generations of expert officials. The education of the rising generation of higher officials in the spirit of the national and national socialist rising will become much easier and more perfect the earlier the young administrator starts his future career.

In doing away with the existing civil service in Prussia, the realisation of the leader's thought in administration is made so much easier. The civil service from now on will be

---

[1] Referendars : young barristers who, having passed their first state examination in law, practise in a court without emoluments, thus qualifying for their second professional examination for the post of ' Assessor ' ; assistant or lateral judge. The German legal system differs from the British, inasmuch as junior posts in the judiciary are awarded more on a competitive basis and therefore judicial rank can be achieved in the early forties.

represented by trusted men,[1] but these representatives of the service in future will not be allowed to have a say in the political life of the civil service.[2] From now on a new state exists and this state takes more care of its officials than the old one ever did. I will not be surpassed in the care I take for the official placed under my control by any representative committee.

The government will watch especially closely the re-installation of a strict, upright and thrifty administration in the boroughs and county councils, who in future will subordinate themselves to the welfare of the state and of the Reich. In this direction of a strict and clean administration we have already taken measures, and special anti-corruption laws have been enacted. These measures have cleared up first and foremost the ' cousin economy ', which in some parts of the country has become unbearable. This law prohibits the one person from having a seat in the council, on the bench and on the county committee. This multiple office holding is apt, through conflict of interests, to render a straight and clear decision impossible and is therefore not allowed. Also, in the interest of authority and discipline, no paid official, workman or any employee of a council, shall have a seat in that council. A thrifty administration, which is in close contact with its population, can achieve much through the scaling down of its paid members of the county councils and the substitution of created honorary posts. The county system has for too long been an eldorado for giving jobs to friends and for putting people into office who, at election times, have been useful to one or the other. To clean this up will be one of the first duties of the government.

A clean, thrifty and conscientious state administration

---

[1] *Vertrauensmann :* Man, who in office, works or factory represents the workmen or the staff in bringing complaints to the management. Under the Social Democratic government, these men were elected by ballot from among and by the workmen, who at that time were members of the Verband or Trade Unions. Now these *Vertrauensmänner* are selected workers or junior officials nominated by the Government. In a broad sense—shop steward.

[2] Under the Weimar Republic, with over fifty political parties in the state, one never knew what exact power was in the hands of these minor officials. While under the existing system Nazi politics naturally enter into the domestic life of officials, they at least know that they cannot give offence to some political theory held by the representative, which may result in dismissal. Hypocritically or sincere, nothing can go wrong if they are avowedly Nazi.

will also be assured now that all senior administration officials, even that grade which up to now has been exempt, are to be subject to probationary service. In order to ensure that the leading places in the councils and committees will in future only be filled by persons of truly national, reliable and upright character, and able officials at that, I will, during the next few days issue new orders for a close scrutiny of their credentials. I myself will make them prove to me that they are capable and of integrity and that they will make their ultimate permanent employment dependent upon one year's satisfactory service.

The knowledge that many of these measures will not be very popular does not sway the government from its determination for one moment, for it sees that, after the sad experiences of the past, they are the only right ones.

With these important and, therefore, anticipated regulations, the reform of local government, especially in regard to the development of the corporations, is naturally in no way concluded. The work will go on. But be assured that the government, in spite of its strict control of the county councils and committees, will not take away from responsible local administrators the love and eagerness to work for the rebuilding of the Reich in their own territory. Quite opposite—we shall encourage them in every way. In order that all local government organisations shall be in a position, naturally with the utmost economy, to do justice to their future business, I will in all my ministries so direct all my energies in order to ensure that the corporations shall be re-established on a sound basis of finance.

Through the new law providing for the reorganisation of the administration, the whole of the civil service has become uneasy. Here, I am afraid, false judgment has crept in. I therefore am able to assure you that the state government is fully aware of its responsibility which, incidentally, this law casts upon it. I proposed, at the conference of the *Reichsrat*,[1] that the fate of the individual official and employee must rest in the hands of the Minister himself. Because this law

[1] *Reichsrat* : The old German equivalent to the House of Lords, having powers of veto. In the Third Reich, this upper chamber has been abolished, and its place has been taken by a newly constituted council of state, which is not executive, but purely advisory.

may strike hard at the very root of existence of the individual, it must be carried through in the most careful and responsible manner. But we have not just made a law to abolish the official who has a ' Party book ' in order that we may instal in his place, others of the same order. He who thinks that to-day it is sufficient to change over from marxist to national socialist in order that unsuitability and inexperience may be forgotten, is sadly mistaken. In the final selection, as far as an official is to be chosen, the party to which he formerly belonged or the badge which he wears to-day, matters little. In these cases I am firmly determined to punish the informer, the slanderer and matters of indiscipline. Official and employee, who inform against their chief or comrades only because they want to move into their places, will not be suffered in future in a clean circle of officials. I therefore once again warn seriously against this because the easily shot off arrow could come back and strike the hunter himself.[1]

I want further to direct your attention to the fact that membership of a party, as long as it is not directed against the state in any way, is in no way a hindrance to a career.

I know that increasing uneasiness is abroad, because to a great extent I have put people of the national socialist party in official posts or have ordered them to be placed at the head of responsible departments in the administration. Gentlemen, I ask you not to forget the tremendous discrepancy that existed when formerly millions of national socialists led the fight for freedom in Germany and yet for a decade were excluded from government posts of any kind. I am sure that it is my holy duty to make good the wrongs committed by the rulers of the ' system ' in Prussia. Apart from that there is the eternal law : He who has fought for and conquered positions shall hold them : He who is willing to build up the new Prussia will in future only be judged by his national way of thinking and by his suitability.

The (new) spirit must also be expressed in the administration of justice. Law must not, as it has been done up till now, rest on its own perception—this would give an abstract justice which would stand by itself and not tied to the people.

[1] German idiom for : ' Hoist with his own petard '.

The fount of justice is the people itself. Its kind, consciously or subconsciously, directed by the blood, draws its effect from custom and descent. Such a living custom is the expression of the conscience of the nation, which is being elevated to a state protected norm. That is the task of the law. The giver of law must not put the arbitrariness of rational abstraction in the place of the rights of the people.

The Prussian *Erbhof*[1] is considered to be a typical right of the people. This usage the Prussian state Germanic justice has kept up, despite centuries of suppression, in the consciousness and dealings of the German peasant and farmer. The indivisible farm, the indivisible family of the farmer settled on his own land will become the foundation, through this new law of inheritance, for the peasant constitution. In doing this, the Prussian state ministry has brought to a logical conclusion the work of vom Stein and Hardenberg, providing for the liberation of the peasants, and which, after the passing of these two great statesmen, was buried until now. This will be a signpost to historic development, attaching the peasant to his land and liberatig the farm people within the Prussian state.

The effectual carrying through of this law in the life of a nation cannot be done by clauses and decrees, but as in all else in a united nation through men and women. Therefore it is necessary to have judges whose intention and determination is rooted in the consciousness of organic blood-relationship with the whole of the people, and whose work will be guided by only one rule—the welfare of the nation as a whole ! It is necessary to make this rule the guiding light for the education of legal students, lawyers and judges. The preparations have already begun for reforming the preliminary work and for the ultimate examinations themselves. The organisation of justice must also conform to the tasks before it. It must be near the people and must not be swayed by any financial considerations. For the

---

[1] This was formerly peasant customary law, more akin to English entail. What has happened in this case is that the Prussian Government has made entail compulsory on every land owner great or small. Thus obviating in any future bad times, non-German speculators jumping in, as happened between 1922–30, and buying up large tracts of land or house property for a mere song.

machinery of its administration is not the end but the means to an end. Closer relations with the people have already been brought about by the affiliation of all the Berlin courts. Justice will best discharge its functions, to secure the safety of the nation and to protect the life of the individual, by quick, strict and just measures. Punishment is still the only deterrent to crime. The penal code as a whole will be the main item under discussion in the Ministry of Justice during the next few weeks.

Justice will go back to the old ways in Germany on the basis of word of mouth proceedings in court. This has been laid down in law and will assure quick and lively judgments, and strengthen the faith of the people in justice. This will only be possible by freeing the judges from administrative work for the more judicial duties of their office.[1]

The same action must be taken in the Probate, Common Law and Bankruptcy courts and also in the Land Registry and Registrars' Courts. By solving the problem as before-mentioned, justice will become a bearer and protector of the nation's conscience. As much as the nation is a living organism, so in turn shall justice form itself into an organism, in which every cell through its functional development will work for the well-being of the whole organism. Security of justice and the peace of justice is to be kept in that way in a truly national common life, and it is the proud task of justice to fulfil this.

Turning now to the organic new ordering of economy. It is important, at the outset, clearly to recognise the basic new idea of the problem to be solved. The reorganisation of economy and its basic reform must proceed in a direction where employer and employee must overcome the idea of classes and must grow up together in a new working unit. The Reich bears the greatest part of this burden and Prussia must use its influence on this in future decisive development, because economic rebuilding cannot take place without taking regard to the political rebuilding of the Reich, the states in the Reich and even down to the counties themselves.

[1] A reference to an intention to use the judges as judges and not as registrars, clerks and bureaucrats.

In addition there are the chambers of Industry, Trade, Handicrafts and Agriculture and they are important starting points for economic reconstruction—and they have all more than a century of tradition. These chambers are under the control of the states themselves—that means that by far the greatest part of them and their economy are under the supervision of the Prussian state government.

The same goes for the German Stock Exchanges. The steady saver, the hard working country farmer and the honest merchant, when it is a question of investing saved money or the proceeds of a good crop, shall be more important than the speculator in future. All speculators who are not conscious of the fact that they have to work for the welfare of the whole nation will have to leave. The reform work in this direction, already started, will go on at high pressure. The Reichs government has turned its attention to the reorganisation of the joint-stock banks and credit houses, and the Land Banks, the Saving Banks, the Transfer Banks and the Clearing House, particularly, are undergoing reform at high pressure.

Activities in the Savings Banks during the last few weeks showed a steady increase in the relaxation of tension, finding expression in an increase in deposits and a decline in the number of closed accounts. All this has the effect of reducing the indebtedness of the Savings Banks to the Acceptance Banks and to the Reichsbank. This is a further indication of a tangible increase in the trust of our economic system. The state government is of the firm opinion that a re-enlivenment of trade and a decrease in unemployment on a large scale depends upon the trust that is being placed on economy and a peaceful state leadership. I myself declare that a peaceful state leadership is absolutely guaranteed. The state government will know how to deal with economic disturbances brought about by irresponsible or unfair dealings in economic life. The fortunate position of the savings accounts has made possible the granting of new credits by the Savings Banks, and this has had the effect of improving the economic life of the middle classes.[1]

[1] Loans to small traders, dealers, farmers, officials, etc., where security is reasonably guaranteed.

Prussia has encouraged the renovation and decoration of house property, without doubt one of the best means to create work. Up to now sixty million Reichsmark have been expended, but further sums of money are urgently needed for this purpose.

In the desire to create new work, repairs and extensions will be carried out on bridges and harbours owned partly by the state and partly by limited companies.

The department of mines in Prussia is pursuing untiringly the investigations of the causes of accident in close collaboration with the heads and the administration of the mining companies.

The endeavours to ease the economic misery in the upper and lower Harz mountains have been greatly assisted by valuable investigations in Lautenthal and by assistance from the state for the mining and metal industry in the Harz. New orders flowing into the mining companies from the Prussian state are also responsible for easing of unemployment.

In all cases our most important task is to make our economy healthy and bring it back to new blooming. It will not come to any flowering though if the individual branches of economy, without taking heed of the immutable natural laws, try to achieve their own aims through artificial measures, through interference with the government or through interference with other measures which are important and necessary to the state. It can only be done by realising inter-relationship of economics in all its branches and that by using it in practical fashion our nation and people, and its thousandfold economic strength, will be brought to bloom.

The national socialist state is built up on the leader thought and based on the ability of the individual. Our economy, too, can only get its utterly necessary impulse by ability, experience, industriousness and through the honourable conduct of business.

One fundamental condition must be held on to at all cost : All that happens must be for the best interest of the state and the common weal. That is the sense of the national socialist motto : Common welfare comes before personal welfare. Neither experimentor nor dilettante must meddle with the fine and delicately wrought work of German economics, which has been built up by centuries of hard work. Everybody should therefore apply to themselves the words spoken by the leader on the 1st May—that all the people working in German economy, if at the anvil or at the desk, at the turner's bench or in the office of director— everyone in his or her own place shall try to work towards the fulfilment of the set task : namely : To force Germany's rise from her hard fate.

Not jealousy, but happy co-operation, is the basis of the boom in our trade and thereby the guarantee for the cure of our unemployment. Economy must have peace in order to work. Away with eternal mistrust. Not backward but forward must our eyes be turned.

A clear basis of justice and authority must also be guaranteed in economics. The head of every works, whether large or small, must be inspired by the greatest responsibility toward the men entrusted to his care and towards the whole nation. Cleanliness must, first and foremost, be restored in our economic system if esteem and credit are to increase. The state government will also take serious steps here if a case of real corruption is proved, and in order that peaceful development can proceed it will put a stop to all unnecessary spying and informing and class animosity. The following must govern the actions of all in economy : Do not abuse your authority and take great heed to your responsibilities. The state will put a stop to the nonsense of the small and very small commissars. The responsibility for any undertaking will repose in the head and not in the majority of a works' council.[1] The harm done to Germany's economy by the past system cannot be repaired all at once, but in future our economy shall be our strongest activity, supported by the power of the state, the will to rebuild in the national socialist movement and the guarantees of law and order which emanate from these.

The tasks of the newly created fighting organisations have been grossly misunderstood—as much by economy as by the members of these organisations themselves. They have

---

[1] *Betriebsrat*. The leader is known as *Betriebsführer*—equivalent to a shop steward.

not been created in order to attack or in any way disturb our economic system. They were organised to work in territory allotted to them in conjunction with the works-cell associations, namely, in the field of educating workers in factories and shops to be national socialists. Their function is not to create new diversity of ideas, but to render impossible of re-forming, under any disguise whatsoever, those groups which have been so justly destroyed by us. In them the economic party (*Wirtschaftspartei*)[1] of unhappy memory shall not see a resurrection under national socialist emblems.

Their task is much higher, much more powerful, for it is world envisaging, and therefore asks for all the strength of leadership of the associations to this aim. The oppositions of class, birth, occupations and interests have brought Germany to the rim of the abyss. We have not torn Germany back from the pit in our terribly hard struggle in order to see these oppositions take form in new disguises. The Prussian state government and more particularly I, as its exponent of the national socialist world-philosophy, will ensure that this opposition of interests, and be it even with a fist of iron, will be brought into the harmony which is necessary for the welfare of the whole people.

In the realm of agricultural economics sums are ready for the technical improvement of vine culture and for the increasing of wine sales. In those parts of East Prussia which have been damaged by rain and rust disease, action has been taken providing for far-reaching replacements and new sowings, for which the Reich has put up one million (marks) and Prussia another million. In some districts of West Prussia, which have been hard-hit by bad crops of fodder, we have taken special action for securing the proper feeding of animals, and in this work Prussia has also taken a prominent financial part.

In connection with this and in spite of it not belonging to the realms of agriculture I would like to say one thing : East Prussia is cut off from us by the Corridor, but it is not cut off from our hearts, nor from our feelings and thoughts. We know what East Prussia is suffering. We are aware that

---

[1] The economic party was closely allied to the Centre and Nationalist party and its leaders were drawn from heavy industry and agrarian interests.

E

East Prussia stands as a lonely outpost and that we have to look after that outpost. East Prussia must know that it can always renew its strength out of the whole of Prussia.

Important measures are in preparation of being framed for the improvement and development of the waterways. In state forestry administration enlarged programmes of work are being envisaged and put in hand. The preparation by the state of means for giving work as I have outlined in my speech has only been possible by the exercise of the greatest thriftiness in the whole of the Prussian administration.

Therefore, at the end of my speech, I come to the specially important question of state finances. The fact that a firm and solid basis is necessary for an orderly and solid state treasury has moved the government to take steps to reconstruct the controlling offices as one of their first official actions. On 24th April it closed the budget for the year 1933, and the budget for 1932, which in any case was only temporary at the time, has been ratified in law. In order that the treasury loan issue shall be clarified the government has decided upon a law governing loan authorisation, whose main purpose will be to restrict credit grants to the existing scale and to free the treasury from the losses of past years. This means that through the operation of this law, the treasury will affect a saving of two hundred and ten million marks. Schemes covering the relief of unemployment in Prussia will cost in all, during the coming year, thirty-nine million marks.

The loan authorisation law, as well as the budget statement, are reproduced in the budget statement and report, the advance report you have already received and which have been published in the state Gazette. For everyone who takes a special interest in the construction of the Prussian budget, the large volume of the advance report and the countless explanations of the special items contained therein give sufficient information, and I would therefore like to omit further mention here, in order not to occupy your attention with sums, the appreciation of which is only made clear by lengthy explanations. I only want to mention that the fiscal year of 1932 will close with a deficit of thirty-eight million marks in the loan account. The new budget for 1933, with a round sum of two thousand seven hundred million marks, is balanced.

This balancing is not only a formal matter which is enforced through circumstances in order that the greatest German state shall have a balanced budget, but I would like to accentuate the fact that the government has taken great pains, through extreme thrift in all departments of administration, to see to it that the budget balances materially too. Income and expenditure have each been budgeted three thousand four hundred and seventy six million marks lower than in the past year.

It must not remain unmentioned that, from the beginning of the new fiscal year, the long-suffering house-owner as well as the property owner will experience vast relief in income and property tax. Taxation in agriculture, forestry and gardening is also greatly reduced.

The personal and material expenses have been reduced considerably, and the number of state officials has diminished by two thousand seven hundred and eighty-nine compared with last year.

The present arrangement of financial measures is for the time being only an attempt to clear away dead wood in the treasury. The close collaboration, which in the financial life of the Reich, states and provinces finds its expression in the adjustment of finances, and which has found great strength in the unification of the political will in all territorial organisations through the national socialist revolution, pro- hibits that the finances of the greatest German state shall be looked upon independently of the Reich and of the other states and counties and their organisations. The form of the whole German finance politic, which lies with the Reich government and which can only go hand in hand with the development of the whole field of (national) economy, is also a deciding factor for the final reorganisation of the Prussian treasury. It is therefore of special value that, following that close collaboration and association, the Prussian Finance Minister should also sit in the Cabinet of the Reich so that he will be able to inform the Reich govern- ment of the financial state of Prussia, in order that the Reich can utilise this information for its own financial movements.

It will therefore depend upon the development of the whole economic position of the Reich as to whether the new budget can be kept to its present scale or how far any alteration of the whole taxation system in the Reich will have to be made. If we are successful, we shall have to decide how to alter the economic structure of the state and also of the counties and municipalities.

That conditions in the municipalities and municipal organisations are urgently crying aloud to be put in order I know, but that the government alone is not able to help them in one sweep I need not explain. For to-day I only want to show clearly the aims to bring Prussia, in closest financial collaboration with the Reich, back to a secure financial position, at the same time creating for the municipalities, a sound basis upon which they may build. As a stepping-stone to this aim, the statistics and measures contained in the budget and report for 1933, together with the management of the loan and credit positions, can only be valued for the time being as the foundation necessary to the shaping of an orderly state economy.

Men and women ! With my explanations I have given you a fair picture of the will and of the work of the state government. The Prussian state government is deeply conscious of the immensity of the task set before it. The Prussian state government knows that it must clear a field of debris and must start to build from the very beginning ; the Prussian state government knows what it means when marxism has been victorious all along the line ; the Prussian state government knows what it means when, for fourteen years, the rulership was in this spirit and was directed from this very place. I know that it is impossible to overcome all these difficulties, which seem ever to tower before it, in a short while, and to bring about that success quickly which the nation badly needs and the government desires. But the state government it moved by the influence of the spirit of these great times and is filled with strength which is given to it by the idea which it is serving. Therefore it is hopeful that it will succeed in leading Prussia out of the misery of the past and upward once more. When you gentlemen help her, and when the whole nation stands resolutely and faithfully behind the government, then Prussia will be one of the strongest props of the new German Reich, newly united by our leader, and will not only exist but will return to the glory of her past, flourish and thrive. The presumption for this has been created by the national socialist revolution. In the name of the Reich government it is my duty, which I discharge with all my heart, to thank all those who have put their all at our disposal and who have sacrificed all so that we may be victorious. We know that our thanks have to go to those old fighters of the national socialist freedom movement, the faithful S.A. and S.S. men, when we now see that our work was successful. To give honour and freedom to the nation was, and still is, our aim.

In the difficult fight for those treasured possessions, in the struggle for Germany's equality, we now stretch out our hands to all those who want to fight with us and work with us.

To-day we are still mindful of the tremendous impression made yesterday by our chancellor in his holy peace confession.[1] We thank him warmly for expressing this will for peace clearly and distinctly, while at the same time representing the honour of the nation so firmly. The whole Prussian government stands for duty and conviction with the whole of the Prussian people behind this declaration of our chancellor. In this festive hour we will too, remind the whole world once more that through the terribly harsh Treaty of Versailles, millions of Germans have lost their means of existence without, however, giving up the cry for life itself.

The German people have a right to live, the German people will live and the German people want peace to live and it will keep this peace. But the German people want honour and freedom! We have not retained German honour through long years of struggle and fight in order to deny it now. Prussia was once created on the formula of honour and freedom and Germany grew out of Prussia. Therefore let me close our confession of reconstruction with the words spoken by me when I opened the Reichstag : Honour and freedom are the fundament of Prussia and Prussia is the fundament of Germany.

[1] A reference to a speech made in the Reichstag, which was considered to be an answer to a message sent out to the world by President Roosevelt, calling for peace among the nations.

A BROADCAST OVER THE GERMAN RADIO NET-WORK DESCRIBING THE FIGHT AGAINST VIVISECTION AND MEASURES TAKEN TO PROHIBIT IT, 28th August, 1933.

COMPATRIOTS ! Ever since the day that I issued the proclamation against the torturing of animals by vivisection I have received a flood of telegrams and letters, all of which agree and expressed great relief that at last an energetic step had been taken to put a stop to this torture. My proclamation, coming as it did like lightning out of a blue sky, came as a surprise to many. For years the struggle against vivisection has been going on. Much was talked about and in scientific and lay circles there was a lot of fighting, but nothing concrete was undertaken. The national socialist government was very clear about its attitude to this problem from the very first—that energetic measures were required—and yet it took months before adequate legislation could be framed. Pending the passing of these final regulations, and in order that animal torturing shall not continue, I have now stepped in with my proclamation and I have made use of the right that is mine, and will commit to concentration camps those who still think that they can continue to treat animals as inanimate property.

The German people particularly have always shown their great love of animals and the question of animal protection was always near their hearts. For thousands of years the German people have always looked upon their household and farmyard animals as their companions, and in the case of horses, as their fighting companions and as God's creatures. To the German, animals are not merely creatures in the organic sense, but creatures who lead their own lives and who are endowed with perceptive faculties, who feel pain and experience joy and prove to be faithful and attached. It would never have been the perception of the people to put the animal on the same level as a dead, lifeless and insensible thing, to look upon the animal as a soulless and unfeeling thing to be exploited—as a means for work, which perhaps one could employ for reasons of mere usefulness and then torture and destroy.

The fairy tales and sagas of the Nordic people, especially the German people, show the spirit of close contact, which all aryan people possess, with the animals.

It is the more incomprehensible, therefore, that justice, up to now, did not agree with the spirit of the people on this point as it did on many others. Under the influence of foreign conceptions of justice and a strange comprehension of law, through the unhappy fact that the exercise of justice was in the hands of people alien to the nation—because of all these conditions, until now, the animal was considered a dead thing in the law. Legal pronouncements gave to the animal owner similar rights to those which he possessed over his inanimate goods. This does not correspond to the German spirit and most decidedly it does not conform to ideas of national socialism. The owner of an animal shall not possess an absolute right over it. We could not understand that the owner could destroy it within his own four walls, just as any piece of furniture, or that he could have tortured it out of mean beastliness, and escape punishment.

Until the national socialist revolution, the frontiers of justice came up to the point where ill-treatment of, and brutality to, animals was punishable only when it became a public nuisance. There had also to be present witnesses and other persons who objected to the nuisance. Then and then only was it possible for the person in question to receive punishment. The draft bill for punishment (for ill-treatment of animals and vivisection) of the year 1927 was intended to break with this state of affairs and was going to make torturing as such a punishable offence ; but in the interpretation it was explained that exemptions would be made, in the case of religious or scientific activities. This of course is a mean and insufficient interpretation, which neither does justice to the basic protection of the animal against torture nor gives any clear line of demarcation as to what does, or does not, constitute scientific reasons.

The casual handing over of animals for scientific purposes cannot be allowed to just any person who feels inclined to make experiments. Experiments on animals for the purpose of defining an illness in human beings, for the preparations of serums and other experimental use, need legal regulation in detail and the keen control of the state. It is a sorry sign of science that during the past two decades, amply protected by the law, materialistic scientists have wrought unbearable torture and suffering in animal experiments. Not only French experimenters, like the notorious Claude Fernar, but Germans too, have made experiments, the utility of which stand in no way comparable with the cruelty employed. Examples from scientific literature of the past describing, without a sign of human feeling or sympathy, tortures of the worst kind, and operations performed without any form of narcotic, observations on burned, frozen or starved animals, prove that individual scientists, mostly alien of the nation, have had their feelings so numbed that it is doubtful if any existed at all, so detailed is their description of the suffering.

Vivisection—the cutting up of a living animal—was used without the application of an anæsthetic. The experimental animals were rats, rabbits, guinea pigs and, what must have hurt the feelings of the nation most of all, the friend of mankind—the dog. In these experiments the belly was opened, the heart laid bare, the brain was chiselled and the limbs cut off in order to observe how the organs responded to such operations and what would happen to the body after the loss of certain organs. It is incomprehensible to national socialists that where in many cases the usual anæsthetic could have been applied with ease, it was often not at all, or, in other cases, insufficiently used, just because the things experimented upon were only animals.

It may remain a matter for speculation as to how far such vivisection has helped in the last decade to achieve an advance in knowledge of the construction and functions of the human body. To-day science itself holds the view that the torturing and killing of animals through vivisection can further our knowledge no longer. These experiments have been more and more discontinued by science. An absolute and permanent prohibition of vivisection is not only a necessary law to protect animals and to show sympathy with their pain, but it is also a law for humanity itself.

It is not only necessary to watch over the work of the animal protection society[1] but to fight thoughtlessness, indifference and brutality to animals and their pains.

I have therefore announced the immediate prohibition of vivisection and have made the practice a punishable offence in Prussia. Until such time as punishment is pronounced the culprit shall be lodged in a concentration camp. I have given orders to the Prussian Ministry concerned to take steps in the quickest way, to work out the draft law and to-day I can tell you that the Reich Ministry of the Interior, which is the equivalent ministry concerned, will pass a law to this effect during the next few weeks.

Vivisection does not cover all branches of animal ill-treatment and torture. Not only scientific torture, but also the ill-treatment of animals in everyday life requires close inspection and legal control. Ultimately, all questions of the law for animal protection will be ordered in model form and from the study of all animal questions, on which experts are now sitting as a result of my decree, will emerge the new regulations.

It will and must be, the tasks of the experts to state individual cases and to decide how far it will be necessary, if at all, to experiment on animals in order to advance the knowledge of disease in humans, to produce medicines and generally to further scientific knowledge. I am thinking in this regard of those pests which attack humans and animals alike and of infectious illnesses and of finding methods for their recognition. If it is impossible to discover the germ of these illnesses by microscopical examination and recourse must be had to animal experiments, then it must be undertaken with the proper use of narcotics and protection for the animals. Blood taking in order to prepare serums from the blood serves immediately in the fight against the most dangerous human illness. The small operation necessary

---

[1] *Tierschutz Verein.*

for this cannot be called vivisection or torture as they serve the great aim of fighting the worst infectious illness. Let us for one moment think back to the experiences of the war and what irreplaceable help serum was in the fight against gas gangrene and tetanous. If the drawing off of blood is carried out in a responsible manner, the animal does not suffer any harm, for it must be remembered that in special cases human beings give their blood for transfusion to help another human being.

When animal experiments have made it possible to dis-cover in the pig, Germanin, so called after Germany, and which is the only medicine which helps in the treatment of the terrible sleeping sickness, and as such has gained world recognition, it can be readily understood that tests for its reliability must be carried out on animals. But these experiments have to be carried out under rules governing protection of the animal and with the prescribed anæsthetic.

Medicines that are made from the organs of animals, like Insulin—the most successful treatment for diabetes—and for the production and sale of which the civilised countries of the world to-day are struggling, are by their nature not capable of testing without recourse to animal experiment.

Scurvy, the leading illness of all forms of malnutrition, could only be found and its reactions recognised through experiments on animals. Such experiments will, I hope, further our knowledge in the field of nutrition and help us to go further beyond.

I will not add to the examples already given. They are witness to our successful work in science, but in this work all experiments on animals which are not really necessary must be stopped, and all action in this regard must be taken with the utmost care. General and local anæsthetic must not only be given to human beings when operated upon, but in the same degree and with equal care to animals when they serve the cause of science and humanity. Animals which are specially attached to us like dogs and cats must not be used for any experiments when other meaner animals are available and which will serve equally as well. The rat, a parasite which has to be destroyed in any case, is surely not as susceptible to pain as our domestic pets and is most certainly not worthy of our sympathy—but, if used in experiments, the same care and the same forbearance must be observed, and here too experiments will only be allowed in so far as they are utterly necessary for the good of humanity.

The limited group of persons which will be allowed to make such experiments will be that small circle of scientists who are in charge of serious institutes, thus ensuring that such experiments will be made which prove a cure and a help for suffering humanity. But here too the state must supervise and have the right to step in when misuse of the animal is found. For teaching purposes the picture and film can be used as fitting substitutes for animal experiments.

All these individual items will be cleared up by the scientists whom I have called together in conference to examine the problem and who, in due course, will make their proposals to me. Purposely I have invited those scientists first of all who for years have fought against vivisection, in order to give them the opportunity of laying before me in clear and concise form their conception of the constitution of future legislation. For many years there has been bitter opposition between those who see this necessity of animal protection and those who want to use animals carelessly for the purpose of serving the human race, and it has been an eternal point to quarrel over. Surely it is not possible that everyone who studies medicine believes that he can enrich his knowledge by making his more or less happy experiments on any animal that comes his way.

We will solve this burning question. We will bring about a solution through this new decree made by me and, in doing that, we will have installed peace in part of our German cultural life.

Unnecessary, harmful vivisection and animal torture will disappear, and only necessary animal experiments, properly supervised, will be allowed, thus bringing unity in our domestic life.

AN ELECTION SPEECH AT KIEL, 28th October, 1933, when the German people were asked to confirm the German President's decision to announce to the world Germany's withdrawal from membership of the League of Nations and from the Disarmament Conference.

M Y dear German compatriots ! I think that not one of you would have believed that we would have to prepare so quickly for a new election fight. On 5th March we told you that it was important to arm for the last decision. The whole fight then was directed against internal politics, to the inner development of strength for the awakening. In that hour we called upon you to decide if you wanted to return to domestic well-being once more. When we call upon you to-day to stand together once more as a whole people, this time it is for a tremendous manifestation of our will of resistance, as a nation. You shall decide this time whether we shall remain helots, or whether Germany shall have free will in its foreign affairs. That is what you are asked to decide. Just as the 5th March brought victory and decision in our internal affairs, so, we hope to God, we can make the world see on 12th November that a new Germany has been created.

On 5th March we beat our internal foes, smashed the party state and destroyed the parties and their existence— on 12th November we will prove to the world that out of internal unity has grown unity on foreign affairs too.

Compatriots ! We have called upon you often, and again and again millions and millions have shown their faith in us time and again. To-day, when we seek to rally the whole nation, it is important that you should all be clear on what must be the deciding factor. To find that we must look into the past ; not the past of the last eight months and what has happened in that time, but how we stood before that time. A nation can only arise anew, only then can its strength grow, when it realises the danger that threatens it. To-day we decide the fate of our nation and all must know on what the decision must be taken. Therefore let me draw briefly for you all the threads and connections once more. Parliamentarianism ! What is it and what does it really mean ? The individual man, the leader, they mean nothing, but all at once the whole nation is expected to bow before the cowardice of numbers. Naturally, cowardice can never lead to any heroic decision. Secondly, there was the perfect twisting around of the concept of authority and subordination. In parliament there was only present a responsibility that went downward—it was the twisting about of the conception that authority has always to proceed from above downward. So it had to come about that in all cases cowardice sought a solution in compromise, but it never found it. So we (Germany) became a state of parties—the November system. But where marxism is victorious, a nation breaks in pieces—where communism takes the rudder of state, a nation is destroyed. Marxism and communism grow from the same root. In their destroying habits they are the same. The deciding factor is that marxism will always build a bridge for communism. I have the holy conviction that Germany would never have lost the world war had marxism not existed in Germany. Germany, once a flourishing country, was made an absolute field of debris in that way.

The class fight tore the people asunder. But while we hold Marxism and communism responsible for the class war, we cannot hold the middle classes[1] completely free of guilt.

We must understand and differentiate between matter of second order and matter of fate. There are decidedly certain fundamental questions of a people, about which there can be no two opinions. In such matters, for instance, the German worker cannot and must not hold a different opinion to the farmer. When, for instance, the one half of a nation believes that private ownership is proof of cultural progress and the other that private ownership is a form of

___
[1] Bürgertum.

refined theft, then a rift appears. Then no one can rally a nation in an hour of emergency, because the one half will trip up the other half. When one-half of the nation is impeding the remainder it is impossible to expect the strength of a nation to show itself. One can think at variance in minor or technical matters, but on the broad question of fate there can be only one basic thought. Either it is right —then the people have to subscribe to it. Or it is wrong, and then the whole nation has to oppose it.

The raggedness of Germany during the past years degraded it into a state of perfect unconsciousness. In this land the heaps of varied interests formed—here the cow-dealing thrived.[1] The proletariat cried : We are the children of socialism, and the middle classes answered : We have rented nationalism ! and when one looked closer, then one could see that marxist socialism was a lie and that the middle class nationalism was a business proposition in disguise. The natural outcome of all this was that the one half saw in the word ' Nationalism ' an opportunity for middle class business advantage, and that at the mere mention of the word ' socialism ' the other half got a ' goosy ' feeling down their spine. So have both groups degraded the meaning of these, which in reality have high and noble meaning, until they became complete distortions without equal. Then came a movement that threw both these groups into the cauldron of a united *Weltanschauung*. For the one is necessary for the other. Life without both conditions present is unthinkable. During the time in which these two ideas were being melted down—in this time a nation was reborn. We have not made bridges between the proletariat and middle classes, we have destroyed both, in order to let a new nation arise with new ideals.

The result of this class warfare on the one hand and the demands of the middle classes on the other led, in all fields of our common life, to disastrous ends. If one looks at our economic life, one sees exactly that never before has a nation known so much misery as Germany during the past few years.

A nation from which peace is stolen must sink down into

---

[1] German opprobrium for sharp practice.

economic misery. In the past we have all experienced the most grotesque phase of this economic misery—the greatest crime that a government committed against its people—the inflation, which destroyed completely the prosperity of the whole nation.

When they say—inflation is a natural law—then I will answer : No ! it was the meanest ' sharper's ' trick ever. Here the Jew has proved and excelled himself as the ' wire-puller '. The work of marxist socialism was to make the people dissatisfied, to make them unnational and to stamp them body and soul as proletarians.

But it was not out of unemployment that this plague of economic misery came. It grew out of ' character ' crisis of socialism. When a doctrine preaches to the people all the time that work is a curse, how then can one make that people strong in the zest for work and how can one make them work joyfully ? Under conditions like these the proudest nation becomes degraded to a nation of paupers. But the German workman will not beg. The German workman wants to sit down to a table laid with the food that he has earned and not someone else. Who can comprehend the misery of soul of the unemployed—how he despaired of his fatherland. Who can blame them for destroying, when, after all, all that they once had was destroyed by others. We will thank God that there was one movement that was ready to take these despairing ones into its fold in order to make out of their despair—iron and steel for reconstruction.

Once a nation allows its history to be destroyed and falsified—once it permits the memory of the great ones of its past to be besmirched by ridicule and dirt, then a nation pollutes its own wells, out of which it could have drawn new strength.

The Treaty of Versailles has taken all our freedom. But a nation does not lose its freedom before it first of all abandons its honour. Strangers can take its freedom, but only the nation itself can cast away its honour. When we stamp Versailles as the day on which Germany lost its freedom, we must also search for the day on which Germany broke its honour. German honour was bartered away in the woods of Compiegne. It was there that a so-called German abandoned German honour. He was no soldier but a parliamentarian, who sold German honour. If at that time a common soldier, instead of a politician, had gone quietly in his greatness—gone as a negotiator—Germany would have had better terms than it had through this low haggler.

Then came the time of political helplessness and the madness for fulfilment (of the Treaty). In the midst of this madness of fulfilment the people awoke in opposition. It was a fight which will be described in history as tremendous. It was a holy fight for the soul of the German people. It was a fight of ideas. In the darkest night, Adolf Hitler shook the German nation out of its delirious dream. He found people who followed him. Slowly, growing like an avalanche, the movement grew and youth hurried to our banners.

We have suffered—we have bled. We did not know family or private life any more. For us there was only one thing, the fight for the German soul. That was our revolution. We were fanatical in the extreme in our love for the people and in our hate against the opposition. That gave us the strength to overcome all in the end. In the end came victory. We had fought and struggled for this victory. With the victory and assumption of power came a new chapter. We asked for supreme power not for the sake of power, but because we needed this power in order to be able to save Germany. The power once in our hands, we were firmly resolved to beat the communists once and for all. For that I did not need the Reichstag fire. I was resolved from the beginning to tear out communism by its root.

When the leader called me to the leadership of Prussia, he gave me the task to cleanse Prussia and to perform the building up of the state. That has been done and further work is in hand in order that I may purge the tremendous Augean stables of Prussia. A tremendous work, however one looks at it. Take a few examples : The rôle played by the police in the November state—on the one hand it was the beaten one and on the other hand it had to beat[1]—with

---

[1] A peculiar way of describing the impotency of the Prussian police, intending to illustrate the corruption in the force. Conforming with the policy adopted in the whole of these translations, English idiom has not been substituted for the German.

that I finished at once. It was my duty to do my best in order to form a powerful instrument for the state. But when one builds a new house, one must take care that the marshes underneath are drained off. Following this principle it was necessary to instal anti-corruption departments. We have proceeded upon the principle of not only finding the smallest criminal, but to hang the big ones before the little ones have been caught. That too has been done. Further it became important for cleanliness to be introduced into public life. It was important to instil once more the sense of security in the nation. The security and the morale of the people demanded the punishment of criminals. From now on the motto goes : As ye spill blood, so shall thy blood be spilled ! The success of my tactics confirmed them. Since we reign in Prussia only one murder with robbery has occurred. The gentlemen of the underworld have realised that their ' protected clubs '[1] avail them nothing, but that at last a bit of clearing up has been done which will do away with the scum of humanity.

The most tremendous problem crying out for solution before all others is that of creating work. Every single person must help here. We must bring back the German people to work and bread. We have led the fight for honour and freedom—but we have also promised to fight for work and bread.

A new spirit wafts itself through Germany and at its head stands the Leader. Wherever the fight is hardest, there he is in front. Wherever the heaviest burden is to be carried, he carries it alone. Out of this spirit, the wonderful happened, that a nation found itself—the wonder of the rise of a nation. Adolf Hitler has brought it about and put once more into an outer frame—a united people. Now we have once more a nation with aims, of one idea, with one belief, of one strength and with one leader.

[1] A reference to the fact that many members of the known underworld were members of a certain type of masonic order and that many police officials were also members of the same order and were consequently protected by them to a degree undreamt of in England. The writer knows personally a case where an engineer killed his wife and cut her up and because he was a friend of a Berlin Police Commissioner he only received a sentence of two years' confinement. Owing to the prisoner awaiting trail for a long period his sentence was commuted and he was allowed on parole.

F

This nation will witness and prove to the whole world what strength it can exert. To-day we can proudly say : Farmer, workman and soldier are as one people, for they are the people. The wonder is that we have found each other. All this has happened under the sign of the swastika, the symbol of our fight. All this has come out of our fight. So we must further hold together, to-day more than ever. For while we have destroyed the enemy inside our country, another opposition has grown up around us. The ring has closed in on Germany ! Once again they want to suppress the fatherland and once again Germany shall be declared guilty for all the sins in the world. Apparently we are threatening peace. With what do we threaten it ? We only know that Germany wants peace, that it must have peace in order to live and to be able to rebuild. Therefore it is madness to say that Germany does not want to disarm. Only because the others do not want to disarm do they want to find us guilty in not doing so. We do not fight for cannon —about that we could soon come to an understanding. With us it is a matter for our freedom and our honour, for equality and peace. Therefore we had to leave the Disarmament Conference and the League of Nations. And now once again they curse Germany. But the opinions of newspapers are not identical with the opinions of nations. We have found that a rising respect is being observed in all nations for the German people. Already foreign powers are almost jealous of us, because they have no government like ours to create cleanliness. And with the rising respect abroad, the understanding of Germany will increase.

When Germany marches firmly and united on its way, then the nations around us will realise that their peace is, in the end, only secured when peace lies with Germany too.

On 12th November we will show to the nations abroad that we have become one united people. We step in front of the people. We do not know the fright of the middle class politician for an election—we measure other things than mere party interests. Our Leader can ask of the people great sacrifices. The people only want to know why and for what they are called upon to sacrifice and out of these sacrifices it looks for success. When all this is done, the

German people are ready to lay even the greatest sacrifice upon the altar of the fatherland. That too has history proved. We do not make sacrifices for ourself—we make them for our children—for the future of our nation.

We are no war mongers. We, who have seen war, know its terrors. We have experienced terror and we are not frivolous enough to sacrifice even one single drop of blood. We are ready to do all to get peace for our people. But— we are not ready to sell our honour in exchange for a foul peace.

Two powerful ideas are struggling to-day in this world. The idea of reconstruction and the idea of the Soviet star. The idea of the conception of people and fatherland and the idea for the destruction of Europe. When our idea is victorious, and of that we are sure, then there will come for the whole German people and for the fatherland a new period of expansion.

Therefore, honour the symbol of the swastika. That is the guarantee for a rise. This sign of the sun has brought us honour and freedom once more. Therefore respect the flag. Carry it in front of you, for then Germany will be resurrected for all time.

ADDRESS TO THE REICHSTAG, 30th January, 1934, the first anniversary of the Third Reich, referred to officially in Germany as the Day of Victory.

MY Leader! my comrades! To-day the Reichstag is assembled on a memorable day, for it is a Reichstag elected by tne German people on the 12th November, 1933, and it is here, for its inaugural session. This day, the 30th January, will be in German history a decisive turning point in the destiny of the German people.

A year has passed since that date—a year which seems to us like a decade—so tremendous have been the changes, so tremendous that which has been achieved, so singular in what has happened, for all of which the German people have pledged themselves.

One year of German history but also one year of historic world importance. From the depths, from the valley of darkest night, the German people have risen once more. The German people has recovered its honour and freedom, two things without which no nation can live. My comrades! especially those of you who were members of previous Reichstags, how different is to-day's meeting from those of the past!

Outside the people are crowding the roads, outside the German people demonstrate their joy and they cannot do enough to thank their leader and show him their affection.

To-day, the German people know that in this Reichstag there are sitting deputies who are firmly resolved to follow their leader blindly. And what is expressed by this love, this tremendous faith? Nothing but the satisfaction of the people in having at last one leader and one leadership.

In past times, in the days of parliamentarianism, it was left to the people to decide their own questions and fate.

The people themselves in their own strata of interests had to decide. Their leaders were too cowardly to make decisions for them, for they wanted to hide behind the anonymous idea of majority. To-day the people realise that those exercising the power of leadership have the courage to lead and to carry into effect those things which are considered to be for the best.

The fight was not easy and our unity was attacked from many sides. Again and again they (the opposition) tried to make pitfalls for the weak and the frightened, in order to loosen the unity. It was not successful. With brutal fist—where it had to be—we have thrown back enemies of the state.

Ruthlessly we have proceeded against them, against those who put their own ideas before the interests of the nation.

In future, too, we are going forward in the same way, in keeping with the wish of our leader, against all who try to touch our unity. Everyone, no matter if he comes from the ' right ' or from the ' left,' will be stopped with the same firm resolution. It is now impossible for any group to use the rise of the nation as a means to further their own interests.

The German people of to-day know only one thing, and that is : Their Leader and the movement which he has created and which in turn has created and formed the new German people. And it is only to the leader and his movement that these people lean and reposes in them their trust for the future. This one year illustrates the power of the reform of the Reich—this one year has re-ordered whole ideas. In Germany there is not one solitary federal state left which can do as it pleases. No longer can it be that one law holds good in one state and in another something quite different.

In so far as we have only one movement, know only one people, trust one leader, recognise one authority and one sovereign power—then that is the Reich.

The task set the present Reichstag, therefore, is to go along the road drawn by its leader and to fulfil with all its strength and ability those great conceptions which the leader will order. The Reichstag of to-day is the first

Reichstag of one united *Weltenschauung*, which is greater and which goes far beyond the ideas of all the strange groups composing earlier Reichstags. Now the world can recognise : Just as the people are united, just as the leadership is united, so then are its representatives governed in one whole *bloc* by one will in the form of the German Reichstag.

Wonders have happened in this past year. I do not know how history will later on record this re-birth of Germany. I do not know how history will be able to pass on this wonder to our descendants. I believe that it can only be done by pointing at one man, to the man who has created all this.

To-day, the unity of the people is expressed in the unity of this Reichstag, and we are, all of us, from the farmer out on his land down to the last workman and last little Hitler youth, moved by that warm feeling for the leader to whom we have to give thanks for everything. Our leader, who is to be thanked for not allowing us to sink into despair during a decade of German shame, but who in the years preceding the German awakening, carried the banner and bade us not to weaken—he who always led us forward with his great aims.

SPEECH AT A CONFERENCE OF THE PRUSSIAN COUNCIL OF STATE, Potsdam, 18th June, 1934, dealing with National Socialist state formation.

GENTLEMEN of the council ! after a lengthy pause the state council meets once again, more especially in order to be informed about the plan of the Prussian budget. There is a tremendous difference between the manner in which all past budgets have been sanctioned and the new method, whereby authoritatively and along principles laid down by the leader, all matters are being attacked. When to-day we do not pass the budget in the old parliamentary spirit and usage, so it is necessary and of the first importance, that just those gentlemen who are chosen to sit in the state council, forming inside the state council a close union between the state and the people— are entitled to be informed about the budget in order that they may look into financial matters. You shall see how the means are being used, you shall know which great and tremendous tasks the state government has even now to fulfil and you shall put forward new proposals in connection with the budget.

The contents of this budget show a neat picture of perfected work of the state government. The more general explanation of this budget the finance Minister himself will give to you later on. I would like to keep to the statement that the demand to be thrifty to the extreme and the need to expend in certain most important quarters have been brought into harmony. When we speak of utmost thrift to-day, we have different positions in view compared to those that were once customary. Thriftiness must not end by merely knocking out items schematically, for in doing this more is disturbed than built. The main point is that the present means at our disposal are being led into politically important channels, so that with little much can be done.

That the budget balances is not natural, after we have stepped into an inheritance of ruin. But when it balances, as in this year's instance, when just now means have been made free, which above the material matters, secures the foundation of the spiritual and the material, then special praise is due to the finance minister, Professor Dr. Popitz. Tremendous difficulties were mounting up, which at times seemed impossible to overcome. You must also realise that an orderly control of state administration has been achieved when the budget is presented so early in the financial year. That too is deserving of praise, for in past years we had become used to waiting for months for this to happen.

The political position of to-day does not allow of us looking only upon Prussian affairs, even when such an important item as the budget has to be discussed, simply from the Prussian viewpoint. Since the revolution, the Reich reform started to flow more easily and the task of the Prussian government and the development of all things in Prussia can only be understood if we visualise the great mission that the Prussians have to fulfil in the German Reich—the first fighters and foundation stones of the Third Reich. From the beginning of the taking over of power Prussia has proved to be the pace-maker of the Third Reich.

One must always remember that Prussia represents over three-fifths of the Reich territory. Therefore, the whole work already done during the revolution for the great task and for the creation of the Third Reich, was of fundamental importance. For the manner of working in these three-fifths of the Reich and the manner in which reform was carried through, must naturally, alone by the heavy weight of the Prussian measures, make an impression upon those in the rest of the Reich lands.

As example I need only mention shortly the destruction of marxism and communism in Prussia. The heavy weight of these forces lay absolutely in Prussia and here the fight was hardest. We must not forget that during the days of the ' system ', the Prussian state government was always the high spot of democracy and, more than that, it was social democratic and even communistic. The most important measure therefore, was the reorganisation of the police force.

That the renewal of the Prussian spirit and a reorganisation of the police was basic to the rebuilding of the Prussian state, was clear to us in the first few hours of office. It was necessary, because the police force had been absolutely rotten through and through. During the days of the ' System ', the police force became the means by which the ruling ' gentlemen ' kept the rudder in their hands against the will of the people. The police was the domain of party-book officialdom.[1] If the new state wanted to shape the instrument which was necessary to the safety and welfare of the state, it had to undertake, naturally, a tremendous change.

The creation of the Gestapo was a necessity. The new state has given to this new instrument of state security a great importance, and that importance can be best realised by the fact that the Prime Minister himself is subject to the authority of this branch of administration, because it is of fundamental importance that all possible streams that may be directed against the state shall be keenly observed.

A further task, which radiates out of Prussia into the Reich, was the creation of an early foundation for the renewal of the cultural life. Here, perhaps, the revolution showed most. The perceptions and ideas of the different cultural fields, made clear the difference between the new national socialist state and the last system. The rottenness which had taken hold of everything and especially in the cultural field, was not confined to the purely superficial appearance of life—it had in it rottenness, already attacked the national consciousness of Germany and had already destroyed the German soul. The creation of a new and firmer basis was necessary. Here, indeed, we had to carry stone after stone and build them together. The Prussian Ministry of Culture has in this respect done tremendous work in a large field.

[1] A reference to the membership of various political and sometimes secret societies. The individual was issued with a kind of pass book showing the size of contributions to the funds of the party, and often the book was the means by which the holder drew additional benefit from the party, so that it may be said that certain parties bought support from its members and were thus in a position to demand their support for legal or nefarious business in the state. This party pass book system was not peculiar to any one party, but was common to all parties in the state including the N.S.D.A.P.. Thus as party funds waxed or waned, the membership was proportionately affected.

The Prussian state theatres, too, will in a short while again be the finest in the land and will be able to stand up to the best stages in the world, because here the national socialist spirit has ruled from the very first day on. A further and especially important presumption for the reconstruction of the new state, lies in the aim and security of national socialist justice. Here too there have been great cleavages between our conception of justice and the conception of democracy.

Justice shall not be pronounced in dull paragraphical, blood-strange and race-strange manner, but shall be dispensed in a close contact and lively connection between the man who administers it and the people and the blood in which the people have been born. We must return to a time when there is German justice, to a consciousness of justice which every individual German carries deep down in his heart.

Here a tremendous task lies before us and only a modest beginning has been made. But that a beginning was made at all, that a platform has been built on which the pillars of a new justice can be erected, is specially praiseworthy of the Prussian state government and particularly of the Prussian Ministry of Justice. A corner stone of this erection is the new law of inheritance as applied to farm lands, which has proved as no other law once again, that the conception of the state can be equalised with a lively sense of justice in the people and that as a forerunner of the Reich law administration, proves Prussian industriousness in the territory of Reich reform. At the same time this law proves to be a great work for securing the farmer on his land.

Compared with these activities, other things which the state government has put in hand may perhaps be of no account, for the state machine is a tremendous piece of work in which not only the large wheels go round, but in which the small cogs must function also, if the work of rebuilding is to be successful. As an example I will pick out only one thing. The administration of forestry, which has to be reformed to comply with the need of the people. I do not mention this point merely because it is very near my heart and because I have myself created this new reform, but because, quite apart from pure forestry reasons, it will prove a very important factor in the life of the people and their economic existence. As Prussian laws have been patterns so often for the Reich, so all these measures are intended as the basis of Reich forestry laws and will be prepared with all speed for the Third Reich.

I was given the opportunity to achieve other connections between the Reich and Prussia and they have been of an organic kind. I believe that I can say that nothing in Reich reform has been carried through so lively as just these measures.

After the Leader had given expression to his will at the Reich party day at Nurmberg, that at long last the thousand-year-old wish of the German nation to become united had been achieved, it became Prussia's duty too to do everything that lay in her power to help towards the fulfilment of the will of the Leader. I believe that nothing can further this more than the new firm association between Prussia and the Reich.

So now we have in all and every walk of life created a new unity. With the exception of the Finance Ministry, all Prussian ministries are directed by Reich ministers. But the Prussian Finance Minister too belongs to the Reich cabinet. There has been up till now no unification in the realms of finance, because the chancellor and we have realised that such a thing is of no real purpose at the present moment, for no territory of politics is so difficult, so great in expanse, and so weighty for the future as finance. Also, we do not yet know which way the Reich is going to proceed in financial matters. Recently a new unification has taken place in the economic field between Prussia and the Reich, which stands above the personality of those directing such work.

In the union of these two economic spheres into one rationalised whole, German economics will have a possibility of showing impressionable leadership.

Of great importance is the unification that has taken place of the Reichs lecture ministry (*Unterrichtsministerium*) and the culture ministry. Here, more than anywhere else, was a great gap in cultural affairs, because there was no special department in the Reich for cultural matters and science. In this new ministry all matters have been co-ordinated having relation to lectures, science, and the development of the human being for its future task. The questions relating purely to art, the museums, theatre, etc., which do not properly reach into science itself, have been handed over to the propaganda ministry. In Prussia, however, they are still subordinate to the ministry of culture. Already I am working on a plan to provide that in future all questions of art shall be administered by the Reich minister himself, who will be responsible for all matters of this kind to the Reich.

A few days ago the Prussian administration of justice was amalgamated with the Reich department of justice. Here too, you see development pursue its natural course. There was a danger that the Reich Ministry of Justice, which after all is leading in the compilation of the new statute book, was growing beyond itself. For this reason the Reich Ministry of Justice had to be brought into the closest association with all the departments of justice of all the German states. I am happy that here too the Leader has followed my proposal.

For me it is bitterly difficult to part with my Minister of Justice[1] and you all know just how much a strong national socialist personality can achieve in justice and matters of justice. In spite of that I have, mindful of the great aim before us—the creation of a united Reich—come to the conclusion, together with the Leader, to put hesitation behind us in order to create first and foremost unity in the Prussian justice administration. I do not like to let this conference on state political unity pass without thanking the Minister of Justice Kerrl with all my heart for the great work which he has done. He has already created the most important proclamations, so that further development of justice can proceed along clear-cut lines of national socialism. I was enabled to reach my conclusions much easier, because the Leader has recognised in the Minister of Justice the personality which ensures that in future the same lines for the renewal of the legal system are followed up and which therefore makes us all conscious of the fact that a balance between the authority of the state has been found. I am indeed very glad to learn that Minister Kerrl will continue to serve in

[1] A reference to the fact that, with the co-ordination of law departments, Kerrl, the Prussian Minister would cease to function as such.

the cabinet as Minister of state, in order to stand up with his valuable advice for special tasks.

All state political connections about which I spoke just now have been of deciding importance, but they step into the background when compared with what, in my mind and in the mind of the Leader and in the mind of the Minister of the Interior too, is the most important move in the reform of the Reich—the combination of the Prussian Ministry of the Interior with the Reich Ministry of the Interior, which has been brought about under the leadership of an old hero of our movement, Reichsminister Frick.[1]

The Reich Ministry of the Interior (Home Office) is in future responsible for the constitution ; it will be the Ministry controlling officials of the Reich and will have at the same time the great and responsible function of preparing the details of the reform of the Reich. How impossible it would be to think that the Minister of the Interior could perform such a task if it had no foundation, if it were without lively connection with the administration and thereby in close contact with the need of the people.

I have given up this Ministry only grudgingly, for it has been in the Prussian Ministry of the Interior in particular where, for eighteen months, I worked on tasks of fundamental importance. When I parted with this Ministry it happened because, to my mind, unity in administration was presumptive to pulling through the reform of the Reich constitution and because I knew that after me an old and tried fighter takes over and because I, as the Prime Minister of Prussia, carry now as before, the final responsibilities of all Prussian Ministries.

I do want to take this opportunity to make clear to you all that the idea of giving up the Prussian Ministry of the Interior to the Reichminister was not proposed to me, but that it was my own original idea. I am happy now this unity has been brought about and the basis for reform of the Reich is prepared, and I am happier to know that it is not being worked out around a conference table, but that it is

[1] First Nazi to have ministerial experience, being Minister of the Interior for Thuringia several years before 1933. See Blood-Ryan's *Göring, the Iron Man of Germany.* John Long.

being carried through with living associations with the people and that the thousands of proposals, wishes and woes of the people have found in Reichminister Frick a faithful trustee.

For the councillors of state it will not only be important to learn what Prussia has done in the reconstruction of the Reich, but they will also learn something about the future development of the state of Prussia itself.

It is clearly to be defined that the old idea of the Prussian state has been dissolved into the Reich—that means that Prussia no longer has to fulfil tasks of a sovereign state. What remains is the eternal ethic of Prussiandom. Long ago, the idea 'Prussia' was pushed beyond the territorial and material things into the mystic. This ethical idea ' Prussia ' is no longer tied to frontiers. Where in other lands[1] state virtues like bravery, courage, diplomacy and most of all, state discipline, are being praised, where one speaks of a sound and clean official service, there it is commonly called ' Prussiandom.'

Prussia is well known for the fact that it has produced less artists but more statesmen, who in turn have created the supposition that an Adolf Hitler could at last fulfil the longing of the German people. It is a wonderful play of fate, that up to a certain time it was commonly supposed that efforts of the North would unify Germany—when Prussia was the tremendous peg from East to West—yet now in the end fulfilment has come through a man from the South of Germany, who as the first Leader of a united Germany, creates that for which our people have longed for a thousand years.

In spite of this higher sense, which is not bound to the earth but which springs from the ethical, I know no better Prussian than the Leader. The firmness of his character, his cleverness as a statesman, his personal courage and his modesty—all point out the virtues through which the Prussian official and, better still, the Prussian soldier, have created and shaped Germany. This ethical conception we bring into the new Reich as Prussia's most valuable asset.

[1] Other lands in this case meaning lesser states of the German-speaking peoples.

That is—the Leader has spoken of it so often—in the end the most wonderful and valuable possession that Prussia can give. With that Prussia fulfils its last mission.

Now the new Reich—The Third Reich—composed no longer of Prussians, Bavarians, Wurtembergers and the like —but the new Reich of the Germans stands in the stead of all these and Prussia lays in its hands, its tradition and its mission.

Even when we conform with all the decisions of the Reich reform we must not forget that Prussia is still present for the time being as an important financial and administrative unit. When other places storm and press (for complete unification of Prussia with the Reich), then Adolf Hitler points again and again to the development in the other lands (of the Reich) and cautions patience. On closer inspection it becomes obvious that the question of Reich reform is for the present really a Prussian matter. The other states have more or less ready-made frontiers of future Reich provinces, but the great Prussia has to be dissolved into a number of provinces. When this is done there stands the basis of Reich reform. Growing out of this subdivision there arose the necessity, if unity was to be achieved, to reshuffle the Reich and Prussian cabinets—finding expression in the fact that several departments, because of their scope, were taken over by Reich Ministers. In the other states these adjustments were not necessary. This state or that state may be called upon to give up certain territories—perhaps Bavaria may be divided into two or three provinces, but no state will be like Prussia, which, because of its size, will have to be divided into a large number of provinces. That the Leader has clearly stated and must come about and he has given me the task in the course of the next ten years to complete the equalisation of territories, the co-ordination of the Prussian Ministries with those of the Reich and to divide Prussia into Reich provinces, which will be named by himself.

In the decade which the Leader has given me or in such time, which he now thinks to be longer than ten years—we hope that it will be achieved sooner—as it will take to co-ordinate Prussia with the Reich—Prussia remains a state and will be administered as such. Therefore it is highly necessary that you do not abate your efforts, for now more than ever it becomes increasingly necessary that you make proposals to us, so that the task of merging Prussia into the Reich will be solved as soon as possible. Your work and your tasks have not finished, but I would say, they have become greater and of more importance, because your work no longer stands on a local idea of a state, but is far above it—the higher idea of Germany. This task we have to fulfil.

In the meantime Prussia must be exactly and cleanly administered, as during the past eighteen months. In this coming decade of reform there must be no loophole—no hollow space, the existence of which would be damaging for further development.

The task of the state government will be to see that the machine of state runs faultlessly, as before, and that one day in the future it will, without creating any disturbance, become part of the machinery of the Reich,—but we have all to help in order to bring this about.

I know that one of the questions causing disturbance in the minds of many, is the question of how the Reich provinces will be frontiered off. I believe that I must state two things very carefully in this regard : In the first place we have provinces in Prussia, a number of which already have the form of future Reich provinces. No one will be in doubt as to how the province ' East Prussia ' will look. I also believe that there will be little difficulty in finding an appropriate form to fit the Reich province ' Brandenburg ' and it will also be more or less clear about the shape and extent of the province of ' Pomerania.' ' Silesia,' too, will give no great difficulty. In regard to the others, then of course things become a little more difficult. For the rest, one will of course consider the existing frontiers of the present states when arranging the Reich provinces.

Secondly, I advise, insofar as it is a matter of frontiers, to drop all proposals for future Reich provinces and to look upon the problem from the point of view that no one is better qualified than the Leader to decide the final settlements. He will be advised by a board specially chosen for this purpose.

That will create the necessary peace. The Leader will not consider the individual nor the local point of view, for he is guided by the thought for the country as a whole. So when he is going to create a territorial definition of the Reich, he will do so for the reason that the structure will have to last for centuries—aye, thousands of years.

For the rest, I leave no doubt in your minds that I, as far as I can do something in this matter and am allowed to inform the Leader of it, will always see to it that never again shall be created a foundation so weak that in later years these provinces will be turned into lands again threatening to burst the unity of the Reich. I can already see the seed for such a scattering about in the all too strict frontiers of the different tribes.[1]

When to-day we praise one land or the other (in the German speaking countries) it is because in the past the tribes have been well mixed in the dynastic interest, and it is on these lands that to-day we have been able to form one Reich. The construction and organisation of the provinces must be further handled in such a manner as to preserve the unity of the Reich, independently of all possibilities of development. Another problem in mind is the distribution of the tasks between the Reich and the provinces. This question, by its nature, becomes at once the most difficult and yet the most important. Territorially, the new organisations will stand in the closest connection with the Reich. The Reich must have a sovereign position, with all the authority necessary for a powerful appearance, internally and externally. Providing this supposition is fulfilled, I naturally agree that the provinces should be so equipped as to fit them to carry as much responsibility of government on their shoulders as possible, and so that the provincial governors will be adequately employed. We will also have to beware of a too extravagant centralisation. The German people as a whole, have no time for such centralisation—it does not fit the German people. Therefore, everywhere, as far as it is possible without endangering the unity of the Reich, one

[1] Like Saxons, Bavarians, Rhinelanders, etc.

will have to give to the provinces a certain independence. But everywhere, presupposing the power of the Reich as a basis of unity, the writ of the Reich alone will run. For the rest, in distributing tasks between Reich and province, one will have to consider the financial position of the future province.

The Finance Minister has in mind to explain certain matters in this direction, which will prove that in the matter of currency, to-day there is no Prussian province which is financially independent.

The creation of the new Reich provinces is also bound up inseparably with finance co-ordination and from this problem there already clearly appears the fact that the Reich must, in this sphere, have the right to dictate.

You can be assured that I, as the Prussian Prime Minister, affected as I am more than any other head of state by problems of Reich reform, will lay special emphasis on these things and that the whole state government will be led by me in all its official dealings, with regard to the future development of the Reich and the ultimate development of Germany, to the stage where it will be the perfect unitarian state.[1] Therefore I ask you to take up this task in that same spirit and work within the council of state for the future.

Next to the problems of territorial rearrangement and the distribution of duties, comes the question of the task which the (Nazi) movement is called upon to fulfil for the people and for the Reich. This is of tremendous importance in the reconstruction of the Reich. On this question the Leader alone can speak the deciding word, for in his iron hands all threads run together and must run together. He has the supreme leadership in the Reich, for it is his own idea that we are following when we speak of a united Reich. For that he has laboured for fifteen years. For that he created the supposition for a united Reich, for that he created a united people out of a torn nation. In all this, Prussia will help him and will do its utmost to discharge the duties imposed upon it.

I would not like to conclude my explanations without at least touching one common political question. I come here

---

[1] Used in the sense of centralised.

to a, let us say, important and yet an awkward point. I hear so often : The animation (for the Nazi revolution) has run down, dissatisfaction flickers here and there. When one observes these things properly, then one will recognise that, without doubt, there is cause for dissatisfaction here and there. But these are, after all, only individual and isolated cases, even although they may appear as typical cases. Much worse, however, is the systematic dissatisfaction which will criticise everywhere and everything. We must first realise that it is only one and a half years ago that we came to office and power. Our first experiences then were an impulsive feeling of freedom and a breathing again as after having carried a heavy burden. An awakening after darkest night and looking upon the glaring light. The workman saw that he was no longer ostracised, but that once more he was again a member in the family of Germany, that all the dividing factors had fallen away. There was a buoyancy and enthusiasm, but that was natural. It is just as natural that such an enthusiasm cannot continue as an everyday feeling. High moods must keep for certain times. Then they will echo long and will be repeated. That they will come again and again must be our care. We must take care that the contact with the people does not become lost. By that I mean that we shall not just make speeches to the people when we need them—when they shall vote at election time, but that the people must be able to see us often and to feel the contact. I do not think that it will have to be a matter of appearing before them among masses of people, who in any case have already the spark of excitement in them. I believe that a far better purpose will be served if the leaders of the people and of the movement, not only call meetings, but turn up unexpectedly in different places and inquire into the cares and needs of the people. That I believe to be necessary, in order that the people will feel that we really look after them. On the other hand, we will strain all our strength to remove just causes of dissatisfaction. We must act harshly against those people who cannot become accustomed to the new state and who believe, with their eternal criticism, nagging and whisperings, that they can undermine the new foundation of the state, slowly and surely.

Who has the right of criticism at all ? In my opinion, only the person who is able at all times and willing to make or do better the things he criticised. When people complain to-day that we have criticised in the last ten years all that the opposition had done, we will tell them : Yes, we criticised, but we were ready every day to step to the front and to prove that we could improve upon what we had criticised. For the rest I can see one danger only, which could disturb us in the rebuilding of the tremendous structure which we are about to erect, no matter if it is in the realms of justice, culture or administration : and that is the need for more faith. Once that faith is shaken then the platform on which we are building is not only falling in, but everything will be destroyed.

We can bear everything—we can climb down in difficult times and we can rise again to the heights of light, but the faith of the people must be unshakable.

We have conquered this faith in a heavy struggle and we have had spilled too much noble blood for us lightly to give it up, without a thought

Now a word on the question of the churches. If ever the motto of the great Frederick was true—that everyone should be happy after his own fashion—it must and shall be true now. Adolf Hitler, our Leader, and we old National Socialists, all know one thing—that we will not harm a single person because of his profession (of faith). On the other hand, the state cannot be completely indifferent to what is going on in this sphere. The question to be asked is : Will the Church turn back to its old duty of being an institution supported by the state or will it continue to be the breeding place of criticism, dissatisfaction and nagging. The national socialist state has created one thing, namely, from among the Protestant churches, in view of the necessity of Reich reform, it has pointed the way to a Reich church. The state, very wisely, has not taken the matter into its own hands. After it has stated the norm it has left it to the church to live its own life and to achieve its own unity. I speak not only for Prussia, but I believe that I also speak in the name of all national socialist state leaders and in the name of the Leader too, when I state that we have never even dreamed to lift up the Lutheran, the Reformed or the United Protestant Church above the other or to use the one for the suppression of the others.

It is of no account to the state to which confession or profession the individual belongs. The state will protect all these professions as a whole. And when the Prussian State Church has absorbed up till now, the Reformed, the United and the Lutherans, then I definitely state that these three also belong to the Reich Church and that they are secure there and the state will never tolerate that either of them shall possess different standing in the eyes of the state. On the other hand I would like to warn the priests of the state Church very seriously to bring an end to their eternal fighting, because this fight helps to rob Germany, which up to now was one of the leading Lutheran countries in the world and from whence the ideas of Luther went out to the world, of the leadership that it so far has attained. We ask and require that at last there shall be peace and satisfaction in church matters and that church-goers shall not be further disturbed by these squabbles within the Prussian State Church.

Now to end on a short word of foreign politics. In this field I believe that our Leader has created one masterpiece after the other. When we are told to-day that the one of the other measure is the cause of the boycott by other countries —well, gentlemen, do you believe that countries abroad, just because the Third Reich has appeared, have to take care that this Third Reich shall from now on prosper and flourish economically ?

Only recently we have passed two stepping stones. The pact with Poland and the singularly successful conference of the Leader at Venice, which we hope will lead to glorious work together of the two nations.

So I can see also that foreign politics are well developing a progressive pace. We will not stand still, but will do our work and will not be retarded by anything in our striving to maintain our freedom and our honour. Then we will also overcome our difficulties. When one looks at these things, no doubt can remain that, outside of local and immediate causes, there is no foundation for serious dissatisfaction. The use of new and perhaps more radical methods would lead to hardly any improvement.

It does not lie with us to say if a second revolution is necessary. The first revolution was ordered by the Leader and finished by him. If the Leader wishes a second revolution, we stand to-morrow, if he wants us, in the streets. If he wishes no further action we will suppress every one who wants to make a second revolution against the wishes of the Leader.[1]

That is the idea which everyone must take as his own idea, for about things touching the machinery of state as a whole in its fundamentals, only the Leader has the right to say the final word. I also want to accentuate the following : As much as we would never dare to venture without the Leader to undertake a revolutionary act, so I wish on the other hand, to leave no doubt in the minds of any that we watch keenly and observe all. Further, we will not tolerate that all these things for which we struggled in this revolution, shall be destroyed behind our backs by lower orders or by the purposely misconstruing of legislation. From this perhaps may spring sabotage and it will lie with you to stop such sabotage at the right time.

Often the question is posed to us—what is to be understood by real national socialism ? I would like to repeat to you, word for word, the very sentence spoken by the Leader at the Labour Front Congress : " Nothing else than that for the upkeep of our community, the highest abilities in every walk of life shall be put exclusively at the disposal of the state."

This sentence is fundamental. It is, through the authority of the Leader, who has given us the idea, clearly and thoroughly stated. And now it depends upon everyone to give of his utmost—to fulfil the best and highest tasks for the unity of the German people and the state. This means also the setting on one side of every special wish. I need not emphasise that we expect the utmost from all party functionaries and state officials and that we ask of them that they

---

[1] This is one of the very outspoken warnings given by Göring about this time to Roehm, Papen and others involved in the 30th June, 1934, purge and discussed in *Göring, the Iron Man of Germany*, Blood-Ryan. John Long, Ltd.

discharge their official duties in such a manner as will give a model to the whole people.

When we go along these lines then we shall be successful in keeping the enemy of the state down on the ground to where we have forced him. The danger of communism is just as great as we allow it to grow. It lies with us to limit the activities of this danger. When we will, the danger will be no longer present—neglect it and it will be able to grow ! I do not need to point out what is necessary for the destruction of enemies of the state. By appointing the Reich leader of the S.S.,[1] an old and proven fighter of the movement to direct the Gestapo, the line of activity is already indicated.

Summing up, I would like to say : The national socialist state—or better still—the national socialist movement within the nation, is as much as ever on the march forward.

Tremendous things have been done. More tremendous achievements await us.

The task of Prussia is clear. I have stated it in my explanation and ask you to look upon it as a line which you have to follow and as a compass by which to steer. When we do that then we will reach our utmost aim and no one can do more than to put all his heart and soul into it. That shall be our oath and we will also commence the session of the council of state by showing what we think of the man to whom we are all obligated and who has created for us all this, without which and without whom, we would be nothing, without whom no new Germany could have arisen and in whose strong hands lies the destiny of Germany and its people. Three cheers for our Leader, the great German chancellor !

[1] Heinrich Himmler. Chief of the state secret police.

SPEECH AT THE CONCLUSION OF THE ANNUAL COMPETETIVE FLIGHT ROUND GERMANY, 24th June, 1934.

COMRADES ! After the finish of a very strenuous flight, it is a very special pleasure to me to give the prizes to the victors in the round-Germany-flight, 1934. Last year I laid great stress on the point that the achievement of the individual pilot and his reward must not be over esteemed, as it was in the past. I have asked of you, that instead of striving for individual success you should train in future for achievement in association with others, for relay races. In repeating that request I do not wish to underestimate solo flying. There are two reasons why only relay races are counting for trophies this year.

In the first place, I wanted to create a closer association between the pilots themselves. I sought still further to impress on all pilots, the spirit that in four years of heroic life proved so successful and singled out German flying during the war—the team spirit among the crews.

Secondly, in the national socialist state of to-day, it is of the greatest value that no one looks upon his labours as an individual worker. At last the people have been united into one well of strength, from which alone in the future can we draw our success. In times like these, it is natural that German air transport should look beyond the individual in its aim of united achievement. Joint work must take the place of individual effort. My comrades ! We must admit that after the dissolution of the old German air service it was impossible to carry on the old spirit of comradeship in disciplined form. Most of us were uprooted from our work and the air service remained only as a wonderful dream. The terrible longing for flying nevertheless remained in all of you The new Reich has ordained that flying, even in the other forms of sporting and civil flying—shall rise again. To bring this about we must create the old spirit of comradeship and this cannot be done by the individual, but care for the comrade and the helping of each other will further this aim.

The flight round Germany this year proves that our policy brings success and shows that we have achieved in German flying a new and firmer unity. Leadership and discipline live again. This year's contest was intended to prove that the individual pilot who wears the honourable coat of the Air Sport Union (*Luftsportverband*) works to this end and that discipline has achieved its aim.

This flight has proved to the German people that flying has reached its old form and that it is inspired by the old (war time) spirit, even if it has to work on other grounds. That much has been achieved and now further work has to be done. Youth shall get encouragement and incentive. The young Germany shall be brought up in a passion for flying in order that the German nation shall become a nation of pilots. Other forms of flying are not allowed us, but I have never left any doubt that things cannot remain like this. Germany cannot stand for it ! At this moment, when the Leader himself stands at the head of German aviation, my own task looms sharply before me. Germany will not attack other nations, but she does not wish to be attacked by other nations. Out of all this must come the old demands : As long as other nations own bombers, Germany must possess an air service which guarantees the security of life and of the nation. That at last other powers will have to see. When one speaks of equality, then one means, primarily, that every nation has the same honour. It is natural, and the other powers must at last understand this, that Germany cannot continue to be discriminated against, as it is at the moment by the denial of the right to possess (military) air craft. I will hope that the negotiations with other powers will be successful and bring as a result an acknowledgement of Germany's right to own defensive air craft which will secure her peace. While the nations around us are bristling with arms and possess thousands of heavy attacking aircraft—which are ready to destroy

Germany in a moment—we renounce the arms of air attack in the realisation that we have to deal with the more important thing of real politics. But we will never renounce the arms of protection !

Comrades ! It is not the material alone that decides the fight. If the material alone was indeed the deciding factor, then it would be purposeless to expose you to even the most minute danger. Quality and quantity of material can always be laid down in conference and by negotiation, but what cannot be limited is the spirit of German flying. No negotiations can define this spirit and it cannot be restricted and stated. It is your duty to keep alive this spirit. You have this duty to the sacrifices that your comrades have made in the greatest struggle of all times. We have the right to honour our heroes and to hold them up as models to the German youth. In no treaty is there a clause which demands the destruction of this spirit, but the cowardly fellows who have made our people unhappy for the last decade and a half, have tried to break this spirit. They not only broke up and destroyed readily every airplane—they were also prepared to disarm morally, spiritually and mentally. Now we have exerted our own spirit against this. This Reich stands and must be maintained by our own spirit. To-day's flight has proven this spirit anew. Exceptionally good work has been put in and a number of examples have shown up the pluck possessed by the teams. With pride I realise the dash and the sporting ambition. I thank the teams for this dash which they have shown and I thank all those of you who organised this flight and who thereby proved, that in quiet work and preparation, a model organisation has been created.

It has been a special satisfaction to all of us here to-day that the flight led our pilots to the place where, from time to time, our leader rests from his hard work. In taking the roses to Obersalzberg, we see a singular compliment from German flying brought to our leader. With pride and pleasure, the leader could himself observe your achievements from his house. This compliment is the natural thanks which we expressed through these achievements. For without Adolf Hitler, where would German pilots and

German air transport be to-day? Where would have gone our dream—our longing, if he had not created the new Germany? Therefore, comrades, before I award the prizes, we will stand and think a moment in silent respect for our leader—our beloved leader—our people's chancellor.

A DEMAND FOR THE PEOPLE'S DECISION TO SUPPORT ADOLF HITLER on his assumption of the office of President of the Reich, the title of which he changed to Leader and Chancellor. *National-Socialistische Korrespondenz*, 19th August, 1934.

WHEN grim fate tore away from us on the 2nd August, 1934, the protector of the Third Reich and the President of the Reich, our Field-Marshal von Hindenburg, sixty-four millions of German people in the Reich stood in silent mourning. The venerable old gentleman had held his protecting hand over the nation, which was threatened. In his old age, which is without equal in German history, he had lived a long life, which was filled with duty, and he was able to see his greatest wish turn to reality—the age-old longing of German man, a united people—a united Germany.

So our Field-Marshal could go into eternity peacefully. Without fears for the future of his people, he slept after he had spoken, shortly before his death, with the leader of the German people, Adolf Hitler, who, sustained by the faith of the aged President and ennobled through the faithful love of the people, will from now on receive the inheritance of Hindenburg and also fill his place. The President could close his eyes in peace, for he knew that his work was in safe hands. In peace and security, too, the German people could mourn their great hero, without worry for the future. There was not one single German who was not clear in his mind as to who should succeed in the inheritance of Hindenburg and who should lead Germany in future. There is only one man—who was sent to the German people by a merciful fate in the hardest time of misery and who is chosen to lead Germany to proud heights : Adolf Hitler !

[*Translated and reproduced in English with acknowledgments to* National-Socialistische Korrespondenz.]

In him, we old front soldiers see the man who gave us back our honour—he who cleansed the proud tradition and the glorious greatness of the past, of which Field-Marshal von Hindenburg was the embodiment—from the dross of the things of the ' sub-man' . It is he whom we see as the bearer of the tradition of the deceased Field-Marshal, connecting the great past with the clean and great ideals of the young Germany, as embodied in the movement which he created. And because Adolf Hitler is as much the representative of great German tradition as the tireless, youthful fighter for the future, German youth sees in him the Leader.

As Adolf Hitler, in our national socialist movement, has moulded the spirit of the old soldier with the youthful dash and revolutionary courage to form one common will, so, as the leader of Germany, he has also created the synthesis between the progressive revolutionary spirit of youth and the indestructible tradition of authoritative state life. As the leader of the national socialist movement, he is as well the leader of the German Reich, for movement and state have become united by his hands.

As a true leader of the nation, Adolf Hitler himself has called for a decision from the people.[1]

Next Sunday the German people will stand behind him as one man and will lay their ' yes ' with an eternal oath in the urn : We, the living, have our Adolf Hitler !

[1] *Volksentscheid*—decision of the people—confirmation of, from the. On this occasion it was for the people to agree, by writing " yes " on the ballot paper, to Hitler's assumption of the leadership of the Reich.

SPEECH TO THE GERMAN ACADEMY OF JUSTICE, 13th November, 1934.

WHEN to-day I am speaking at the German Academy of Justice, then I ask you gentlemen to see in it a strong and firm confession that justice as the foundation of security is fundamental to the unity of the nation. Since the trust of my leader has placed me at the head of affairs in Prussia, I have tried hard to restore this perception of justice and this security of justice, which was shaken to its depths when we came to power.

That great juridical nation of the past, the old Romans, said that the security of justice was the fundament of the state. This axiom was distorted in an epoch which has now passed—it was twisted around in the ' night watchman state '[1] to the effect that the state had nothing to do but to take care of the individual in his own private sphere. The people was a thing unworthy of consideration, alone important was the individual with his egotistical aims—he was secured and protected by justice. We national socialists recognise the importance of justice to the orderly communal life in the state absolutely. To us the individual is not the primary consideration, but the united community of all people. Therefore we call ourselves socialists. Our state was created by the leader for the people, so that the people can live. Our state therefore is not one of self-purpose, but means to a purpose. The national socialist state has the ambition to unite its racially related people into a national unity, into a peoples' unity.

But there is no community of life among people without justice. This is a realisation which our Germanic forefathers had already achieved as the basis of their thoughts and

[1] An opprobrious reference, similar to the English vernacular ' old woman ', implying infirmity, slothfulness or talkativeness.

dealings in political affairs. A thriving life among the community—a healthy life in the people, is only possible when the life of the individual, their manifold relations between and with each other are ordered, when there are firm lines to follow, when laws direct the many wishes and exertions, so that a great sound order is created, which is directed for the life and welfare of the people. Therefore, from the very first day of their assumption of power, national socialists have placed accent on the character of justice in their state and have created and substituted new laws for the insufficient and out-of-date statutes.

Gentlemen ! I know that one can over-reach the foundation of law as such. I want to say one thing beforehand : Not justice as such is primary. First the people were in existence—then the people created the state and the state created its laws for the community of the people. Out of this we can always see again, that always and ever, the people come first and that only out of the people can the state and justice rise and take shape.

Of course, we have not started with a constitution on paper, when we came to power, like the Weimar republic, which was in a great hurry to set bloodless theories to paper and which were strange to the nation. We leave these things to organic growth. We have tried to solve urgent questions of community life through legislation, and have, in doing so, substituted national socialist juristic assets for a great many remainders of justice. Laws which do not fulfil their purpose remain dead letters. Yes. Which even injure rather than help, if the guarantee be not present that they will be everywhere and at all times executed in the sense and for the purpose for which they have been created.

The state must see to it that the laws are truly executed and expertly administered ; it must guarantee to every member of the peoples union—to every single German the purposeful and orderly handling of the law. The first thing is security of justice. Only then can the strength of the nation unfold itself and come to be a blessing, only then can grow among the German people the close united love of people and fatherland. Through trust and through the proper understanding of each other and through the helping of each other, the people's unity can take on substance. When every German can live in the certainty that his person is respected and given protection in the great community, when he knows that first and foremost his honour is being protected, and that which he has acquired through work and that which he may have inherited from his fathers, is secure —then indeed we have justice.

Gentlemen ! The past epoch never acknowledged the foremost and sufficient means for the protection of honour, while all other things were protected. Every encroachment by the capitalist kind could find the protection of the law, but there was no protection for the honour of the individual. The newspapers tore and tattered the honour of the individual. Buckets of dirt could be poured over people even in the highest positions. Honour counted for nothing and when a man who knew in his heart that his honour was his most cherished possession, took the means of self-defence of this honour into his own hands, then he was sent to prison as a common criminal. Therefore legal protection of personal honour is one of the most important points in juristic security.

Security of justice is therefore the basis of every national community.

That especially goes for the national socialist state, which is governed by the spirit of the old Germans—the form of life related to German race along the lines of the feudal followers' law. This form of living consists not in fear and suppression, but stands firm because it is the contrary to despotism and arbitrariness. Its foundation is the exchange of faith between leader and followers. The order of this state is founded on an unshakable belief in this state idea and on faith and trust.

But there can be no faith of the followers, if every single person out there on the land does not know that the leader is always active through his chosen organisations, to fulfil the eternally living claim for justice—of putting reality into the law and bringing fulfilment in that law.

Every single follower has the right to make this claim. But he has not got it of and for himself—not because of his egotistical aims—but he possesses it as a member—as a part of the band of followers, as a part of the community, for which the state exists at all and for which laws are only made. The right of the individual to demand orderly execution of laws can never over-ride this communal claim. Here the claim finds a frontier which, for national socialism, is impassable. It is quite out of the question for the national socialist state to use its organisations and its powerful means, in order to protect him in his aims who seeks to obtain something that is harmful to the nation. The landlord, who in hard-hearted fashion, unscrupulously seizes the homes of poor people, has lost the protection and sanction of the state for his activities, for even though he may appear to have law on his side, he is working against the fundamental law of national unity. You all know the sort to which I refer—the cases are absolutely shocking and from the humanitarian point of view, the activities of these people are not understandable. I assure you that I will proceed ruthlessly against them in order to put a stop to this sort of thing.

Justice must be as purposeful as the state, and no state which wants to be true to its kind and purpose will allow itself to give protection and encouragement to those who, by their dealings, are working against the fundamental thought and purpose of the state. The past liberal state allowed itself to be used in this way most shamefully. In doing so, it made the people unhappy and led it to the edge of a precipice. But I decline to stand protectingly in front of anti-social exploiters and usurers, for whom there is no room in our national community.

Every single person has the right to claim the protection of the law, but only as long as he moves about inside the community as a real compatriot in the truest sense of the word. He who by his deeds puts himself outside the community, he who is proved as having fought against the national interest, he who betrays the state and thereby the community, puts himself outside the law and loses his right to protection. The state created its laws in order to guarantee the life of the community, and not to give help and protection to those whose aim is to undermine and destroy the state and the community of which it is the embodiment. I know, gentlemen, that in judicial circles offence will be

H

taken at my remarks and you will say that justice must remain justice—even the criminal must have justice and he must be judged through competent laws—that only the competent court can sit in judgement on him and that only the state can intervene with its power to do away with anti-social elements within it ; that any interference with legislation by the people comes within the category of lynch-law.

Without doubt you will be right, fundamentally, but I would like to draw your attention to one thing : These things have been done already in distant times. At that time, when everyone carried in his breast the feeling for justice so much more stronger than to-day, there was a thing known as the ' ban '. One put to the ban certain anti-social elements and one spoke them free as a bird,[1] and in doing so one placed them outside the law.

This ban not only empowered the courts to execute him, but it gave to every man the right to do so. For killing a man one could not be punished in law, because the other, through the ban, was not a thing in law and was therefore without its protection. Our early ancestors declared such enemies of the state as peaceless,[2] while in the middle ages they were put to the ban. We also turn out these disturbing elements in the state and have given form to the idea of justice by reviving the old law in more human form, yet retaining, and indeed modelling on, the old germanic idea of outlawry.[3]

But we must take care, as I mentioned before, that we do not over-reach justice and thus destroy the feeling for justice in the people. Laws must be so framed that they find approval and echo inside the individual man and that justice does not simply lie up in the clouds,—perfectly incomprehensible. Laws must not be thought out in judicial dryness, but they must be always full of blood and content and demonstrate a lively connection with the people. I believe

---

[1] *Vogelfrei*. This meant that a person put to the ban, usually of the Emperor but sometimes by the Pope or lesser king, for any offence ranging from treason to heresy was fair game to be shot at by all who came across him and that he was an outlaw.

[2] Doomed to live a hunted existence.

[3] *Ausbürgerungsparagraph*—more fittingly described as disenfranchisement act.

that it would be healthier if justice itself could be framed by the people themselves—that is by representatives of the people—and then that justice used by lawyers who have ascertained the wishes of the people, rather than by jurists who are just dry-as-dust experts.

He who is a true member of this national community and arranges his dealings and doings in accordance with the written and unwritten laws of the community—and the unwritten laws are mostly the oldest and, morally, the deeper fundamentally—he has a claim on the state, which must see to it that the trust which he reposes in it will be appreciated and that the trust will not be misplaced—that he will have justice.

The German has always been a just thinking and feeling person. To him, law and order are prime necessities of life. It is not just chance that one of the most germanic poets, Heinrich von Kleist, created the figure of Michael Kohlhaas, who was a fanatic for justice, and who pressed for his rights out of his own convictions, to the utmost. Kohlhaas saw in his ' right ' an important part of his life. In every German there is to be found a little bit of Michael Kohlhaas. It is also remarkable which anecdote of our most germanic king, Frederick the Great, is best known and most often recounted. It is the story of the miller of Sanssouci.[1] The king shrank from the thought of calling the miller to the Star Chamber, for he was the protector of Prussian justice. He did not do so, not because he had no power to have his wish observed, but because he possessed the feeling for security of justice and because this feeling and respect for law was greater than his personal interest in the small mill. So at all times the German has a deep and sincere longing for justice. We know that we cannot satisfy this longing absolutely ; we are

[1] The miller had a mill directly in front of the window of the king's working room in the palace of Sanssouci and its clatter frequently disturbed the king at his work. One day, when Frederick could bear the disturbance no further, he went to the miller and offered to buy the mill from him, but the miller refused to sell, saying that he had inherited it from his father and his father had received it through a long line of peasant proprietors. At first Frederick was furious, but when he returned to his study and thought the matter over, he saw how right the simple miller had been and refrained from either bringing him before the court or ejecting him from the mill, which latter course would have been, in those days, more kingly conduct. The mill stands to this day near the palace and is used as a refreshment kiosk.

human and are therefore governed by human errors, passions, confusions and mistakes, but we must never omit, in all our dealings, to come as near as possible to the absolute satisfaction of this longing. The most perfect law, the best intentions, and the most wonderful organisation, will not prevent some people being dissatisfied by justice. That lies in the nature of things. Such instances will, and must, only prove exceptions and these isolated cases will not jeopardise the security of justice or the feeling of security in the law.

In spite of everything, there are cases to-day in which fair-minded citizens believe that an injustice has been done them, when it appears that a decision of the state affects their rights. But when one looks closer, one sees the mistake of this conception. The person in question fails to see that everything does not happen for his benefit, but for the sake of the nation. It is an absolute and inexorable outcome of the law of the community that sometimes even the decent individual must suffer for the good of the community. It is unbearable in any healthy and natural national community, if the decent patriot is to be obsessed by the feeling that he is defenceless against certain attacks, that his security lies in the arbitrary decision of unauthorised persons. That would mean not national community, but arbitrary rulership ; it would mean not the strength and joy of life which had been fought for ambitiously, not trust and belief, but paralysing distrust and fear. Such a state of affairs must be ruthlessly done away with. Therefore already, in March of this year, I have uncompromisingly, without regard to the position of the persons involved, adopted my own measures, when I learned that in Stettin, innocent people had been unjustly treated because of empty suspicions. How unbearable this can become, when a compatriot has to fear for his own safety and for the safety of his family, just because he is seeking in a lawful manner to obtain his just rights. He who has a well-founded claim on justice must make known his claim in the approved fashion, against whoever it may be directed.

It is also impossible—I remarked upon this already, on the 12th June, in my speech to the public prosecutors of Prussia, in a manner which cannot be misunderstood—for any person who holds high office or a leading position in the state, who uses it as a means to upset the laws of the national socialist state,—and in so doing, injures the Leader down to the smallest compatriot,—to go unpunished.

Furthermore, it is impossible for the law to apply to one section of the community and not to the other, for no one section shall enjoy a better position than the other. Such a condition would bring about a rift in community life which could never be bridged and its continuance would prove a deadly germ for every kind of justice, and also for every sort of community. A community consisting of a variety of classes is really built up on trust and respect, and this is only possible when all, really all, parts of that community are safe in the certainty that the law is equal for all. This idea of equality, however, is different to us national socialists than the liberal idea of equality before the law. It makes no difference to the lower classes in its application, but it affects the others. We do not want to hang the small fry and let the big fish go scot-free. We want to put our hands on those who did the most damage particularly. The Leader has given expression to this fundamental of national socialism in his nine points, which have been explained in a classical manner.[1] That does not mean that all laws at all times have to be considered without regard to the special conditions inherent in each individual case. The organisations of the state charged with the administration of the law and the control of justice must always have before them the reminder that they do not just apply laws for the sake of law, but that they discharge their functions in order to do justice. The sense and spirit is more important than the letter of the law. Here again, I would like to strike a note of warning against the exaggeration of justice. When I am told that justice is eternal, that everything could crumble, but not justice— then I can only say that justice changes daily.

How often does it happen that what was right yesterday will be wrong to-morrow? In single instances law may be altered, but one thing remains permanent ; not the letter of the law, not the letter of justice, but the feeling of right—

[1] A reference to that section of the official programme of the N.S.D.A.P. dealing with war profiteers, usurers, loan capital, race and the more particular aspects of capitalism.

that remains eternal—the feeling, the longing for what is right, and belief in justice. Therefore it must not be exaggerated in law and decree.

The moral right remains eternal.

The eternal right—the moral right, has been for centuries anchored in the bosom of the human race. It grows from father into son and is therefore born of the blood of a nation. Therefore the race and blood related peoples have their laws and understand them. You would hardly find people in the South Seas who would understand nordic-germanic justice. What is justice to them and understood by them as such, is incomprehensible to us and is frowned upon. Blood speaks its own language. The basic language it knows is a language of justice fundamental in a connection and union of all race related peoples.

One often hears : The world may disappear if only justice may remain. No ! The law is senseless when the world has disappeared. Should one law disappear, then another can be made, but when the world vanishes everything sinks. Or one hears : Nations may disappear. No ! Nations are primary and carry their laws unwritten as their holiest possession in their breast.

Gentlemen, we have seen terrible injustice done in civil law.[1] Go out among the people and ask them if the civil law, which grew out of the capitalistic focus, did not secure the rights of the profiteer and imposed itself upon the little man. This branch of law will never be understood by the people. It insults their inherent sense of justice. The people cannot understand why someone should dig out of the old forgotten tomes, a statute which had been forgotten to be repealed, and thus, by virtually creating law, perpetrates an injustice. Listen to the Homeric songs of two pleaders and you will understand what is law and what is twisted justice. A healthy and clear justice must really be represented by the individual himself. In true justice there is no need for a pleader. I am secure at court, not through the special ability and eloquence of my pleader, but alone through my right with which I am standing before the judge.

Gentlemen, what a dreary picture present-day justice,

[1] *Privatrecht.*

even now, presents. What a thought—when everyone knows that he can only obtain his right if his banking account is large enough. What hope for the little man, when he knows that he cannot go to an appeal against the primary judgement because he cannot foot the bill. The little man already knows that his opponent with the fatter purse and the longer breathing space is bound to win any action. What have we not experienced so far in this matter of capitalistic profiteering. If anything should be free of cost to all, then it should be the representation of true justice in the national community.

Gentlemen ! Do not hold it against me that if my suggestion was followed, we would have a flood of cases and that the judges would be swamped under. I am of the opinion, gentlemen, that this apparent danger could be omitted if you punish a person who brings an action carelessly. You would then arrive at the same speed as at present, but with greater justice. So I am hoping, and I am convinced that the national socialist state, and particularly the creation of this Academy of Justice in the national socialist spirit—will bring about fundamental changes in this dreary territory (of law) and in so doing will strengthen and promote the feeling for justice as fundamental to a real people's community.

Gentlemen, there may arise circumstances, both at present and in the future, in which the application of the existing laws brings about great injustice. The use of the law in such cases must not be purposely omitted, for the judges and the administration are bound to the law as if it were the written will of the Leader, and consequently, any deliberate omission or deviation from the law would be injurious to the people and would bring about injustice and a sense of insecurity in justice. But, in such cases we must expect from the organisation entrusted with administration of the law, that they find opportunity to enable them to be merciful and to find a way out in extenuation. For instance, I found it to be unjust that a man, who during the early months of our taking over power, out of excess of zeal, offended against the then powerful laws and was executed by those laws, which were intended for application in normal times.

Revolution means fighting, and revolutionary fighting, sometimes out of necessity, leads to lawlessness. No nation on earth can sit in judgement on us, because during the time of this struggle, here and there things happened which could never happen in peaceable times. Revolutions in other nations lead to disorder and licentiousness. The national socialist revolution has been carried through with tremendous discipline and lawfulness. Therefore it seemed to me madness and in opposition to ideas of true justice, to punish those who, out of zealousness, may have become too hot-blooded in pointing to the laws which they themselves helped to create.

Arising out of this, I have empowered the Prussian Minister of Justice to abolish by law, penalties for certain punishable offences, which had been committed during the struggle leading up to the foundation of the national socialist state, that is, before 15th June, 1933,[1] and I know that these measures have proved a blessing to many, have hindered much internal injustice and have helped the national socialist fighter to keep his belief in the faith and justice of his leaders. The Leader, in the meantime, has declared the revolution to be at an end. We have fought our way to an orderly structure. By his amnesty decree of 7th August, 1934, the Leader has once again shown his mercy in a noble-hearted fashion. He who goes against the law, deals a blow at the will of the Leader, deals a blow at the movement, the concept of state and against our philosophy (*Weltanschauung*). In doing so, he injures his most holy duty of keeping faith with the Leader, for obedience is implicit in the faith of our followers. He also strikes at our national unity, which is sustained by the will and spirit of our Leader. This applies to all—to every compatriot. It is not possible that an individual who has earned distinctions for service to the state and the people, can now place himself above the law because of those distinctions. That would mean the end of all security of justice—that would mean naked arbitrariness, bringing in

---

[1] This date corresponds with the official end of the revolution. Hitler, in a proclamation to the Nazi movement, said in effect : " The revolution is over —back to normality," and proceeded to break down the power of Roehm and the S.A. by sending the whole brown shirt army on indefinite furlough. After the purge of 1934 he reiterated that the revolution was ended.

its train the end of national community. We pure national socialists, during the long years of struggle, have learned from our Leader to serve the cause unselfishly and disinterestedly only because of one thing—the great holy love of the German people—the German national community. We have not fought to gain advantage over others. If we had done this, we would not have earned the name of honest fighters, we would not have earned the respect for us and for our fight—which to-day we can demand, and which we do demand.

For us in our fight only the law of our Leader is important, the great law which means : ' To do everything for the people, in every task to think only of the people and its community.' If we forget this law, then the events of the middle of this year, which stand out in shocking clarity, point to where it leads.[1] The harsh and conclusive action of our Leader was then necessary, in order to avoid the destruction of the security of justice, and in order to rescue the national community, which was threatened by it.

Gentlemen ! How much has this greatest act of justice been misunderstood abroad. How much have they tried to expound the view, that here in this instance, arbitrariness ruled, and that we have executed without resource to courts of law and many other things further. Gentlemen, for the German people this chapter is finished. Through the word of the judge of that hour, the Leader, who declared that in that hour of danger, he alone, the Leader chosen by the people, was the highest and only judge of the German nation. The relief of the whole nation, its agreement with what was done and the enthusiasm shown for the Leader in those days, was a clearer testimonial for the feeling of justice than anything else would have been. Therefore I once more ask the judges and public prosecutors to deal with the position to-day with special tact. You all have a most important task, which is very difficult, but also terribly necessary. We are still, that is most of us, thinking back to the long years of fighting against a state which we have now overthrown and whose laws we do not recognise. Because of this, there lies slumbering in some of our fighters, the feeling that they were

[1] 30th June, 1934.

treated unjustly by the past government and that the injustice was inflicted by judges still in office to-day.

Gentlemen ! You might just try, for one moment, to put yourself in the shoes of these little fighters and from that you may realise the importance of the task you have before you in trying to keep the national community together. On the one side, you must let the strict letter of the law speak, while on the other hand, you must not abuse the authority which we have given you. It has happened with certain judges, that they in their hearts refused to recognise the national community, or refused to acknowledge the national socialist state, and they inflicted the utmost harshness of the law, especially against national socialists. Much of our work which we are doing in the rebuilding of the state, much of our talking and preaching in order to strengthen the feeling for justice in the German people and in order to lead justice back into its old channels of security, are being destroyed if injustice causes the individual in our movement to think : My punishment will be of the hardest, not because of the deed I have committed, but because I am a national socialist and it is not I that is sought to be hurt, but the movement. Well then, I say : if this temper gets about, a dangerous spark is being lighted and if ever I should have the feeling that this is being encouraged purposely, then I say that this comes within the realms of treason. If the individual, through the judges holding firmly to the letter of the law, even if the law says it ten times over and even if the judges may say it ten times over, that the sentence is being pro-nounced because it is demanded by the statute, although to the judges and to the mass of people it appears to be against their sense of equality, feels that in ignoring his plight his Leader has deserted and betrayed him, and that he is to be hunted as in Brüning's time under Groener, just· because he is a national socialist, then of course justice has disappeared and with it the individual's belief in justice.

There, I say to you all, that it lies in the hands of you judges and public prosecutors to build up, in conjunction with us, the new security of justice, from all angles, but in the national socialist spirit. National unity, gentlemen, asks for unselfishness. It also asks for faith and helpful understanding of every single person by his fellow-compatriots.

Gentlemen ! Once more I come to an important chapter of the liberal past and of the past system. Misplaced humanity and false mildness only help to undermine the conception of justice and security in justice. Read the records of judgements given in the courts against the worst type of criminal, against murderers and robbers and you will find, no matter if the crime was done with the greatest brutality and cunning, that in the main, pardons were issued, but at the same time nothing was done to help those people who fought for their freedom. While they could be shot at or murdered from some hide-out and nothing done to protect them, one by one murderers were being pardoned. Such a condition naturally undermines justice. There you can no longer speak of the feeling for justice in the people and security is destroyed once more for another reason. Put yourself in the position of a taxi-driver who is asked at night to drive into some dark lonely suburb, not knowing if his fare is a decent man or a murderer. Think of yourself as a bank messenger or a postman, who knows that his colleagues are butchered without the murderer being executed. No ! gentlemen, misplaced leniency has at all times destroyed the security of justice, and has undermined the state itself. Just as much as one must not pronounce eternal condemnation upon a person who has once fallen, as much as one must always and in every case reform that man and make of him a respectable member of the community, one must draw the line somewhere—for somewhere there is a frontier which cannot be crossed. He who has no respect for the life of another and murders his fellow-man for ridiculous gain or to remove him because he stands in his way, he has lost the right to live. Is it justice or in conformity with a sense of justice, that these murderers for gain shall be a burden on the tax payer, living as they do behind prison bars ? I think not, gentlemen. This is where leniency is misunderstood.

Therefore, from the first day onward, I have sworn ruthless measures against all those who, out of self-gain and anti-social proclivities, disturb or endanger the community. On principle, I have refused mercy to persons who have spilled blood—who have murdered. And the success ? Look at the statistics. Compare the murders with robbery before we came to power and now, and you will then realise that in one month alone in the year 1932, there were more murders with robbery in Berlin alone than in the whole of Prussia in the complete year 1933. I am of the opinion that this record speaks plain language, and indicates to us what has to happen if we are to guarantee security of justice for the nation.

No person in the nation can feel safe if the murderer of a bank messenger is being pardoned. Not one of us can have a sense of justice, if the man who first raped a girl, and then murdered her, is to escape the punishment for his deed. No ! Here again the eternal longing for right that is lodged deeply in the breast of every human being finds its expression. It is the real and true sense of justice and is the foundation of any national community. Therefore I have refused to pardon many cases of anti-social elements, who by law and through justice have lost their heads. Therefore, I have put a stop to the ridiculous nonsense of the alleged pathological case, and the method of treatment of criminals who have been influenced by wrong unhealthy human ideas, and I have seen to it that punishment is punishment once again. I have demanded from my officials, again and again, that they do their duty ruthlessly, without care for their own person. Their duty is to work entirely with all their might to safeguard the national community, and to ensure that every member of that community is protected in his person and is secured his fair measure of justice and can live in it himself and for the benefit of the community.

The national socialists have no understanding of overpoised law puzzles. We deny rights to naggers and informers and we will not give them the opportunity to enlarge their bothersome and dangerous leanings. We do not call it security of justice, when the state places all its powers and organisations faithfully at the disposal of those who fight against the state and its purpose. To us that is no security for justice, but a crime against the nation and its community. We will do everything to serve this community, in order to secure for every member of it a place in which to live, freedom of life, security of life. We will guarantee joy in work and life, and the right to live and work as a member of the community. That becomes the embodiment of justice, which has always lived deep down in every German human being, and which we understand. This security of justice we will once more strengthen and stabilise for everybody and for all comers.

In the fight against false justice and lawlessness, Adolf Hitler has created the Third Reich. As long as everybody takes care that it goes into history as the Reich of Justice, with the old Prussian motto *Suum cuique* (every man his due), all will be well.

A SPEECH APPEALING FOR THE WINTER HELP
FUND in the Krupp Works at Essen on 4th December,
1934, in which the blessing of national community is
the theme.

MY dear German compatriots ! It is a peculiar feeling
to speak on a Sunday morning in a hall, which on
other days of the week is devoted to work and
creation, in the heart of a place, which proves as no other,
what German work can do in the creative sphere. And here
in front of me you all stand in unity, who live, year in, year
out, for your work, duty and service to the factory. And
believe me, if this is a change for you from the monotony of
life and as such may be remembered by you, it is for me
equally a change ; it is an experience of strength and power
such as you probably cannot imagine, for out of all you
thousands of workmen comes the strength which we need
to work for and serve the people. We are one—leaders and
followers, and that must be strengthened still further, so that
the leaders stand in the midst of the people, that they lead
the people and that they talk over with the people the great
and important things which have to-day become matters
of destiny for the German people.

In past times of the ' system,' compatriots, you were often
asked to attend meetings. But in those meetings there was
more often than not a whipping up of hatred or else the
talk was about economic difficulties. In long speeches, small
matters of no importance were made much of. They always
forgot that there was the nation standing in the grip of a
ruthless fate. That it was solely a question of to be, or not to
be, for the German people, and that no one could be an
exception, that they could never rescue Germany by telling
one class or another that their limited programme was the
foundation for the reconstruction of the whole nation.

Today we do not come here in order to speak to the people about the water rate or the dog-tax, but to tell the people again and again what a great wonder has happened in a newly risen Germany, and to drive home to all that we must faithfully care for and keep this holy possession of unity in our nation, so that it shall never be robbed from us again. To-day we stand before the whole nation, in order to put questions before them for resolution, questions which are not important to one class or one profession, but which have become matters of destiny for the whole nation. Therefore, compatriots, I am here to-day in order, once again, to render an account to part of a nation—to you—of what has happened and in order to point to the road along which we have to go in future. To-day's meeting is held under the auspices of the Winter Relief, and that, comrades, is not merely any sort of welfare institution. It is not a question that we are organising a sort of bazaar or jumble sale. No ! We want to make it clear to every single person that the winter help is a matter for the whole nation, from the leader down to the last of his followers. And on this name winter help, accent must be placed on the word ' winter '. When you look abroad, you find that they harp upon one theme —you will come again and again across one sentence : ' This Winter of 1934–35 will prove to be the testing time of national socialism. In this winter it will break down completely, for it will not find strength to live through the winter. Should it succeed, then we must make up our minds that national socialism has won the race.' We will prove to everybody that we will win the race, because we have the nerves to go through the winter too. We will make it clear to them that a time of upheaval has come and that we do not help in the sense of alms, but that the winter help has become a duty of the nation and of every single human being in it. For this winter help shall do much to alleviate the inheritance of terrible suffering that we have taken over and it shall do much to build up new things. But, compatriots, we must clearly realise that in the long run it is not just a question of material things. I am convinced that the material things will be forthcoming, in response to the appeal of the leader. But we have a matter of much more

importance. It is a question of realising that the winter
help is in the end only the outward and visible sign of inner
unity in the nation. Not quite two years have passed since
we came to power in the government, and yet, compatriots,
even those who do not want to recognise us, must grudgingly
see and admit one thing ; that a tremendous number of
happenings have followed fast on the heels of each other,
that a lot of things have been done and that we have never
lived so intensely as we have during this time. There arose,
without the individual noticing or feeling it, a brand new
world. One often thinks back and says " Was that only a
year ago ? " " Who was Brüning ? " " Who was Scheide-
mann ? " All those are long since forgotten, because over
them rose a new nation, in the throng of this happening,
this wonder that they all had found each other once more.
A new nation has arisen and with that a new life has started.
Courageously, we are ready to destroy the old ruins and to
erect thereon a new building as a home for our nation.

So this work is really nothing more than the deep realisation that we have to stand together, because one alone can't
do it. We could only achieve the things we did because
Germany is once again united. Believe me it is no megalo-
mania, it is a great heartfelt pride which makes me say :
" Our nation is the greatest the earth has ever seen, if its
full strength is only gathered together in one hand." Its
achievements were such that the other nations, in order to
be fair, had to show respect. Where, compatriots, does world
history show another example in one nation withstanding
the whole world for four years ? Even to-day German
heroism is not forgotten abroad. It will always remain so,
as an impression that cannot be wiped away—aye, for the
whole world to reflect upon how this nation once rose like
a giant. One day this collective strength will recover for us
the cup of victory in the race of the nations for a place in
the sun, because this nation is disciplined and possesses
the will to work such as cannot be found in any other.

But we must always remember and realise that only a
nation which is bound tightly together, in which the individual feels himself tied closely to the community, in which
he does not stand outside, as a cipher only, but lives once

more as a human being like his fellow men, can solve such a difficult problem. Has not this idea of unity been trodden on during the time of the 'system', and were matters before the war much different in this connection? It is most certainly true that social democracy and communism preached the class war to the classes. But did not the other side first of all create the cause for the class fight? Did not the middle class, in the conscious casting on one side of the workman, drive him towards the jewish alien whisperings? If they had first of all felt the same blood relationship, if they had seen in the other first of all, the man of the same blood in the same race, and asked him afterwards which occupation he had—a question which is absolutely unnecessary in the face of the main points of race and people—then the class war would have been impossible. Then the huge rift would have never occurred, which cut the German nation up into many parts.

Out of this disrupted condition, misery had inevitably to grow. How did unemployment come about? How was it possible that millions of compatriots were without work? Was it really the fault of all those many crises—the world economic crisis, the raw material crisis, the export crisis, etc? No! They all have been disturbing to economy, but they have never been the main cause of unemployment. For I have merely to ask, although the crisis is not relaxed in any way, why have we today brought millions of compatriots back to work and bread? Why did just that party which professed to care for the working man, throw them all into misery? Compatriots! If one took from you—from every one who works—the ethos[1] of work and the honour of work, then the ultimate end is unemployment. For if the thesis is laid down that work is not a blessing, but a curse, if one tells the workman : " You are outside the community, you are cursed, you are proletarian because you work with your hands "—then it is only natural that from the very beginning the basis for creative work is destroyed. So we experienced the disaster that a state, which was

[1] Göring used the Greek *ethos*—character. It has been retained in the translation to prevent any ambiguity creeping into the construction of the sentence as a whole.

I

governed by the opinion that work is dishonourable, broke apart in the end and was overwhelmed by misery. The unemployment benefit was then the last resort and the last straw, to which they clung. But how long could they have carried on in this condition ? How could the situation have been held if the unemployed rose by one million, another million and so on, until the remainder who worked diminished more in number than those who were without work ? Here was a matter for us to find new ways from the very beginning. We had to see to it that the unemployed workman was not degraded to a receiver of alms and to beggary, but we had to realise that we all had a duty—to put in and wager a last stake for a common aim, which led to the point at which work was respected once more, and to give to work the foundation which it needs to be effective. If it is not to remain only a catch-phrase that every German really honours work, compatriots—and if it is also not to remain lip-service, that every German confesses that the meanest of his race is nearer to him than any of the rest of humanity and foreign countries—then there will be real unity. But these things must not remain mere phrases. Every compatriot must have the urge to help in him, for we belong together. He must feel : " My leaders take care, work and create for me, and while they work for me, they work for the whole nation and its welfare." Therefore we have put away from us the sentence that to help is to give alms —alms given by the mercy of those who have been chosen by fate and who have been endowed with more earthly possessions than the poorer compatriot. No ! This winter help has become a national duty. For look here, compatriots, all those who today are without work, who must suffer hunger and misery—they want work. We still remember this terrible misery of the unemployment.[1] We know how everyone dragged themselves about, tired out, from place to place. We know how the young man, who stepped into life with high thoughts, seeking to storm the world with his young strength, came home at last, tired out and hopeless, because he was again and again refused,

[1] It is possible that Göring used the article purposely to stress his own recollections of the time when he was so long without work and resources.

and because he was still without work. Who can still speak of material things in face of this memory? We know what their souls were like and how they despaired of life. Therefore we must make good the wrongs of the past.

And think, comrades, if Germany was attacked today, as has happened in days gone by. If enemy powers sought to destroy German possessions, do you know that I would say to the middle classes who had always adopted the point of view that the workman does not matter? I would say: " It was the masses of German workmen who, as infantry in the front line, defended the German fatherland." Even the man without any little possession was called upon to take up arms and to help protect the property of others. But we must not be mistaken. The German would never have achieved that spirit and enthusiasm, like the German infantry men possessed, to withstand the enemy for four years, if he was obsessed by the thought that he was defending the property of some other individual German. No ! He did his duty, because he felt that the property was in turn, again the possession of the whole nation. That thought sustained the whole nation.

When we go to work on the winter help today, the words ' Possessions oblige ' must stand out in front of all else.

Possessions oblige, for one cannot do what one pleases with one's possessions, no, one must place them at the service of the whole, and, I can well say it—here it is an old tradition. The name Krupp is well known in the world, because it is a works which is used for the nation, which supplies to the nation its needs for its security. So possession obliges that one places it at the service of the whole, and in doing so, one wins the moral right to demand from the possessionless that he shall stand for the whole as well. But one can never call upon a nation to put forth its strength in the final throw, in the hour of need, when one does not care a jot about the compatriots during the time when need does not knock at the door. It has all been so terrible, that millions of people were put into one category, who grew to hate others in different walks of life, just because their kind of work was different or because their possessions were nil.

Men cannot be expected to be patriots in time of need when they are treated as cyphers in prosperous times.

No ! One can only expect a loyal nation when one is conscious of the fact that to demand the life of the compatriot one must see to it that his means of existence are safeguarded. The right to work is a holy one. The nation has simply got to adjust itself to this idea, and if it finds it difficult, it must find ways to overcome the obstacles and thus ensure the loyal co-operation of the individual for the good of the whole nation.

And so the winter help becomes, in this deeper sense, not alms, not mercy or charity, but duty—an iron duty. Every person can sacrifice something. It is not the amount of money, but the size of the sacrifice that counts. One mark might mean more to one man's pocket than a hundred thousand to another's. The winter help becomes more powerful when each person starts to think : what I give now forces me to go without something, cigarettes, cinema, chocolates, no matter what it is, but whatever I give I shall miss something else. If he thinks like this he knows that he has done his share. He knows that he may have very little, but of that very little he has given.

Without being demagogical, one can definitely say that in this question of sacrifice, the poorest classes have borne most, comradeship among them has always been strong. Even when the people were miserably poor, they gave to the still poorer ones a piece of bread. But how many have been turned away from the doors of the rich—without a crumb. That, compatriots, must force disunity upon a nation, but our winter help will prove to be a touchstone for restoring unity in the people, and we say with pride ; looking upon the nation today we can see that it has become a nation. A true national community has overcome what once rent it apart and broke it into a million splinters. I ask those who today think that they have something to grumble about : " Do you want the old times back ? Do you again want to entrust your destiny to those parliamentarian jabberers who, in seeking the fulfilment of their own aims and needs, saw only the narrow politics of their lives ? Do you really wish to see again compatriot incited into fighting compatriot? If you think that it is right, as communism teaches, that everybody who possesses anything must give it up, then in the end no one will have anything left and then chaos is bound to ensue.

As long as the world exists, compatriots, nothing will be equal. As long as the world remains, there have to be differences, and there will be differences over the possession of spiritual, as well as material, things. That a man has more than his fellow means nothing. The deciding factor is what use a man makes of his possessions, be they talents or goods—and if he uses them for the good of the nation. Minister of state or the man who drives a crane—no matter who it is. What matters is how they do their work, for I hold that a workman, who in his own little world does his duty, is of greater value than a minister who has only his own welfare in mind and who ' wangles ' things to suit his own interests. We saw it in the war, comrades ! Did it matter that one was richer than the other, when all stood side by side in the same dug-out? Do you think that the bomb which hit here or there—which tore apart bodies indiscriminately—do you think that it inquired if the one had money and the other not? If the one had brains and the other not? There destiny walked its own road and there it was proved that we were all alike before God. No one shall be preferred (in the Third Reich) unless it shall be that preference which will ask of the Leader that he shall stand before his followers in the hours of danger. That is a destinction natural in a leader and the people are the judges as to whether a leader adequately fills his rôle.

Therefore I ask once more : Where did all the strength disappear during the time when everything was dull slime of instigation? Where did it go? How much did the individual person feel? Baffled, he opposed all questions that were of importance to the nation. Now we have the new people's union with its new tasks and aims. And you see, German compatriots, that the German people have always remained good in their inner kernel, and that the German people are able to reach a final goal was proved nearly two years ago, and I say to everyone : " Let all those of you who have sacrificed some little, put yourselves in the place of those hard-working and poor compatriots who have given us proof of what it really means to sacrifice for the welfare of the whole and you will understand what I mean." We have always said that a nation can only live when it secures the foundation of its nutrition, that means when the farmer is secured so that he can raise his crops and which are needed for the nourishment of the people. But the farmer has to thank the labourer—his colleague—that he understands the nation's need and works with him in a spirit of sacrifice. That is heroic and therefore the farmer must realise, on his part, that there is a duty imposed on him to provide for the poor and needy. Everyone must take care that he is not led into the belief that he can make a profit out of the misery of the poor. We will take stern measures against everyone who endeavours to endanger the food supplies of the people, whether by selling too dear, or through artificially bringing about a food shortage, or by usury, and he will soon know that he is an enemy of the nation.

But I cannot and must not, demand sacrifices from only one section. Where there are sacrifices to be made, then it must be made by everyone to the fullest measure of his capacity. Only then will it be possible for sacrifice to be understood, and that all are ready and willing to contribute their quota and will be prepared to make further sacrifices. Believe me in one thing : We are quite clear in our minds that we are only at the beginning of our work. We have, as one might say, stormed the enemy's position and cleared it. But we now have to consolidate the position and enlarge it. We have already been successful in giving back to the German people its honour and the German nation knows once again what freedom means ; we must also fulfil the other promises we have made. To secure once more work and bread for the German compatriot. You may believe me when I say that we are working on this problem with all our might and we devote our thoughts to how this can be brought about. We suffer terribly when we know that the position does not allow of the German workman receiving the wages which we see as his fair due. We know that as yet this is not possible, but we must work hard and strive to see that the German worker, as soon as possible, has a better basis in life and that his lot will soon be a happier one. While complete improvement may not be possible in this generation, the German worker can be safe in the knowledge that his children will benefit and that his work, sacrifice, suffering and sufferance have purpose and have not been in vain.

In life it is not only a matter of material things. We leaders, who have not struggled just for a voice, have always preached that we want to bring about better relationship within the nation. Yes, it is no empty phrase, it is a passionate call from the heart. We struggled for the soul of every compatriot ; it is the soul alone we want, for it alone has value and constancy. From inner conviction and out of an innermost force, the individual shall feel one with the people. Then those, who even today, through enticement, passive resistance or even sabotage, try to hinder the building up of a better and happier Germany, make their dark business for nothing. We know to our greatest sorrow that today not everyone is national socialist. We know that in some places there are still bitter and infuriated enemies, who only wait for the opportunity to show their enmity. There are still sitting about in offices, Centre Party men who are furious when they think that they have to play second fiddle ; but under cover of the national socialist movement, they are brooding and plotting to bring harm to the movement whenever they can.

It is impossible for one to talk all the time of Christian love for one's neighbour under cover of the black coat[1] and yet at the same time conspire to disrupt the people and tear it apart again. It shall be made impossible for them to go on working under the protection of the national socialist movement and working against national socialism. We want domestic peace. We are tired of struggle and hatred. We know that only the people themselves can reach the last goal, which is power united in the people, and they have finished tugging and tearing at each other, as has been the case. Germany was bound to become weak, rift apart as it

---

[1] A reference to clerics and Catholics of which the Centre Party was composed.

was. Germany slowly drifted into a state of torpidity, from which it seemed impossible to arouse itself. Yet we have done it. For not even the biggest grumbler will gainsay us, when we state that today, respect for the German human being in the world has become different once more.

Compatriots ! Think back a few years. Then politics were made in the world without reference to Germany, in fact, on the whole they were negotiated ' on its back '.[1]

Today no world politics can be made without Germany. All at once the words ' Berlin ' and ' Germany ' have recovered their ring. One now knows that Germany is no longer a nation rent apart and a nation of cowards, given over to pacifist thoughts, willing to surrender itself and its rights. One knows that it is not just a question of nicely walking into Berlin any more. It has become known that it would be a bit difficult to try it again or to try to torture Germany to death. No ! We are once more a power, and we have become this power out of ourselves and not through cannons ; through the moral strength which has always proved to be the most effective in all worldly matters. Germany must be reckoned with as it is today. The German living abroad need no longer be ashamed of the fact that he is a German. Ask your friends who live abroad how they feel now that they belong to a nation which is respected, feared and strong.

See how it has always been held against you that you are militaristic and warmongering. They are wrong. Only a nation without honour and which is defenceless is unpeaceful, and when an English statesman declared a few days ago that an unarmed defenceless nation is a provocation for disturbing the peace, then he may please think that what goes for England, goes for Germany too. We, too, are of the opinion that a nation without honour and means of defence has also become unpeaceful. We have felt it in our own bodies. We have felt that we have been without peace, internally and externally. Today we want to secure the peace and the world must know again and again :· Only

---

[1] A catch phrase, growing out of the practice of the Roman slaves who carried their master's writing tablets on their backs and who were forced to bend when the master wanted to write. Used in this instance to connote serfdom.

a Germany of honour can be a guarantee of world peace. Only a German people of freedom will keep this peace and will know how to keep this peace. Therefore, we demand for ourselves the same rights as the others possess.

Possessed of these rights, we also know that because of it, the other nations will find the hour for a real understanding, which is always possible between the equally strong, but never between the weak and the strong. We see it so often. The ex-service men of all nations who have stood up to each other in the tremendous struggle, have come to understand each other. Why? Because they came to respect each other. No one can tell the French ex-service man, who stood for four years fighting the Germans, that ' the Boches are cowardly dogs ', for they have experienced if we are cowardly dogs or not. They know exactly that it is not true. They know that with our nation they must find an understanding. But then of course along come the politicians, and twisters of right and wrong, and they think that they are able to distort and turn around these healthy and sensible ideas. One can speak to a French ex-soldier, for he will have the feeling and understanding for an agreement among the nations.

A few weeks ago I had the opportunity to speak to the aged Marshal Petain. There is a soldier. He is a nobleman and he understands how to respect the honour of Germany. With people like this one can come to an understanding, but not with a party leader or politician, who see only their own poor business flourish in the disunity. When the great white nations cannot find each other, then they can look forward to their twilight. The white people are chosen for the leadership of the world, and the white nations must realise and respect the mission among themselves. They must not exclude from their comity the most able and talented nation—that is impossible and against nature. We have rebelled against this and we will make issue against this until our dying breath. We do not want war, but we want our honour. We will not discuss this with anyone in the world—that is certain, for honour is the foundation for the re-building of the nation. Only he who has a sharp sword at his side has peace and quietness. It is not that he agitates for war. No. When one is defenceless, others are animated to attack and rob him, but if he knows that he can defend himself, then peace will be secured to him and with that, peace in the whole world.

The world today has to be satisfied with the fact that Germany is no longer rent asunder by classes and parties, and it must recognise that it is a strong united Germany of Adolf Hitler which stands before the world, in which it demands its place, along with every other nation of honour.

And this German nation will have its future, for we have seen how lucky we have been in achieving the wonder, that mind became victorious over matter, and that Germany has risen once more out of darkest gloom to a new life. We will not rest until this victory is brought to its conclusion. In that you may believe me, compatriots ! They may tell you what they like, they may even lie to you about your leaders. But look at our life. It is a life of work and sorrow. Not our own sorrow. We need not have sorrows in our daily life, and yet the sorrow that lies upon us is a thousand times greater and manifold than yours, for we worry not for ourselves, but for the whole German nation. Believe me, in Adolf Hitler and ourselves, our souls are filled with the urge to help you as far as possible. Our lives are our own no longer, we have no private life, but that does not matter. We are Germany, and you are Germany, and all that is the only thing for which we would all give our lives. They may say many things about us (the leaders). We all have our faults, but no one can say that there is anyone living who can surpass us in the passion of will to do good and to help the people. Adolf Hitler, day and night, knows only his people and the cares of his people and in the far-off firmament gleams the goal—the happiness of his people. So, therefore, he who dares to destroy the faith in the Leader, he who tries to undermine the faith of the people in the Leader, is a criminal. For such people not only spoil the relationship of the people to the Leader, but they destroy the people themselves. In enticing the people from the Leader, they are enticing them from Germany, for Adolf Hitler and Germany have become one unit, and inseparable.

The faith of the followers in the Leader, the trust of the Leader in his followers, together form the foundation on which the new Germany has grown up. Therefore, today, we will remember this man to whom alone we can give thanks for everything. He has given us new faith, he has given back to us trust, and has shown to us what it means to be faithful once more. Therefore three cheers for our Leader, Adolf Hitler, the Chancellor of the German Reich.

THE PEOPLE AND ITS LEADERS HAVE PASSED THE TEST. An article in the *Völkischer Beobachter*, 30th January, 1935.

FOR the second time the hours of our last struggle have lengthened into years. We live again the most difficult moments of great strain before the attack, and we have the same impressions as on 30th January, 1933, when the nation became overjoyed at knowing that at last the door of freedom was opened.

On that day there started for us national socialists the more responsible time—in which fate claimed from the new leadership that it should fulfil its aims and thereby justify the trust that had been placed in the movement by Germany, and which Adolf Hitler had in his co-workers.

It is with satisfaction that we can say today that people and leadership have passed the test. Under difficult conditions and in difficult times, Germany has recovered, through its Leader, Adolf Hitler, the fount of her strength. When we speak of the achievements of the last year or two, we must thank, first and foremost, those unknown collaborators of Adolf Hitler and recognise their achievements. For everyone of us knows that we could not have done the work that we did if the people, wakened to new strength and courage by the Leader, had not stood behind us, ready to take up duties and make sacrifices, whether they were members of the party or not.

The Leader has asked for four years in which to complete the huge plan of reconstruction. Two years have passed of those four. And they have been rich in happenings and work, and it is well worth looking back upon them, and to gain from the experiences we made, and to look forward to

[*Translated and reproduced in English with acknowledgment to : Völkischer Beobachter.*]

the great job that is still before us in the years to come. The year 1933 was the year of wild tempo—of a revolution that blasted its way. In all walks of public life new ideas took root and grew steadily onwards, especially those ideas which had been suppressed by the timid parliamentary government of the past.

The complete finishing off of the secret enemies of the state presents a new main task, which must be undertaken with ruthless harshness in short blows in rapid succession, in order to keep the path clean for national socialism.

In 1933 there was a lot of planing, following which, heaps of shavings had to fall. In this or in that instance, some of our fighters, spurred on by the enthusiastic will to help, may have over-reached themselves. On the whole though, looking at the situation broadly and taking the long view, the words spoken by our Leader this year are justified, namely, that no revolution has been achieved in more disciplined fashion than the German revolution of the year 1933. The great scheme of clearance made unpredecented demands on all colleagues of the Leader. It has also burdened us considerably in the field of foreign affairs, but his great speech in May tore apart the finely spun net of emigrant lies and proved to the countries abroad that not the lust of conquest, but the naked will of self-preservation, drove the German people to this deed of freeing themselves. After the wild tempo in the early days of the revolution, the year 1934 brought us quiet solid work. Great stress was laid on the social tasks. The law for ordering national work is pursuing a further progress which the 1st May, 1933,[1] had started with a festive beginning, namely the winning over to the national socialistic cause and for the work of the Leader, that section of the people who have been enticed and who resisted us.

The progressive measure for the fight against unemployment, the happy development of private enterprise and the consolidation of common finances in state and community, are further signs of the time. We have also been able to make less and less use of the draconian measures which

---

[1] The ordination that in future the 1st May (Mayday) should be a public holiday as the day of the German National Socialist workers.

were necessary during the first years of our fight, although the police have still got to be very watchful in the observation of enemies of the state. That national socialism has not lost its original firmness and harshness, was proved by the hard blow struck by the Leader when he rescued Germany from the ambitious plans of wild mercenaries.[1]

How much the struggle for the soul of the people has been successful is shown in the splendid result of the referendum of August of last year, which, after the death of the venerable Field-Marshal, confirmed the Leader in the office of unrestricted leadership.

This work has borne fruit far beyond the narrow frontiers of Germany. This has been proved in the Saar plebiscite, a few days ago. But it also showed, most of all, on what short legs the lies of the emigrants and separatists stood, and proved how little power their lying has today in the outer world, and compared with this, how firm the unity in the German blood-community proves to be, now that it is brought to the consciousness of all German people by Adolf Hitler.

The contours of the new state started to show themselves domestically, more clearly in 1934. The historic act of 30th January, 1934, providing the law for rebuilding the Reich, finished completely the existence of individual states. In work which was purposeful, the year was employed in preparing Prussia first of all, as the foundation for the re-arrangement of the new Reich. In this direction, particularly, lay the union of the Prussian ministries with those of the Reich, which will make impossible for all time a continuance of that main fault, of the dualism in Prussia and the Reich.

After the greatest hindrances of the past have been removed, and the new foundations of the state laid, the coming two years of Adolf Hitler's four year plan will serve for the enlargement and development of the foundation already put in. It has been stressed repeatedly at meetings, that the arrangements for the new provinces will be put through in the near future. I dare say that in the more important areas the state is sufficiently organised and its

[1] 30th June, 1934.

absolute power established—this has happened not long ago with justice—and that soon the autonomy of the rest of the states will come to an end. In that there will be most important questions arising, and, more particularly, the position of the Reich in relation to its member provinces will take shape. The leader has indicated the direction things are to take, in his speech at the party day of last year, when he announced that flourishing, and not empty, provinces shall be created. The ancient problem of the German formation of the state has now come to a head, and we national socialists have learned from history. We will not fall to the faults which led in the middle ages to the downfall of the Reich, but we will also take heed that we do not pattern ourselves on Western revolutionaries, and equalise too greatly, the manifold life in the German lands, in too uniform a way. We shall also not bunch together all decision in one place only. The experience of the Saar plebiscite has clearly proved that, in spite of cleverly thought out barriers, the call of German blood to German blood, which has been wakened through national socialism, is stronger than the foreign political drum-fire and gas attacks of traitors. This experience will not be neglected in the restoration of the Reich.

We national socialists are proud to be able to work under Adolf Hitler during the years to come—to work on tasks as have not been approached by the German people for centuries. We are positive that the fire kindled by the Leader will further point the way which leads to a better future.

In the historic days of January, we have the propaganda week[1] of the national socialist press. Our press, too, has been given new tasks by the Leader, following upon our coming into power, and our victorious battle against the opposition. These tasks may seem strange to them at first, but they have to live into them, as much as we all do in our new work, which the trust of Adolf Hitler has given into our care.

Just as during the years of opposition, so in the times of re-building, the national socialist press has stood the test and they have created, in their own field, a perfectly new

[1] *Werbewoche.*

form of life. I realise the valuable and understanding collaboration of our press in the rebuilding work in its whole expanse. They have understood how to be silent in the right moment—and that too is most necessary—and to speak at the right time, in a language that the people understood. In company with the rest of the press, the *Völkischer Beobachter*, as the central organ of the movement, has the additional job to work along lines such as will secure in a lively fashion that nation and leadership will further be inseparable.

AN ARTICLE IN THE REICH PARTY DAY EDITION OF THE *Völkischer Beobachter*, September, 1935, on Honour and Freedom.

'HONOUR and freedom are the basis of a nation's life.' This natural law the national socialist party has tried again and again to engrave on the heart and brain during its fourteen years of struggle. Adolf Hitler has given meaning to these words during his struggle for Germany, when our fatherland was bowed down in weak helplessness, when a criminal 'German' government was ready to cowardly hand over the weapons of defence of Germany to the enemy.

When, at that time, the Leader went to work to free Germany, the most courageous would not have believed that in the fifteenth year of the shameful Treaty of Versailles, Germany would have its resurrection. And it strikes one more than ever as a wonder that, already, two years after the beginning of the national socialist revolution, German freedom has been restored and that, therefore, the German shield of honour is cleaned of the smallest particle of dirt. We all are witnesses of this historic occurrence. Every German man is able today to serve his nation in uniform. The German nation stands firmly founded there, created by the Leader and his movement, resurrected by the sacrificial struggle of German men in a long tiring fight against inner rottenness and external suppression. We will never forget, in our pride of the newly created army, that we owe all this alone to the swastika. Not one of the new battalions, regiments, ships and aeroplanes would be here but for the victory of the brown storm troops of Adolf Hitler. Therefore, and justly so, the Leader has invited his fighters of the

[*Translated and reproduced in English with acknowledgment to : Völkischer Beobachter.*]

movement to Nuremberg this year for the ' Day of Freedom '. Let us on this day realise to the full the historic fact
that Germany is once more free.

The dream of youth—the hope of the nation has been
fulfilled. Every German man wears once more his arms
with pride. He bears them in peace, and he knows that
there is nothing more beautiful and greater than peaceful
work in the re-building of the nation and to serve the state
in peaceful work.

But he does carry them in the natural readiness, always to
step forward to defend people and homeland.

Germany is free once more, and all German men are
again in the position to protect the fatherland, women and
children, against every attack. Germany stands once more
with equal rights among the nations, in the air, on land
and on water. Our leader, Adolf Hitler, has saved us from
the fate that Germany should be unpeaceful and without
honour, and has prevented us from suffering as a nation of
slaves. With justifiable pride, every compatriot can say to
himself that he has contributed to reaching this great aim.

For me, too, it is the greatest experience of my life, that
the Leader has nominated me as the man who has to create
the new Air Force. The German workman, most of all, can
proudly look back in satisfaction to the work done, which
he helped to create, in order that the freedom of the nation
might be re-established once more. Once more the German
workman has proved a shining example to the whole world,
for without his work, sacrifice and untiring readiness, the
great deed of freeing Germany would not have been possible.

We all of us realise the great task which confronts the whole
of the German people. To secure the newly created army
against all dangers and to keep the newly wrought sword
sharp and clean. In doing that there will have to be further
sacrifices and fresh heavy efforts, but the German people
will take that upon themselves readily, yes, even joyfully.
For in the sign of the restored freedom, there is again sense
in the fact of working for the fatherland, and, if need be,
to bring sacrifices to the work, in order that the future
conditions of the nation are secured. Of course, many
things had to be put on one side, due to the tremendous

happenings brought about by the re-building policy of our Leader—the work for internal unity, the fight against unemployment and, lastly, the successful conclusion of the struggle to achieve the new army. Many things are still waiting attention.

But, just on the day of German freedom, we feel how very small those are who grumble about this. They only show that they have not been touched by the reconstruction policy of our Leader and of its tremendous experience, which has become the foundation of the new life of our nation. Just the Party Day of German freedom will teach the people to see things in the right order of greatness. This day lifts us right out of the sorrows, which, however, still linger in the heads of small-minded or evil-minded people. He, who is weak from fear and can only see the present moment, only every-day life, is called upon today to lift up his eyes to that overwhelming greatness which has already been completed by national socialism. Then he, too, will realise that the ever-surging forward national socialists will in due course, and at the right time, properly order those things which are today not quite up to the standard of our ideas. The new Germany is strong enough not to be afraid of any task. After this year's Party Day we are not just resting with our hands in our lap, but we are going on working for the re-building of the Third Reich, where and how the Leader orders.

On this year's Party Day, all eyes are turned up to him. In this tremendous demonstration of Germany's political strength, millions of free men are once more lifting up their hand to the oath : Leader and fatherland—we are ready with this faithful oath, even if it be with life itself, to stand firmly and truly by it.

SPEECH AT THE OCCASION OF THE COMPLETION OF THE FRAMEWORK of the new German Air Ministry in Leipziger Strasse, 12th October, 1935, in which the theme was the buildings of the Third Reich.

COMRADES and compatriots! All who stand here at this moment will realise that they take part in a singularly grand event, not only for the Capital of the Reich, but for the whole Reich itself. For the first time we celebrate, in the spirit of Adolf Hitler and national socialism, the Richtfest[1] for a tremendously large building.

Truly it is a remarkable building, which already, on the outside, shows and proves by what spirit it has been created. It shows that it is a symbol of the new Reich, but above all this it is a sign of untiring devotion to work and working strength, which has caused to spring up in a few months a building such as this, for which in past years the bickering alone would have taken up all the time. Again it has been proved that to talk is of no importance, but to work and create is important. Thanks to you all, under a strong leadership, a powerful will and untiring work, the first work in stone has arisen in the Third Reich.

In wonderful words our Leader spoke at the Reich Party Day of freedom, of German culture, about German buildings,

---

[1] The German title for this event is *Richtfest*, which literally translated is ' festival of Right ', meaning (*Das Haus ist gerichtet*) the house is straightened. There is no equivalent in English, because the custom is foreign to us, although an instance was reported in the English national press in the spring of 1939, of the workmen engaged upon a new house being given beer and bread and cheese as a form of celebration before the roof was put in. Actually in Germany it is a regular custom for the owner or builder of a new house, to give the building operatives beer and food when their work is finished, which is of course immediately prior to the joiners, carpenters, glaziers, and decorators taking over, to complete the house. On this occasion, a wreath with multi-coloured bunting is stuck on the roof-framework, which is allowed to remain there until the roofing is actually built on. It is a colourful little ceremony, and the wreath referred to is a common sight throughout Germany, to be seen from the railway or when using the roads. It is, of course, an old Germanic custom and is not an innovation of the Nazi movement.

and about German work in the future, and every single one of you, my compatriots, understood the Leader, understood his heart and his will. He speaks in our own language, and therefore we understood him when he called on us to create great things, to cause great buildings to spring up, so that in far off future times, in thousands of years, they will proclaim the will of a nation which has stirred itself out of deepest misery, up into peace and happiness. The Leader said to us : " the more often the material need bears down a human being, the more difficult it becomes to master life, the more it is necessary because one cannot fulfil the wishes and longings of every individual person—that something is created for all, on which they can climb up with brave spirits, and which they can feel belongs to them." It is more so necessary for a state which devotes itself to the bringing about of a people's unity and which wants to solder all people together into one ; this state must prove the great will which is present in the people.

Truly how could one speak more clearly and more distinctly than in stone ? Times have passed, generations have died, nations have sunk into dim eclipse, and yet buildings out of these times are still stretching over to us and warning us that before us there lived generations filled with pride and strength, so much so that they could leave to our world, thousands of years later, such powerful proof.

When today we stand before such a singular building, which shakes our deepest emotions, and when we think of the past greatness of those times, then, my compatriots, you will understand how my heart rejoices at this moment, when I see this building, when I can see and state clearly today that we have spoken clearly in stone—not for today or tomorrow, but as a messenger for all time.

Every single one of you must be filled with happiness and pride to think that you have helped, with your own hands, on this building of German will and strength, on this building of beauty which is not overloaded with ostentatiousness, but which in its serious lines gives true expression to the serious spirit which rules us all today.

The discipline of the people's unity is expressed in the discipline of the architecture of this building. It proclaims your own will, your own ability, no matter to which part you have turned your hand. Nothing can be created if it is not linked up with the other parts and grows up that way. Nothing can last when it is not firmly put together in stone and mortar. When today pompous palaces and great stores[1] behind a glamorous, ugly and overloaded foreign looking façade, crack and show blemishes, although only a few decades old, here a simple building grows up bravely, firmly built, because the people's union is firmly built too.

Comrades ! Wind, weather and storms may blow over us, but we will stand up firmly in our people's union, like this building, which cannot be destroyed even by the forces of nature, because your work and industriousness has built it firmly. So, my German compatriots, the German people shall also not show one crack, in which distrust, jealousy and disaster can build their nest, in order to burst the work which you have seen growing up before your eyes.

All of you who have worked on this building must feel, that nothing is so much a symbol to a people's unity than a building. It was a cultural deed to erect this building. I live only a few yards from this building. From my home I have observed the building grow, and when at night sleep was denied me, I was terribly happy when I heard the hammers ring in hard work, when the shining light from the spotlight broke through my window. That was music of the new Reich, that was the eternal sameness, the glorious symphony, German work. For that I did not grudge my lost hours of sleep, because I could listen to the tune once more, the wonderful tune which our nation had forgotten.

A few years ago this was impossible. Then millions of starving people crept about the streets, workless, and as they had nothing to do and nothing to eat, they (the other parties) gave them and their hungry hearts nothing but dirt, in order to poison them. Where have those times gone ? and today ? Today all are at work again, everywhere the wheels of industry are revolving and on every

---

[1] Referring to the famous Wertheim universal stores—the German equivalent to Selfridges, which is faced in loud pseudo-baroque style and which stands in Leipziger Strasse on the opposite side to the Air Ministry. During the past year the title of this firm has been changed to A.W.A.G. Allgemeine Warenhaus Aktien Gesellschaft (General Warehouse Company).

hand national values are rising. It is truly beautiful to live in times when a building like this can be built in eight months. But let us never forget that it was only possible through this singular organisation of effort, which radiates from the will of the Leader, down to the poorest workman. One will, one spirit, rules them all, one strong urge actuates them all. All who stand here today have brought untold sacrifices to the task, and also those working comrades of yours who are already working on other jobs, in other places, deserve our thanks. You have all given of your best —you have worked day and night and even on Sundays, the work did not rest, but went forward in the same tempo. May those who cling to the dead word and who feel themselves slaves to the dead word, talk about breaking the Sabbath rest. No ! Comrades ! in erecting a building like this one pleases God. He has given us His blessing for this work, otherwise it would not have sprung up, and when we work on holidays ten times, we have created a special holiday work for it. For this work had to rise, not only as the outward expression of the Reich, but also as a necessity for the work of the German Air Force.

This house is also a symbol for the rebirth of our Air Force, a symbol of forward storming spirits, of passionate energy which rules us all for this instrument, which was broken for us at one time, which was denied to us, because it was known with what spirit we would fill it. But we have allowed it to rise again today, so that a strong Air Force could protect the Reich once more. This Air Force must have a home, a centre, a spiritual central point, from which in turn can radiate rays down to the last squadron, and down to the last company. This building is, and shall be, a well of strength for all those who have been called upon by the Leader, and who have the grace to be allowed to serve the German fatherland in the German Air Force, and to serve the Leader. It shall be a spiritual centre, out of which waves and streams of strong spiritual power shall radiate, a union which nothing can break, a courage which can never be shattered, an energy which nothing can hinder and a passionate will to serve the fatherland, the Leader and the people.

But those who are going to work in this house must be filled with thanks and remember that the horny handed German workmen have created this beautiful place for them. They shall remember in thankfulness, that good can only be created where there is goodwill and thought. They shall understand, in thankfulness, that it was only through the people's union, which was created by the Leader, that this house was built and made possible for them to work in. It is vastly different to live in a building which sprung up in hatred, jealousy and envy, than to live in one built with happiness and which has been carried out by workmen filled with love and joy. So in this building, may the people's union between the workers of the fist and the workers of the brain, be strengthened in singular manner and may this unity be a model to all who are going to work in this house. This house shall also be the castle of the spiritual possession of national socialism. May everyone, who is going to work in one of the thousands of rooms, who either reads, writes, draws or studies, creates, plans or organises—may everyone know, deep down in himself, that all this was only brought about because national socialism was victorious, and because the brains of the Leader became the possession of the whole nation. Because, out of the *Weltanschauung* which he has given us, everything that was splintered and torn asunder in the nation—envy, hatred of class, conceit of position, jealousy and presumption —had to be put aside in order that all that was good, hard and solid could bloom and thrive on these ideas.

May he ever be indebted and always thankful and be a faithful servant to national socialism, to those wonderful ideas which have freed a whole nation and given soul to the nation, to those wonderful ideas which the Leader reached down from the stars in order to give them to a despairing, weak nation which was bleeding from a thousand wounds, like a flaming torch. Never must he who works here forget, that the Leader, with his movement, brought light into the dark night with the torch of trust and faith and lighted him to a new future—that he has thus led the nation and allowed this wonderful building to rise in eight months. Truly a wonderful proof of national socialistic ideas. But—

may everyone shamefacedly slink out of this house who does not understand this thought, or who even only in his innermost self sins against the ideas and their purity. May this building give wings to all in order that they can grow above their own world—may it give strength to them, so that when in stirring times great deeds are asked of them, they can achieve great things above their ability and circumstances, through the strength of this idea, which shall radiate from this building—which is a national socialist building.

Here we have a singular situation. Here stands this building, and across the way, only a few yards from us, stands another building—the old Diet—erected in quite another time and meant for another purpose than that for which it was used. Here is work—over there was muddle. Here a lively interest in the people. Over there was nothing but talk and thousands of conflicting self-interests. This putting up of opposite things, compatriots, makes us think hard. I am unspeakably happy to think that I could take away from that building over there, the original purpose for which it was intended—that I was able to make out of this old Prussian parliament a serviceable building once more, and that I was able to sweep away all the parties over there and to blow them into the chasm which divided us all, and which has now closed over parties, position and class and has made us into a united people and Reich. In a few months we take over the building over there. Then we will move into it and take with us our will and energy ; thus we will use it once again for work and for the work of the people.

We are also thinking of another building, which will link up with the new building (the Air Ministry) and which will rise anew on this ground. But while the parliament building of which I spoke just now was given over to empty talk, the other building was one of quiet and faithful work. Where today the new building of our ministry rises, slowly gaining in height, there formerly stood the old Prussian War Ministry, where there once sat the great men of the wars of freedom—where Scharnhorst and Gneisenau worked in the creation of victorious armies. In this building, duty, discipline, obedience and work ruled. With it we take over a good slice of the best Prussian tradition. We will scoop out of its foundation the strength to work just as industriously, dutifully and obediently. So we see the peculiar combination of two buildings, each with different plans in the inception ; but our tremendous building will take them both up in its strong open arms, drawing them both towards it, pulling strength and tradition out of one and pouring new power and new tradition into the other, thus forming out of the whole a new united work—The German Air Ministry, the centre of German aviation and the High Command of the German Air Arm.

My dear compatriots and working comrades ! There may be in your midst still some who creep about here and there, who after all can't grasp it all yet, because they are of another mind, who say " Look how the national socialists erect one luxurious building after another ", but they do not think, and tell you at the same time, how much work has been given to a great number of people in building this house. It is very easy to say, one must not build because it is a luxury—one must not do this or do that because it is a luxury—but to allow our people to starve to death, is that a luxury too ? There will be many among you who, months or years ago, did not know where to find work and who, in the end, were happy at last to get some. For the German person, especially the German worker, does not like to beg or to live on alms. He will work and receive his just due for his work. Because, therefore, the Leader has resolved to build, wake things up to new life, work has been created, and today we see around us happy and satisfied faces. It is very easy to find fault with everything. It is easy to criticise. It is easy to dig up the minor faults and to be silent about the great achievements which lie beneath them. It is no luxury building that stands here. No. It is a building of work and hard fulfilment of duty. This building is the homestead of the spirit which animates the German Air Force.

Today we are celebrating, in festive spirit, the completion of the framework and we are awaiting with joy the hour when this building will be finished. And so today, at the finishing of the frame, so for the future and all times, a feeling of thanks shall fill us that we are allowed to work inside the building. A true and deeply felt feeling of thanks to all you who have helped to build it.

Once again I would like to say to all of you who helped to build this new home, that we thank all of you—you who have planned it, created it and built it, no matter in which part of the house you have worked. Just as every single one of you feels that he has taken part in this building, so I am just as proud to think that I could watch the growing of this building from the very first hour. Let us thank God that this building was allowed to be erected without our having to mourn for any great accident. Let us thank God and ask of Him that He will in future too lend His strong protection to the work which is meant for the people, until the building stands firmly and securely.

Warm thanks fills us most of all to the man who laid the spiritual and national foundations of this building, who created first of all the supposition for a new Air Force to be created, who created the hypothesis for a happy and able nation to be united once more. To the Leader our thanks, from the depth of our hearts. In his spirit we do not want to work for the injury of anyone. We do not think of foreign conquests or adventures, but we will also see to it that no one harms us either. The Leader spoke words at the Bückeberg which filled us pilots with joy : " The German Air Force watches over the strength of an able and industrious nation ", a sentence, comrades, which makes us truly indebted to the future. Yes ! we will keep watch for the Leader and for the Nation up above, and this building was erected the better to enable us to keep this watch. It lies with us, with all of you, to see that this which is stone will be glowing with our will and filled with your unbreakable spirit, to be what our Leader called us, ' the strength of the nation—the watch of the German people.'

That we swear to the Leader when we call : Our Leader, the chancellor of the German Reich three times *Sieg Heil*.[1]

---

[1] In translation : luck for victory thrice over, this rather loses its force. Often *Drei Mal Sieg Heil* may be taken as ' three cheers ' purely and simply.

A SPEECH AT THE SILESIAN PROVINCE DAY, 26th
October, 1935. Dealing with the relation of Party and
State.

THE foundation and ideas of party and state, which
we national socialists represent, and about which I
am going to speak to you to-day, form an important
part of the great building programme of the German people
and the Reich. While we hear much about the collaboration of these two powerful factors of the Germany of to-day,
party and state, it is abroad, and not at home, that doubts
are thrown upon the possibility of their reconciliation to
each other. The more we hear from the distant talks upon
this theme, the more there seems to arise in the two an
opposition, the open conflict of which, so it is prophesied,
will be the ruin of the national socialist state. We ourselves,
who are well informed about all such things, know that
they cannot come in conflict, because the state was created
out of the party, because it is filled with the ideas of our
Leader and the movement and because in the first place,
it is composed of those men. The state is the highest form
of expression of existence—it is the organisation of the life of
our people and, as such, of the movement and of the party.

The national socialist movement grew up in opposition
and in the fight against then existing state order. In the
Weimar republic, it only saw an opposition, and it stood
against it in a ruthless fight, until such time came for its
complete destruction.

The ' November ' state was immoral and it therefore had
to disappear. It was the form of expression of the Germany
of that time, of its then leadership, which was immoral,
bad and cowardly. We had to do away with that leadership,
in order to restore to the people a proper leadership, which
taught them to think once more heroically. So we destroyed

the state, or rather the 'system', of Weimar of 1918, in order to erect in the people a new organisation, a new leadership, in the conception of the new state, and we have now formed under this leadership a new people. During the days of opposition we had to suffer a lot, because we were pointed out as enemies of the state, and because they tried to make us out to be anarchists in our ideas. We have always stood up against these lies ; we have never been against the state as the state, we only fought against it, because we wanted a clean state and a strong state and in order to destroy an unclean system.

At the moment of ruin and breakdown, when misery and dire need was ruling everywhere, when Germany was stamped with shame and disgrace, and when every human being dispaired, despaired in their conception, and thought that they were wrong—in that moment the Leader lighted the torch, which was followed by a few at first, then by thousands, hundreds of thousands, and in the end by the whole nation. The banner, which flew in front of the first fighter of the national socialist movement, the swastika, for which hundreds of national socialists gave their lives joyfully, is to-day the symbol of our state. It is therefore natural that we cannot stand in opposition to the state of to-day, for we cannot punish blood of our own blood and harm flesh of our own flesh. This state we have built. It was erected in the high atmosphere of the national revolution, when the swastika rose for the first time on government buildings. To this state we swear allegiance, because it is filled with our spirit ; this state we serve, because it is the state of our Leader. There is no opposition. There is only the division of tasks into different territories of work, where the individual has to fulfil his duty and work in order to serve the whole. We must not forget that we have destroyed one state in which the foundation was egotism, which is in opposition to national socialist principles. We must not forget that we destroyed this state, and with it the miserable distinctions, and that in the end, through the co-ordination of all those organisations which fill the common life, grew the co-ordination which justifies the totalitarian claim of our movement. It is natural that we do not want to split.

A movement which is based on a general outlook and common view, cannot let others take part control of it, it must grasp all and fill all. A party which represents a *Weltanschauung* is intolerant as long as it does not reach its goal. Following these tactics, naturally we can take the one course or the other, but basically there is only one straight clear line. We alter the tactics sometimes, but we hold on to the one unshakable foundation line, and therefore the victory is ours.

In the moment of victory, it became natural that next to, or with, the national socialists, there was no room for any other political organisation. We had a duty, which the future of the nation demanded of us—to go forward ruthlessly and in intolerance. It is quite normal for me to invite individual persons, as members of the community, to me, in order to place them in key positions, in which their particular professions may be valuable, but I cannot and must not take up whole organisations as such, but must break them.

Often I hear it said : ' This co-ordination ! ' Certainly it may appear boring here and there ; here and there certain misunderstandings may have taken place and have been even tactlessly handled. But that has nothing to do with the main principle. We understand by co-ordination of organisations that all things running through, and which form the common life of, the nation, must be brought into harmony, so that life can play its part with as little disturbance as possible. All this must be watered by the same spiritual ideas, and must be fed by the same root.

It was very natural that everything which did not ring true had to be dissolved. We do not mean to say that everything was bad ; but the time for many of the things was past, they simply did not fit into the new order of things. If perhaps someone wants to raise the matter of the dissolution of the parading student's corps and say that it was a point in the programme of the national socialists, he is on the wrong path. It was necessary to dissolve an organisation which did not fit into the national socialist people's union and which would neither feel at home there. That does not deny that there have been times when the existence of these organisations was justifiable, even serviceable.

So our new state was created, and at the same moment, when Adolf Hitler stood at its head, the opposition, or rather the irreconcilable elements, and the fighting of the parties in the earlier state, were brought to an end. The Leader declared the revolution to be at an end. He pointed out in a few words the danger which lay in a few fantastic madmen hoping to go on with the revolution, for the sake of a revolution, and to carry strife into all eternity. He closed the revolution at the same time as he announced the unification of the state with the party. To-day, state and party are one, but there is a kind of division, inasmuch as the duties of state and party are distributed in a proper fashion. Many of you witnessed the final demonstration of this year's Party Day at Nuremberg and were witnesses to the words of the Leader, when he gave us our lines of direction in the questions of state and party ; therefore a mistake appears to be impossible for everyone who is well minded. Those who are still making mistakes, wished purposely, from the very beginning, to act against the state and the party.

In a very few words I will repeat what the Leader has laid down as directions for our work, and in some cases I will voice my own opinion.

The party has the duty to set high aims for the national work of the people—the aims that were born of the national socialist point of view. It has to bring public life into tune with these aims and to keep it there. It has, and that is the more important task, to train the leaders of the future and to place them at the disposal of the people when called upon to do so. Lastly, it has to recruit the people and to bring them up as national socialist compatriots. In the more important matters, steps have been already taken— in fact, directly after we came to power. You have only to remember that leading posts in the state are filled by leading national socialists. In order to realise the distance of the (immediate) past to a few years back, one has only to think on what has been created in affairs of state by the men in the movement, and remember the speed of our times.

As the first, I put purposely the new freedom of our armed forces. Without trying to be boastful, we national socialists can declare that it was our work. The courage for such a decision could only be possessed by our Leader and his national socialist followers. When to-day we are happy in the possession of that army, then we shall not forget, even if I have to keep repeating it, that without the victory of the swastika there would have been no battalions, cannons or aeroplanes. I have given orders in my own department, the Air Force, that when leading men of the party appear on the flying fields, the troops are to remember that it was the struggling of these men which made possible their being there, and are to show these men the necessary respect.

To-day, after our victory, we are happy to be able to give the necessary means to the army and to supply the necessary personnel, and we are happy in our knowledge that, under proper leadership, the sword, which alone secures the safety of the nation, will be kept sharp. We had to experience in the years of shame, that when the sword is broken, peace is stolen, and when that is so, honour has gone. To be defenceless, means to be without peace and honour.

When we wanted to restore our freedom and honour, we had to have for its protection the German sword, which was forged by the Leader.

Furthermore, I would remind you that the thousand year old craving of the German people has now taken shape. We are at last one Reich and one people, having overcome all that the centuries had parted from us. While German brothers and lands fought each other and while German mercenaries fought each other on foreign battlefields, the rest of the world distributed the possessions among themselves. Germany went home empty-handed, because the Reich was not even geographical, but only an idea in world history.

What seemed impossible to statesmen in past times, the Leader and his movement achieve, because they had the faith of the people. When, in earlier times, people used to say that Germany did not want to be united, then our answer is that the German people always sought unity, but their leaders and rulers did not want it.

I am very proud that the Leader has appointed me as the Prime Minister of the greatest of the German states, and declared to me clearly : I put you there, not that you shall become another conservator of the old Reich, but that you shall be the liquidator of the old Reich and that the new Reich shall grow from and out of all (German) lands.

We Prussians can justly claim that the work of Prussia in history built the foundation for unity of this Reich. When some people came to me and said : " When you have unified the Reich what will become of Prussia, what will happen to you and the Prussian government ? " I answered openly and clearly : " What happens to me, and to all this, is the most unimportant thing in the world, if only one Reich will stand." The value of the creation of one co-ordinated Reich is best shown in the reaction abroad. I believe that the statesmen abroad see much more clearly than we do what it will mean, when in Germany there will be no longer millions and millions of powers and energies posed opposite each other, but closed together in one strength. We owe our thanks to the Leader that we now possess what other countries have had as their advantage for hundreds of years. It would be easy to speak here about all the details of the important work and successes. What tremendous work alone lies in the fact that millions of Germans have no longer to live on alms, but are able to feed themselves through the effort of their own work. These workmen felt it bitterly to be kept by alms and in a state of beggary. It was not so much the material side of it that mattered, but our workmen's souls were depressed to think that they were excluded from the communion with working people. That this is a fact one can see in the will to sacrifice in our workmen, who with every energy without example, and with heroism, toil at the terribly hard task of re-building and re-armament, without first thinking of the material gain. No workman in any other country would undertake this work for the small wages that we are still only able to pay to-day, just because it is necessary. Let us be happy that the German worker has re-discovered his own people. When to-day the German people again enjoy the harvest of their own work, then it is all in connection with our own work in the movement.

L

Many came again and again, during the past year or two, and said : " Look what you have set down in your programme. Now that you are at the head of things, we suppose you don't want to recognise the awkward things any longer. For instance, what has happened to your race clauses ? When do we see action ? At the Party Day this year these people, too, have had their answer. Through the Nuremberg laws, important points in our programme have been completed and they have been set up as corner-stones in the re-building of our Reich. I have at the same time, by order of the Leader, founded the flag law,[1] and you all know that I did this out of my inner convictions and out of my respect for the old victorious black-white and red flag, which once fluttered over battlefields. Of course, every town and province will have its own symbol, which to them is a badge of their own tradition, but it is only a colourblind person who does not see that the colours of our Reich are black-white and red.

It is very natural that the badge for which we fought, the emblem of victory, should flutter over Germany. That is a sign taking us back into the best times which Germany ever knew. There is certainly nothing forgotten in any territory and there will be nothing overlooked. But it cannot all happen at the same speed. The tempo of the march is ordered by the Leader, and by no one else. He who does not like this must go.

The national socialist movement to-day has its grip on all compatriots. In its hands are film, press and wireless and in these lie all matters necessary to grip the people, to enlighten it and to instruct it.

All heads of the movement are placed in office as leading officials and in future the movement will work in every field, and will thus ensure a uniform conception in the principal places. But when the Leader calls upon men who have not come out of the movement, then we national socialists must have enough understanding, to see the reason of the Leader. If he thinks that he can trust these men,

[1] From March, 1933, by order of Hindenburg, until this time, the old war flag of Imperial Germany flew side by side with the swastika banner of the N.S.D.A.P. This decree introduced the law governing the present official standard of Germany.

then we must also give them our trust, for the Leader has a better knowledge of humanity than all of us together,

In the municipalities, in the provinces, everywhere, the party can be of service. It can provide unit Leaders and advisers. Nearly all provincial leaders are also at the same time the heads of some official department ; they are also men of the state administration. It is most important of all to remember that from the Hitler Youth Movement alone will come the future leaders of Germany. This is a deciding factor, for we must always remember, that we are only the first generation, which has started—most of us already advanced in age—to grasp the ideas of national socialism. Everyone of us is richly packed with the baggage of old times, we have all had to throw off a lot of it, the workman as well as I and everyone else. We were burdened with a wrong upbringing, no matter if it was born out of marxist class hatred or middle class conceit of position. We have all had to throw a lot of it away to make room for new ideas.

We are the first generation. Because one or the other of us can do things quicker or slower than the other we cannot set a measure and a standard for all. From our generation we cannot claim that we are the finished product, for we have gone too long on different roads. Therefore it is impossible for the present generation to think and feel one hundred per cent national socialist. Those who are *Pimpf* to-day[1] will, please God, sometime be completely national socialist. To work towards this aim is our holiest task. The work of tutoring these youngsters is perhaps the most important task that we have to fulfil. On this the movement depends for its future, then movement and state will stand firm. To this we must give all our energy and exercise great care that in the next generation, perfection ripens slowly.

Therefore it is necessary that all districts of the party shall stamp indelibly on the youth the idea that this state is our flesh, that it belongs to us, and that we have to work

[1] *Pimpf*, name for the very small Hitler youth, boys about the age of English Wolf Cubs in the Boy's Scout Movement, sometimes also known as ' *Wölfchen* ' (' little wolves ').

for it as we work for the movement. Every single youth has to be made conscious of this fact, so that in due time his will will become firm and in the end will lead to that harmony visualised by the Leader.

The time when the movement thought it had the right to correct things in public life is over. The leaders of the movement are everywhere at the head of affairs, and have arranged all these things. The whole party machinery is being re-organised, and it will be placed at the disposal of the state, in unselfied discipline, for the task of the unification of the Reich. Those who do not keep in step with the time ordered by the Leader, be it in the party or in the state, must be eliminated. Every one can assure himself that the Leader will go his way unswervingly. Therefore, following upon the wish of our Leader, we intend to deal seriously with those who think that in individual action, lust for notoriety or even well intended enthusiasm, they can act without discipline. Naturally, there are still some people at work, who came to us because they thought that national socialism was quite different to what it really is—who had some fantastic and muddled plans, and who now think, in their misconception of our work of blood and earth, that they can get the fulfilment of some romantic daydream about Thor and Wotan and other things. And this brings me to our position in relation to religion and the Church.

He who has gone through all these years of struggle as a national socialist has proved that he has the power of belief, which is tremendously great. It would never have been possible to have brought about the re-birth of Germany, and to experience it, if they had not been filled with the deepest belief in the Almighty, who blessed this gigantic work. Therefore, he who says that we national socialists are atheists—is a liar. When we are said to be fighting the Church, then I must clearly state that it was the Church which started this fight. We are standing on the defensive. We have not attacked the Church ; we have declared to the Church that we stand on the grounds of positive Christianity. When the Church, in spite of this, denies us, then it aggresses us and has driven us into the defensive. The

Church must understand one thing : never has national socialism failed when on its defence. We have always and ever been active, when on the defensive, and it may have happened, here and there, that incidents have occurred which were not in keeping with the orders of the Leader, disturbances which have only been possible because we ourselves have not been left in peace. It is no use for the Church to tell the people that we are connected with the devil, for we can prove to them that we are not. They cannot substantiate their tales that we are hide-bound in superstition, because we have good causes to throw superstition in their faces. The Church can be sure of one thing. If it will only be content with national socialism, then we will be peacefully contented with the Church. It lies with the Church alone if it wants peace. We, the movement—and most of all the government and the state—have never attacked the Church. We have promised the Church protection and the Church knows that it possesses this protection in its fullest measure.

Therefore we cannot accept any reproaches. Movement and state want a people who believe, and therefore we neither wish nor seek a fight with the confessions. Quite the opposite. The Leader has far more important matters to engage his attention—things of world importance—which he would like to see brought to a conclusion as soon as possible. But, on the other hand, we must not forget, that only four years ago there were in the Centre and in the Protestant parties, people who used Church and religion for their own political ends. We must remember that these parties, whose representatives preached belief to the people all the time, in reality went arm in arm in the Reichstag with the God-denying marxists, to achieve identical aims. When the Church to-day tries to lead its fight against us by spreading the tale that we hold anti-Christ views, and that this is confirmed in national socialist books and magazines, then I declare openly and clearly that we national socialists know only one book, and that is Adolf Hitler's *Mein Kampf*.

On the other hand, we decline to forbid any serious investigator and seeker after knowledge his work, because the Church does not approve of his activity, and because his researches may disclose awkward matters. National socialism declines to work against spiritual fighters with the stake and the inquisition, as was done in days gone by. National socialism stands aloof from these matters—it awaits developments—each one in the field to which it belongs. That every national socialist knows, and it would be a good thing if all in the Church would know it also.

We national socialists have no longing to mix up in domestic matters of dogma and in quarrels over confessions. We want freedom of spirit and freedom of belief and we want to keep it the same as Frederick the Great saw it : ' Every one shall be happy after his own fashion.'

We also do not wish to see other parties celebrate their resurrection, disguised in the brown shirt. For instance, we have no desire to see the economic party, working through certain organisations, reappear in national socialist costume. On the whole, we do not feel too happy over a too strict division and association. We only see our movement as a whole—the German National Socialist Workers Party.

When I repeatedly see to-day how our race programme is being played about with, in order to make better business, then I would often like to say : " You belong to the economic party, take off that brown shirt, you have made a mistake." Where in a Berlin street there are six Jewish clothing stores, and only one German, and when six days later, after every one has stopped buying at the Jewish shops, the clothing in the German shop rockets to double the proper price, then the German proprietor's place is with the six Jews, for it is a most un-national socialist action to play on our holiest views (race programme) for personal profit. In future, we will direct our attention sharply to these things, and will wipe out those shops which are trading in such a fashion.

The same thing goes for those who think that they can improve their own conditions, arising out of a bad position, by driving up prices. The frightened ' rabbits ' who hoard food, who are worrying that they won't be able to fill their bellies sufficiently, when they hear a whisper that something is scarce, are in the same category. The duty to the nation does not end when they affix to their door the plaquette, ' common welfare goes before personal welfare ', and then slip into the back door with the hoarded food.[1]

Everyone should be an example of this slogan, otherwise the people will never benefit from it. The care for minor and personal interests must remain secondary considerations.

We have always warned the worker that he must not judge every government by the amount in his wage envelope —the grocer, not by the size of his daily till-roll—the industrialist, not by the height of his dividend, and the farmer, not by his egg and fat-stock prices, but they must all judge by the manner in which this government creates for the whole people the future of the nation. That should be the measure of their judgment, and that is the task of the men who have been called upon by the Leader to work on the education of the people, and to care for the lasting welfare of the people, not only in regard to the winter help, but in every question.

The men of the movement are responsible, not so much that they just alter a matter, but that they see to it that the leading men in the party get to know about all problems, and to put them right. That is the work for which I ask. A special eye must be kept upon the works and factories and on the workmen. I have repeatedly received reports that here, too, things are not what they ought to be. The workers' leaders have not yet learned to use the great freedom and responsibility which we have given them, in the right manner and to the proper purpose. We only judge the factory owners and workers' leaders by the way in which they associate with the workmen, and not by the magnitude of their contributions to the winter help funds. This compounding for the responsibilities of leadership we do not want, and this practice was better suited to the times that are past.

[1] In the national socialist state adhesive paper plaquettes bearing various legends are sold in aid of, inter alia, the Winter Help Fund and it has become the practice for all classes to stick these on the main door of their dwelling. In appearance, these plaquettes resemble the coloured religious tracts given to English Sunday School scholars. It is a common sight to see front doors plastered with these slogans—the greater the number the more fervent the owner—at least outwardly. They are sold every month and cost only a few Pfennigs.

Nothing makes us happier than when we see that everything is in order, and that the works leader has realised his responsibility and task as leader, and that he is a real national socialist, going with his men through thick and thin, not just at a factory outing or beanfeast, but in everyday life. This real closeness which should be existent between leader and followers, will be the standard by which we will come to judge factory owners and factory managers.

These are the things, the custodianship of which we have given into the hands of the men of the party ; the enlightenment of the managers and workmen and the reporting to the national socialists, who are at the head of the life of the state, so that they may take steps through the powers given them, where enlightenment and education seem no longer possible. In the fight for Germany's future, the men of the movement have to lead the whole people and to stand in the van, and I am convinced that now, as in the past, they will acquit themselves accordingly. No one shall tire himself out in small-minded quarrels—that is not decent or in accordance with the ethics of national socialism—which have grown out of lust for personal revenge or personal ambition. He who does not understand national socialism can naturally not occupy a leading position. But he who proves himself and he who has taken up our aims and ideas seriously and who works accordingly—with him it does not become a matter of the date of his entry into the party, but what he can achieve for the movement and for the people.

We are moving towards difficult times.

Germany has become strong and many do not approve of it. The Leader works day and night, in order to secure peace for Germany. But it is not on us alone that peace depends. We are prepared to keep at bay everyone who disturbs the peace. If the people should be called upon in an hour of destiny, then it must be a strong people, able to withstand the rigours of this difficult hour. That is the task of the men of the movement, and also, they have to see that scarcity of food or other commodities will not cause the people to hang their heads down. We must and we will do everything in order to prevent crimes like the hoarding of food or the forcing up of prices, but we must all recognise one thing as being essential : The re-building of Germany, the cost of re-armament, the purchase of raw materials and the possession of foreign exchange (*devisen*). The foundation stone of the Third Reich rests on a tremendous basis—it is called trust in the Leader ! The Third Reich was created on this basis, so under all conditions it must be maintained, with not even the minutest crack appearing.

He who sins in this regard, is guilty of the greatest crime, for he commits high treason, and in doing so he puts the axe to the roots of our very life.

It does not matter whether we like the nose of the other or not. It does not matter if the one grumbles or swears, as long as one is not too sensitive about it. But to the Leader there can be nothing less than unceasing trust, thankfulness and pledged devotion.

Every one of us lives through difficult hours, in which decisions have to be made, and in which one is not too sure of oneself, and in which one listens to other people who are not too well intentioned. Should we ever come to such a position in which we may be tempted to weaken in our trust, then let us look at the Leader, and with his shining example before us, take new strength inside ourself. His strength will impart itself to us, if we do the right thing and trust him—when we follow him and when we try to do as he does. When we are obedient to his will with the discipline of the free man, then our goal will be reached : the happiness of our people, the greatness of the nation and the glory of the Reich !

SPEECH AT THE FESTIVAL OF ST. HUBERT.[1] Held
on the Hainberg, Brunswick, 3rd November, 1935, with
the theme : the leading National Socialist motto :
' Common welfare goes before personal welfare '.

GERMAN hunters, German compatriots ! For the
first time since the foundation of the new Reich, it
has fallen to me to organise a meeting for German
huntsmen in this venerable old town. The government of
Brunswick and the town of Brunswick, along with the
hunters, have prepared for this meeting in grand manner,
and in doing so have made Brunswick, as they did in earlier
days, too, through the building of the Reich Hunter's
Court, the middle point of the German hunt. With great
interest, a firm will and with much love, we will now proceed
with the first meeting and discuss those matters which
are urgent and necessary. Apart from discussing the current
legislation which the new state has created, we have also
to place on a firm basis the fundamental rules of the organisation, in order that the German hunt and German hunters
shall come into alignment with the aims and objects of our
wonderful movement.

In the years immediately following upon our taking over
power, much has been done to improve the German woods
and game laws. Under the determined leadership of the
state, laws have been created which serve to maintain the
different kinds of game and to conserve our forests. Both
these things are inseparably connected.

Forests and heaths and the things that live in them are
put there by God, and do not belong to the individual, but
to the whole nation. We will translate the highest motto
of our movement, ' Common welfare goes before personal

[1] The patron saint of hunting and hunters.

170

welfare ', into hunters' language and will say : " In the creatures we will honour our Creator ".

As we have broken new ground in our legislation for the protection of animals in general, it becomes a natural and special duty of German hunters to look after the game which, to-day, still lives in German forests and heaths. Let us thank fate that it has preserved for us a noble piece of nature, and let us take care that our fatherland will not be exploited in this field of existence—as in many other states.

Our wonderful Germany must keep its variety in nature, for this gives to the hard-working compatriot joy and love for the homeland, accompanied by the possibility of recreation and collection. From the economic point of view, also, the wild, which is here entrusted to us, is a valuable national asset. I believe that the tremendous contribution of German hunters to last year's winter help work has proved conclusively to the people what an important factor game has become in the nutrition of the whole nation.[1]

That all our hunters should have taken such a prominent part in this great work of assistance for our poor was only natural, and I know that I need not thank you for it particularly. I also know, that should I call upon you again this year, then this time you will excel yourselves. But when the German hunters, on their side, fulfil their duty, then they have a right to expect that every German compatriot shall do his duty also, in order to make this work possible—that general well-being should take first place in our interests. It must not be that one person does not allow game to feed or graze in the German forests. Game too has a right to live, for God has created it. The upkeep of game must not be rendered impossible through heavy claims for damages alleged to be done by the game.

Communism and marxism have always been enemies of the hunt and of nature. From this cause alone our position is clearly defined, for we know that marxism and communism brought nothing but ruin, to everything, and everywhere.

[1] It has now become an established custom for the German hunters all over Germany to give their December 'kill' to the winter help organization, and the statement above is a reference to the inaugural year's contribution of venison, game, etc.

Because of this also our position in regard to the German forests, game and hunt is more than ever defined. To watch over them becomes a self-apparent duty. We also expect the self-same realisation and recognition of duty from all organisations, ranks and compatriots.

How can we protect nature if the main object everywhere is the lust for profit ? When everybody believes that he has to cultivate every bit of ground that exists in Germany, then he destroys the wells of beauty that nature has given us, for he who thinks that these things are unnecessary only proves that he has already been suffocated by coarse materialism.

If we would destroy everything that is in any way connected with ideals, then the nation can no longer intercede for ideals and can no longer strive after those ideals. Therefore I reject the idea, put forward by some people, that a thing must be destroyed because it has no apparent material value or purpose ; for some things are often matters of great purpose and cannot be exchanged for pure gold.

I must demand from the organisations and also from every individual compatriot that our forests are treated as if they were valuable possessions, given to us by God Himself, and that the creatures which live in them are treated with that love of which they are worthy. The forests are not created in order that one should go in them and make a bedlam of the place. Forests, to us, must become places of devotion —one can even ask that they shall be considered as Cathedrals of God. I am of the conviction that this meeting will help much to place matters on such a footing, which the national socialist conception of nature, its treasures and its beauties can demand from us, as the keepers of these treasures and beauties. To you I give one warning ; remember that our ancestors demanded of the hunter that he should possess spirit and character ; that he should have courage, care, bodily ability, ideals in thinking and love for his neighbour. That shall, and must, remain so !

Hunters who only shoot for gain and who count the ' Bag ' in hundredweights, must be prohibited from hunting. We need hunters who feel deep down within themselves the responsibility of placing the upkeep of the preserves before everything. I therefore demand that the German hunters shall subscribe to the moral idea of national socialism, ' For the individual, nothing—For the whole German people—All '. Hunters' Heil ![1]

[1] *Wiedmannsheil*—this is not a new word in the German vocabulary, neither is it a nazi word, but an old German greeting. When one meets a hunter in the road or in the fields, one offers him the *Weidmannsheil*—luck to the hunter, and he will respond with : *Weidmannsdank*—hunters' thanks.

ARTICLE IN THE *VÖLKISCHER BEOBACHTER*, 30th
January, 1936. S.A. Special Appeal edition. ' Adolf
Hitler's Fighting Troops.'

THE appeal to the oldest political soldiers in the
service of the Leader, on this 30th January will be
of special interest to all. From all over the Reich
representatives are arriving in the capital of the Reich, in
order to demonstrate in a tremendous march the harmony
of the political will, and which the fighters of the national
socialist movement will effectively make known.

Our old fighters of the S.A. have the right to proudly
represent hundreds of thousands on this historic day in the
Capital. We in the S.A. and S.S. have all stood up to our
baptism of fire, and are proud of the fact that we belong
to the fighting troops of Adolf Hitler, all of whom, from the
very first hour onward, have defended the flag of the movement with courage and bravery, and have borne it to
victory.

To-day, also, these storm troops carry the banners of
national socialism in the battle-tried hand.

When the Leader, during the early years of the struggle,
entrusted to me the control of the S.A., a time of hard work
and proud joy commenced for me. In a time, when all had
become discouraged and cowardly, or lazily mourned the
times which they thought were lost to them, the wonderful
years of pre-war Germany, there grew up in the S.A. men
a spirit as hard as steel, and they knew nothing but Leader
and Fatherland.

We carried the experiences of the Great War in our hearts
and in our minds, we were born out of the experiences of
the fight at the front line, but we did not live on beautiful

[*Translated and reproduced in English with acknowledgment to :* Völkischer
Beobachter.]

memories and traditions, which were misunderstood. We never stood in aloofness, on one side—we never referred to the deeds which we had accomplished in the past. No ! We grew out of the experiences of the hard fight and we hated the traitors of November, 1918. We loved our Germany, and our Leader, who was to us Germany, even if nearly the whole of the nation did not want to know anything about us. Hatred has made us strong, but love gave us the strength and the faith to cling on till victory came.

The S.A. men of Adolf Hitler were no nationalist middle class clubmen, but they were also not homeless mercenaries. The old S.A. men were tough fighters, real active revolutionaries, but they also knew discipline and voluntary obedience.

There did not exist for them any special interests, or politics—for them there was, and still is, only one thing— the will of the Leader. That was, and is, the S.A. of Adolf Hitler, the fighting forerunners of which, the old guard of which, had its baptism of fire before the Feldherrnhalle, and stood up to it splendidly.[1] This was the spirit in which the S.A. fulfilled its tasks during the long years of struggle. There have been times when ambitious fellows tried to misuse the S.A. and to besmirch its name and reputation with traitors' deeds. All these shameful attacks have foundered—they were obstructed by the loyalty of the S.A. men, who stood up against the deserters.

Never, during the years of fighting nor during the years of re-building, has the S.A. man been unfaithful. Every national socialist fulfils his duty on the place where he stands. No one must think himself higher than the other, and every organisation is worth as much as the other ; everyone has the opportunity for promotion through special deeds. In faithful comradeship, with the other branches of the movement, the S.A. has fulfilled its duty during the time of fight. Shoulder to shoulder, all national socialists have fought and won. And so it shall remain in the future. The care for it, and the responsibility that the S.A. shall also always in future stand as one man, is in the hands of one man, that

---

[1] Munich *Putsch* 9th November, 1923, see *Göring, the Iron Man of Germany.* H. W. Blood-Ryan. John Long Ltd. P. 90 *et seq.*

old fighter of the S.A. and now its chief of staff, Lutze,[1] who is the guarantee to us that the S.A. will fulfil its duty in the old spirit.

So, on the anniversary of the historic 30th January, we see again the old political soldiers of Adolf Hitler marching by in the same spirit of our old fighting call : ' So far the fear and death so near, good luck to you S.A.' ![2]

[1] After the execution of Roehm, 30th June, 1934, Lutze was appointed in his place as chief of staff of the Sturm Abteilungen.
[2] *Die Furcht so fern, dem Tod so nah, heil Dir S.A.*

SPEECH TO ONE THOUSAND FLIGHT-LIEUTEN-
ANTS IN THE GERMAN AIR FORCE ON THE
DAY OF THEIR TAKING THE OATH AND
RECEIVING THEIR COMMISSIONS, Berlin, 20th
May, 1936. On sacrifice, fulfilment of duty and
comradeship.

MY young comrades! First of all I greet you! I
have ordered you all here to-day because I want
to talk over some of the most important points
with the youngest officers of my Air Force. I have called
you here to-day so that from the very beginning of your
career you are clear about the way in which the compass
is set, and on which you have to direct your course during
your future soldierly life.

With enthusiasm—of that I am convinced—you have,
my young comrades, reported to the Air Force. You have
been very clear in your minds that this is a very special
soldierly occupation. You have known that you are already
called upon in great measure, in peacetime, to show what
you are made of; for no arm, in peacetime, demands so
great a sacrifice and calls for so much character and initiative
as ours. Your military duties have been explained to you,
and you are clear in your minds that it is upon those duties
that you are expected to build your whole future life. Next
to these routine duties there are, above all things, the
soldierly qualities which are required to be shown in every
officer and which gives him, in the long run, the right to
be a leader of men. There are three qualities which count
and which are age-old virtues of the soldier.

I have spoken already to some of you on these matters,
when I have been visiting one squadron or another.

They are the virtues of comradeship, the fulfilment of
duty and the readiness to make sacrifices—three virtues

which the soldier must make his own as a matter of course
—three virtues which I look for especially in the members
of the Air Force.

Comradeship—my comrades, you are all still very young
and, I hope, still very rich in enthusiasm. It is so very
natural that the human being shows himself in youth more
uncompromising than in more mature years, and out of
this need for compromise in life there develops very soon,
sympathy or antipathy. A friendship or comradeship is
formed.

I hope that you all possess the realisation at the bottom
of your hearts that one can only achieve something when
strength and energy are not directed against each other,
but when they are turned to united effort. This gathering
up of energy is achieved in true comradeship.

Just think about this yourselves. Why is it that the com-
radeships which were formed during the war have held firm
with people in later years—why is it that men are drawn
to each other in times of service—part in civilian life—and
still remain comrades when they meet again ? The main
reason is that all soldiers have the same conceptions. The
aim for all is the same, the foundations are the same, and
the work is the same. There are no opposing elements,
there is not one section representing this interest and another
representing that interest. All have the same interest—
service and sacrifice—and thus is formed, because opposition
of interests do not exist, the comradeship and the marching
along together in the same direction for the common cause.
This is the basis for comradeship, which is all-embracing
and such as we cannot find in any other occupation or in
any other walk of life—only in soldiering.

You will grasp what strength can lie in such a comradeship when you try to probe deeper into the heroic fight
which our nation fought during the world war, when you
investigate more closely individual human destinies, the
destiny of the little man right in front of the dug-out ; not
into great conclusions but into the strength of character
of the individual fighter, into their sufferings and yet their
wonderful great times. Then you will realise how often
this comradeship idea proved deciding, deciding not for

the few men who were soldered together, but deciding for the tasks which were given to them to undertake.

It is only natural that in a division, and particularly among the officers, where this spirit of comradeship does not rule, however perfectly trained they may be, duties cannot be discharged satisfactorily and it cannot fulfil its function. Therefore, those who do not follow the common interests are always disliked (in a military unit), especially those who pursue their career from an egotistical standpoint, who look upon their occupation as a soldier only from their own ambitious point of view, seeing in it only a means to an end, and thereby serving only their own purpose. We must all strive to put our own ego in the background and only see our own duty in front of us. That duty is called : Service for the Leader, people and Reich !

When you all see this as the original aim and purpose, and when you all strive to achieve it to the exclusion of all personal interests, then the ground work has been put in, providing for the growth of a spirit of strong comradeship.

Understand me well, my young comrades ! Man must have ambition, but it is important that he uses it as a means to an end and not that it shall become avenues for his own ego. Milksops, who have not the ambition to step forward in an effort to distinguish themselves, I have no time for. Only through healthy ambition can the highest deeds be achieved, but the ambition must not aim at personal success, but at achievement for the benefit of all. Ambition must work to this rule, if it is to remain a healthy means for driving onwards.

It must not, however, overrun everything, so that out of silent, misunderstood ambition, jealousy, grudges, discord, and in the end, hatred, may grow. That we will leave to other occupations, which out of their manifold interests pull against each other.

We want to bring ourselves to find a well of strength in united effort and comradeship, which will strengthen the individual in his hour of trial. You will learn in later life, often enough, the value of comradeship, and as they draw closer together you will find the bonds of friendship giving you a strength greater than your own.

Why do I demand comradeship so strongly?

Because I know the great strength that flows from it. When the whole Air Force knows only one will and advances in closest contact with each other, then when the danger is greatest I shall know what sort of thing this corps is capable of, because I know the strength which springs from comradeship. There, my young comrades, I ask you to further this aim ; stand together, respecting in the comrade, the comrade. Stand by him, even in the bitterest hour of your life. See in the life of your comrade things of greater importance than your own, and, in the long run, that will prove to be for your own good. A squadron will be rotten to the core if good comradeship does not obtain. Educate each other. Grind yourself down ; damp down that which you see in others, that which has the appearance of false ambition. Further everywhere the feeling of closest relationship. Become real comrades in the trust of each other. Secondly, the fulfilment of duty has always belonged to the soldier in every nation. This is, perhaps, because the soldier does his duty less for his own ego and less for his own advancement than for the advantage of the whole. This is the most wonderful thing of our soldierly occupation. We are not existing for ourselves, but we are one of a unit and work for that unit, which we call people, and set our all at stake.

It is a different matter when someone is working for his own gain, in order to enlarge his banking account, or works towards some other personal goal, than when he does his duty actuated by the feeling to work for a great aim which stands above his ego, and to which alone he only feels as a servant. There is, therefore, expected from the soldier the highest form of duty, because it is a wonderful duty to serve the fatherland, not on its own account, but for the future of the nation. Therefore, we demand from the soldier the highest fulfilment of duty and a readiness for sacrifice to the bitter end.

You have wonderful and splendid examples before you when you read the tremendous military struggle of the nations and when you start to investigate the individual cases of destiny. We must take the supposition that the soldier fulfils his duty as something absolutely natural and we must demand it. When, in spite of this, I try to add to it—when I call to you to rise above the measure of devotion to duty as a soldier and to improve upon it as soldiers of the Air Force, only then, when the Air Force achieves outstanding deeds, will the future of Germany be secured. The duties of young officers in the Air Force in peacetime are perhaps more arduous than in the other branches of the army, by virtue of the fact that more inner discipline is called for ; he is trained more in the ways of danger, and danger stands nearer to him than to the others. That alone demands strong nerves and inner strength, calling for a greater depth of character, and in the end, an additional fulfilment of duty.

It is now my ambition to instil in you this high additional feeling for duty, because only then can we look for greater achievements arising out of this feeling, for only when the armed forces are so trained, and prepared in peacetime, can it expect to achieve deeds in more serious times. When in peacetime, for example, you always fly blind, even in the heaviest weather, at night time and in fog still continue to make your routine service flights, then that calls for the greatest conception of duty—for it is much more cozy in bed—that means harnessing character to the task and fighting with oneself. When it comes to the more serious matter (of fighting), then the fruit of such fighting with oneself is vividly shown in the accentuated conception of duty. The closer a battery, squadron or company is tied together in this spirit, the clearer becomes the individual task, and the more the individual officer probes into his duties and into their fulfilment, the greater will become the effect of his work in serious times.

I therefore once again direct your attention to my appeal. Think about it yourself, and reflect upon the mission for which you have been chosen and think about it yourself, when I can say that I have the most disciplined, the best trained and the highest powered Air Force. That lies more in the realm of character and will of the individual than in technical equipment. The machine is dead, it only begins to live through you, through the strength which you give her, through your power and, most of all, through your will.

It still remains a fact that a bad machine with a good pilot, beats the best machine with a coward sitting in her.

Here, too, my young comrades, you have shining examples. Think about, and look into, the former lives of these examples —then you will realise that in the long run it was always the utmost fulfilment of duty and a proper conception of their duty, which inspired the Boelckes, the Immelmanns, and which led the Richthofens to their undying deeds.

Thirdly, this fulfilment of duty must rise even to readiness for sacrifice. That again is a thing which singles out the soldier from any other sphere. To be ready to sacrifice means to bring one's own self and all that one has as a sacrifice for something, out of which one can expect no personal gain or pleasure, but that that which is offered up goes toward the good of the community. I urgently advise you all to take the example of the last few years, which has become to us something holy, and not just an empty phrase. When I speak of readiness for sacrifice, there awakes in me a memory and I think back twenty years. I see before me all those who were ready to make sacrifices and those who daily made sacrifices—those who stood in the morning next to one, full of joy of life and whom, in the evening, we laid to peaceful rest.

It is no empty word ; it is no empty phrase. We were ready to be sacrificed. Some made the sacrifice and others were passed over by destiny, but the readiness was present in all, and that readiness distinguished the German army in the greatest of all wars. As long as the Germans are ready to give their lives, at any hour for their people and their father-land, so long shall we stand unconquerable. When ideas and thoughts creep into our minds which suggest that readiness for sacrifice is an unwise quality, thoughts which push the individual interests into the foreground, and forces the community to take second place, and when the whole nation becomes eaten up with such ideas, then the nation is soon finished. Thereof, too, my young friends, recent history is full of the most gruesome examples. This readiness for sacrifice I demand from you already in peacetime. I know that I could avoid sacrifices, I know that I could reduce losses to *nil*. That would be possible if I demanded nothing from you—if you only became 'fair weather' pilots, who had to try out nothing and, therefore, achieved nothing. It would be very simple, but you would then be a crowd who have forgotten your honour, and not soldiers. You may be convinced, my young friends, that it is something very terrible for me, when I see in some of my morning reports that this or the other young comrade has given his young life for the fatherland in the midst of peace. You may say that I just sit there at my desk and sign such a report.

Well, when you get a little older, when one or the other of you will have the responsibility for the lives of thousands, perhaps hundreds of thousands, then you will appreciate that there can be no heavier burden for the soul than to have to say to oneself " these sacrifices have been made because I asked for the highest, and in spite of these sacrifices and these dead, I have to continue my demands ". My dear young friends, for this one must have strength of soul, such as you to-day cannot yet comprehend.

Understand me, I do not demand it because I am ambitious to be the leader of the best Air Force. I demand it so that the eternal life of our nation can be continued. So you must look upon it, and so you have to be ready.

No sacrifice has been made in vain.

And that, again, is a wonderful and splendid thing in the Air Force—that we are always ready, in peace as well as in war—to show that we can make sacrifices.

Therefore, I am sure and convinced, that when the Leader calls you at some time for the highest effort, and for your full stake, that you will be ready to risk your life. Every human being shall love his life, and especially you young fellows shall do so—you shall be happy in your life and enjoy it. That is why you are young. I wish that you shall do so, but when the destiny of the whole people is at stake, then you must be ready to put your life at stake, because everyone knows that the future and the lives of millions of descendants will be secured.

Therefore, when comrades go from among you, honour them and keep their memory green. Do not weaken because of these sacrifices, but take fresh courage and strengthen yourself from the sacrifices which, alas, your comrades had to make.

Those are the three cardinal virtues which have to distinguish the soldier and, in greater measure still, the soldier of the Air Force. This already is so through the special training of the members of the Air Force, and has become so because of the special task of the service, both now and for the future.

Now when these three virtues—loyalty to duty, comradeship and the readiness to make sacrifices—are the fundamental virtues of the soldier, they become more especially the virtues of the national socialist, because national socialism can only be thought of as a militant thing. It was born out of the battle thunder weather of the Great War. It was brought to the people through a fighter, a simple soldier of the war. National socialism is the highest standard of soldierly behaviour in common life. National socialism gives to the individual German the wonderful world conception (*Weltanffassung*) and world views (*Weltanschauung*) into which he can fit his life, and in which he will find best everything that grows and blooms inside him. National socialism is a *Weltanschauung* which is tailored to the German measure—for the Germanic race. Perhaps, at some later date, it will be defined as being, after all, only the re-birth of the best Germanic spirit in a world of materialism. As much as I demand of you to behave as soldiers, I demand of you also that you belong to this world conception with all your heart and soul, which, after all, has made it possible for you to be soldiers—officers and especially officers of the Air Force. For that, too, you have to remember an unshakable truth : but for the victory of the swastika, there would be no Air Force to-day, just as there would be no German freedom or German honour. Only the terrible hard fight, into which the simple people threw themselves and for which they abandoned their all, has created, during the past decade, the platform for the new Reich, the platform on which a strong, better German army could grow. Therefore I ask of every soldier in the Air Force, and especially the officers, that he takes up the study of these points of view, for in the end the (National socialist) *Weltanschauung* is the compass needle of his life, by which he has to steer his course.

You have been thought of by a national socialist, that is by the greatest of all—the Leader, and you have been created by one of the most enthusiastic national socialists— by me. It is only natural, therefore, that we can only be national socialistic if only because of the fact that unity of thought of the highest aim achieves the greatest power.

I could find no use for a squadron, which in the most important matter of our conception, splinters to pieces. He who believes that he can't bring himself to think our way, he who is smitten by blindness or by a wrong upbringing or through false influences and wants to put himself against our ideas, must, as a decent fellow, take off the uniform and take the consequences.

Before the war, we gave our oath to the king and were therefore allowed to wear the king's uniform. It was unthinkable that one of us should have, say, the ideas of marxism in us and still continue to wear the king's uniform.

So now, no one can subscribe to another political philosophy and wear the uniform of Adolf Hitler and swear the oath to him, when he must be sold, body and soul to Adolf Hitler. I would not like to find any among us who have come to us from different reasons and who have taken the oath out of convenience. I do not mean that everyone of you has to have a great national socialistic past. What does matter is that you take a loyal and decent attitude to matters which are of importance to the state. For instance, I cannot inside myself be an opponent of national socialism and declare to the outside world, or perhaps even believe it myself, that I am loyal to the state. That is not possible. This state has been created out of national socialism and is national socialistic. When I long for it so much, and say to everyone of you that you must be through and through national socialist, I do so because I know how very necessary this standard line of thought is—in fact, it is just as necessary to you as the compass which keeps you on your course.

I have told you already that you were created through the victory of national socialism. You know what great sacrifices the people have made to achieve this, and from this knowledge alone you will know how to conduct yourself with the people. Before the war—that is, before your time, there existed a conception of life which divided the people —there were the ' possessing ' ones and the ' unpossessing ' ones. There was a huge gulf between them. One called the poor, the simple ones, the broad masses—' the people ', and if one wished to be refined—' the plebs '. But one never thought that oneself was of the people. They, those arrogant ones, they did not fall from the sky, they also came from the people, from the same blood, and from the same spiritual stuff. Thank God that this has now been overcome and that it is now only the very old, calcined, ossified old gentlemen who still seem to live on this idea. No. We all came from the people. It must be your greatest pride to be sons of the German people. You must be proud of the fact that you have German blood running in your veins, and that you are allowed to belong to this people, with its wonderful history and its still more great future.

To-day we do not have arrogance—national socialism does not know arrogance—it also does not know the conceit of rank. From this idea, handed down to us, you must all free yourselves. Just as we are firmly resolved to take over all the virtues of the old army, we are just as firmly resolved to free ourselves from all this superfluous stuff, which at one time added to the weakness of the then army. It was a misconception to lay so much stress on the honour of an officer—the idea of the position of the officer was all wrong —and, lastly, far too much was thought of his rank. The occupation of an officer is no special rank. The officer is a part of the people, and the possession of this so-called rank does not entitle its holder to assume with it arrogance. For if we would start like that, then we could not blame any other ranks for displaying a proportionate amount of arrogance. You have not to carry within you the importance of your rank, but the importance of being a soldier, and the greatness of being German ; and into this Germany, where at one time class hatred and conceit of rank tore the people apart and made the country weak, has stepped to-day the community of the people.

Compare these things to-day with what they were years ago, and remember what a wonderful experience this awakening of the people has been. Therefore, my young comrades, it is your duty to do everything to strengthen and develop this people's community ; to put away from you everything which could weaken this community. We see in everybody only the compatriot. It does not matter how he earns his living, it only matters that he works. The rest is only pure accident of fate. The one was born under one set of conditions, the other under another. It might well have happened that an accident occurred to your parents while you were still being educated—they might have lost their money—then you would not be sitting here as young officers, but would be standing at a factory bench behind a lathe or sitting over account books in an office. Such accidents of birth or position do not give us the right to be arrogant to those the life of whom fate has shaped differently to our own.

I do not ask you all where you come from !

I have on my staff, officers specially selected from among the common soldiers, and have learned to respect them as real men. One may come from the poorest of conditions ; from the most insignificant family, yet in truth he carries in his rucksack the marshal's baton. How much he may make out of himself in life depends entirely on him alone. To-day, nothing is a drawback. Conceited appearances of accident have been wiped away, the individual man is tested and stands, as a result, on his own value. And with that all weaknesses fall away which once contributed to the making of cleavages within the officers' corps itself. Therefore I desire, and command of you, that you take the people's community, created by the Leader, as an example, and that you become part of it—and that you count more valuable the poorest compatriot, than perhaps the richest and most prominent foreigner. Only when all of us think and feel like that will we become an unconquerable people's community.

You need only to study the last war and its end. The weighing up of all those imponderables—people's souls, people's opinion, people's feeling, will make you realise how deciding these imponderables are, and you will then further realise how much depends upon one thing : How the nation stands together in the fight. The time has passed when one said : " We will go into a jolly old war and come home in a few months' time laden with booty ". The nation has not much to do with war, some say ! No ? To-day war is a matter of life and death for every single one. The old man, and the baby in arms, are all just as much in danger as the soldier. The bombs do not ask and do not care. Therefore, we must be made out of one piece and out of one political philosophy. This is important, because in an hour of need, the whole nation has to work and deal uniformly, so that in this difficult hour the one part of the nation does not again throttle the other part to death, and make of it spoils for the enemy.

We have experienced it. When we came back to the people, hatred was flung in our faces. Down with the cockade ! Off with the shoulder straps ! The officers were made free game for all. Why ? Because the people were torn apart by different conceptions and political views. That cannot happen when the people are one united whole. This chapter of German shame which we have experienced must be closed for ever. To-day the people must be united, and must remain so.

I have the ambition and the determination to see my young Air Force stand within the people, and become the darling of the people. I know how the people think of the Air Force to-day. The people are proud of you. I can really say it. Perhaps they are proud of you because I myself am tied to the people, and am deeply rooted in the people, and am loved, and respected by them, and so they have included my Air Force too. That must remain so, comrades ! We shall be proud to think that the people give so much, and sacrifice so much, for us.

You stand in the minds and faith of the people as a defensive body, to which fathers and mothers like to send their sons most of all. The people know that the Air Force is that arm of the defence forces which will protect us most, and which will not allow our children to be murdered or the fruitful German land to be torn to pieces. This people has faith in you and you must justify this trust. That must be your pride.

When I speak of trust, then I must also speak of that trust which must be among you. From this so much depends. You must have trust in your leader, especially in me, your highest commander, just as I trust you as the bearers—the fulfillers—of our thoughts and mission. This trust is the firm basis on which we stand, and everyone who tries to shake this trust commits a crime, for he shakes to its foundation our young Air Force.

Only in blind loyalty to each other will we be able to master all our difficulties. You must trust to me to deliver to you at all times the best technically perfect material that we possess. The best that our inventors have thought of —that our constructors have designed and that our workmen have built, will be delivered to you as fast as it can be turned out from the factories. The speed of production rises from day to day and by every hour.

Our machines are as modern as those of the others. They are better ! The organisation of every Air Force in the world cannot by a long way reach up to the high standard of our own. We can say this without conceit. So have faith. We give you the best we possess. I have said already, that it is not the machine, but the man who sits in it who achieves most in the end.

I am not going to demand of you anything that I could not do myself. My life lies open before you—what perhaps I may have to demand of you one day, I have already given. You are not led by a coward. I can rightly say that I have never been a coward and I will never be one, whatever other mistakes I may have made. Therefore, the Air Force itself will never be cowardly, but will be of that same hardness of which my will has always been. I am not going to demand of you anything that I know cannot be done—anything that I myself would not be ready to do—and what all of us would be ready to do and what is absolutely essential to the fulfilment of our tasks.

I understand you ! Thank God I am not gone past the time when I can understand youth. You are young and it is my will that you experience this youth inside yourself.

Youth must possess joy and happiness in life, and I desire
that you should be happy and thirst for life. You can rely
on this : I will not obstruct any one of you (referring to
promotion) who just kicks over the traces in youthful pranks.
I prefer that to having place hunters and lickspittles in my
corps. Remain always so that you can look me in the eye
with open countenance. Then you will have done the right
thing. I do not ask the impossible of you. I do not ask you
to be model youngsters. I like to be magnanimous. I understand perfectly well that youth must be served, otherwise
it would not be youth. You may go and play tricks ; for
that you will be rapped over the knuckles.[1]

But that is not a deciding factor with me. What is, however, is that you are decent fellows—who are, in short—
men. You can fool about as much as you like, but when
the engine is running you have to be ' regular fellows ',
courageous, and driving all resistance to the ground. That
is what I demand of you. Be heroic daredevils !

I have said once before that I have before me the ideal to
possess an Air Force which, when the hour strikes, breaks
like a choir of revenge on the opponent. The opponent
must have the feeling that he has lost before he has even
fought you ! To that end you are trained already. Your
task must get so much into your flesh and blood, you must
be filled with it so much, that when the time comes you
know your job exactly. You must master your work and
blindly live for your duty.

Take your task seriously ! He who thinks that he has
become an officer in the Air Force for the sake of killing
time, and who is not ready at all times in the hour when
I demand it from you all, to stake his all at once, had better
choose another occupation.

I must have the conviction that I have fighters under
me, that I command young men possessed with iron determination for the deed. To prove ourselves through the
deed and to advance to the deed. That shall be our healthy
ambition.

---

[1] This is the nearest English equivalent for ' *dafür werdet Ihn dann etwas auf
den Kopf bekommen.*' If Field-Marshal Göring spoke this sentence in English,
however, he would most probably say : ' For that you'll get a thick ear.'

To-day you can be proud again to be Germans. What that means you cannot perhaps realise quite as much as we older ones, who have lived through the grey times, when we had to be ashamed to belong to Germany. You can be happy beyond measure to live in times like these. Read the history of our people and you will realise that no time has been so great, so powerful and so full of tasks as ours. You must feel very happy that you are allowed to work in the completion of those tasks. We are all very happy, every one of us, to be able to labour in this great work and to find a part in it.

And now for the last, my comrades ! As soldiers you have given your oath, you have sworn it to the Leader. You have named him in this oath by name. With that you have effected the closest contact that is possible between men. You have entrusted your life to the Leader—have given it to him. You have sworn to follow him to the death. This oath shall give you always in your life the closest relationship with the Leader. You shall feel : ' I myself am tied to my leader, directly and closely. The highest bond, the oath, ties me to him '.

I need not tell you what this oath means. It is, after all, the highest thing possible. With this oath you have voluntarily entrusted yourselves to the Leader, as his followers. Loyalty was the most prized possession of our ancestors. It shall be our highest possession too ; Faith in the Leader and loyalty to the people.

My young comrades ! Take to your hearts what I am about to say. When at your work, look into yourself, and later in your life, sometimes look over the past, chapter by chapter and then remember that to-day it was my greatest wish to give you for your future life the best that I could give you. Then remember that this hour had the purpose of drawing us closer together, that you belong to me as much as I will belong to you. Then, believe me, life will lie before you, great and beautiful, and worth living. My warmest wishes go with you all. Be men ! Be worthy of Germany !

SPEECH AT THE BERLIN SPORTS PALACE, dealing
with the problem of the Four Year Plan, 28th October,
1936, and which was broadcast to the nation.

MY dear German compatriots! The Leader has
clearly and simply stated at Nuremberg a matter
of the highest importance—why he has set before
the German people a second Four Year Plan.[1] The Leader
has ordered me to pull it through. Here, before the whole
German people, I am going to show to-day the way in
which we all can best solve these problems.

What is the second Four Year Plan? I will embrace all
its aims in one sentence. The maintenance of German
honour and the maintenance of German right. A clear
aim. We know to-day how far German honour and life
are secured, and we also know that, in the second Four
Year Plan, Germany must be placed on a sound business
footing, through the expansion and strength of German trade.

It is the purpose of my speech to explain my future
activities to you. We National Socialists do everything
before the eyes of the people, with the people and standing
in the midst of the people. Therefore to-day I want to
explain to the people the way it can, and must, help. My
authority comes from the Leader and I am to assume full
powers in order to obtain unified direction of the great
national aim.

The starting point is the position of to-day.

The first Four Year Plan shows great achievements. We
all know and the whole world knows, what it means now
that Germany has won back its freedom and the right of
armed protection, and is to-day defended by the steel wall
of the will and power of our new army.

[1] When Herr Hitler became Chancellor in 1933 he asked for four years in
which to improve conditions in Germany.

Who does not remember the miserable conditions in agriculture at the time when the Leader called upon the farmer to fight the great battle of increased production? To-day the farmer sits once more secured on his own ground. Hand in hand with the battle of production went the great fight to find work, the greatest which a nation has ever fought. Nearly seven million unemployed had to be brought back into work again, and bread had to be given to them. This task is nearly solved.

Who does not remember the terrible misery of unemployment ; the time when the tired man wandered from door to door? He started every morning with fresh hopes, and each evening he came home, hopeless and in despair. To-day, millions are in work and earn money again. Industry started to flourish once more, one factory after another was re-opened and the gruesome position, when the wind howled through the windows of decaying and derelict factories, was done away with. Everywhere again the rotating of wheels and everywhere again the clanging of hammers on anvils ! But foremost, and that in the end is the foundation of all things, during the past four years German honour and freedom have been restored. So the saddest chapter in German history is closed—the pages of shame and disgrace are torn out and we have put behind us misery and need. The new chapter was opened with the motto : Freedom and honour are the fundaments of the German Reich !

It was only natural that these internal political achievements should also have outer political success. Once, Germany lay torn to pieces inside, unconscious, while on its back the other nations united. Germany was the paying slave for the whole of Europe. To-day Germany is again a great power, united, strong and armed, with which the world must count.

I pointed out already what great achievements have been made in the economic world, but it is just in this field that still more has to be done ; it becomes important to strengthen German trade and industry in order to make Germany independent. In no territory was greater sin committed than in this one. Started at Versailles, like an unbreakable thread, the ruin of German trade went on

N

down to economic barrenness and breakdown. From that point it went down to where the misery started that we all know so well and which most of you have already forgotten again to-day, because our recent achievements are so great that this nightmare seems to lie in some remote past, and we do not remember, and we do not like to remember, this terrible horror.

But what the Leader—what the movement—had to create in order to bring about these changes, must be always pointed out. German trade and industry, plundered and exploited by the Jew, and beaten by the marxist class spirit, delivered the German workman over to the misery of unemployment. That was the most destructive power for the lives of the German workers. Tremendous achievements, therefore, were necessary for re-construction. Now I ask you and ask all compatriots : " What has the movement promised and what has it kept, in those four years ? What has it achieved " ? and we can always answer, proudly, " a wonder, yes, a great German miracle has happened in those four years ".

Between the past and to-day lies a huge gulf. In those four years, through the collective strength of the nation and the genial leadership of Adolf Hitler, through leadership in party and state standing together in a common front, great things have been done. But we must not rest on our laurels. We are obliged to work on and to expand our power to the utmost.

The international and political situation gives Germany no peace. On these issues we have to be clear. We must understand that, even to-day, no one likes us to have our place in the sun—we must understand that no one helps us forward if we do not help ourselves.

We have grown out of our own strength and we will go forward on our own strength. We will not be hampered by the lying reports in foreign newspapers, which endeavour to show up conditions in Germany in a wrong light. In these newspapers one can read that in Germany the people are in for a rotten time, because a new Four Year Plan has been announced. They almost reproach us for not having adequate supplies of raw materials, and that we want raw materials and that we wish to participate in the good things of the world. Therefore I say : " Yes ! we want part of it and we will have part of it ! " Is that a cause for reproach ? Do they want to reproach us that we have not enough nutritive products ? Is it a disgrace that we have not got enough raw materials in our land ? The world can indeed be happy that we try only by peaceful means to seek that which is kept from us. We have no colonies. After an unlucky war they were taken from us. They declared to us that, if we wanted raw materials, then would we please buy them with gold. We would be only too glad to pay in gold, if only the gold had not been taken from us. It is just irony. First Germany is plundered, is made to bleed itself white, and then it is told : ' what do you want with colonies ? Pay with your gold ! ' ' Give us back our gold and we will pay you with it.'

We will, if possible, create from our own resources the things that are kept from Germany. That is why we must exert ourself. If that is supposed to be a weakness of Germany, then they will have to get used to the position, and correct this view, as well.

We Germans have worked hard during the last four years to keep our nation in food. In spite of our not having raw materials—in spite of all, Germany is a land of order, satisfaction and cultural re-construction. We know exactly, and the Leader said it at Nuremberg, that, in spite of the exertion of all effort, Germany cannot be completely self-supporting.

In Germany there are, after all, 136 people living to the square kilometre. If we had only a portion of the colonies, which other lands possess in superfluity, then there would be no need at all to speak of the need for raw materials or food produce.

God has given us our Germany as it is, and we will administer it as well as we can. We are aware of the cause of the shortage of things, from time to time, during the last few years, and we know why foodstuffs cannot be had plentifully at all times of the year. The Leader has told us that, too. We have had the good fortune to give work to millions of people, so that they are earning once more and can buy food with their own money. Because of this, the consumption of essential food has grown and the increase cannot easily be satisfied—but it has been satisfied up till now. What has to happen now? We can only produce some of the things, even if we increase our agricultural production. Certainly we will do all in our power to increase production. We will call upon the Nutrition Board (*Reichs-nährstand*) to do all in its power to get the last ounce of produce from the German soil. We will try to improve the land by means of better methods of culture and new fertilisers, and we will improve the organisations of distribution, so that the produce reaches the consumer quicker and in better condition. But, through all these measures, it will not be possible to bridge the gulf completely.

Naturally, it will be our most important task to secure the German harvest, at all times. The setting up of various organisations has shown us how this can be easily achieved. The men in the Labour Camps, for instance, can be put to harvesting work from day to day, in order to bring the harvest into the barns. The German farmer and agriculturist must see one thing first of all, and that is what a holy possession the German cereal harvest is, because, through bread, it safeguards the nation's nutrition. For what is more important to nutrition than cereals from which bread is made? German farmers! take the greatest care with that most holy possession of our German soil.

We hear that there will be a scarcity of meat, so we have to reckon on a tightening up in this section of nutrition, too. Here, too, all will happen for the good of the community. We will try to improve conditions under which breeding takes place and provide for the breeding of more cattle. But, remember, there is another thing just as good as meat. There is fish, and when the meat supplies run low, we will take care, in those intervals of scarcity, that there will be adequate supplies of fish.

But our greatest need is fat. We have to import more of this than we can produce, and because of this there is the greatest need for economy. We will, nevertheless, leave nothing undone in our efforts to secure a larger volume of supplies. If everyone helps, and realises that Germany is not rich enough to throw away waste food, but that this waste must be collected and sent to the great cattle fattening centres, then the fat position will become easier.

A most important and decisive factor is that we safeguard the less wealthy and the more hard-working section of the populace, and see to it that they have everything necessary to the upkeep of their strength, thus enabling them to carry on their hard work.

The proclamation of the Leader that, under all conditions, cheap and sufficient fat supplies must be reserved for the poorer sections of the public, must be a holy order, to be kept under all circumstances. We will be able to arrange for this in one supply organisation without issuing food cards, particularly if everyone keeps his head.

It is natural that one has to impose certain restrictions if one wants to do great things, and I am now going to appeal to the German housewife. A great responsibility rests on your shoulders. You must in future always put on your menu those meals the food for which is assured, according to season and which is home grown. It is a sin for one to want to buy just this or that merely for the sake of having it, when one knows that at certain seasons of the year it is not available. The more prosperous households might give thought to that. Some while ago there was a certain vogue, and it was thought very refined, to put on one's table in Winter the tender vegetables which grow abroad, and it had always to be those ' which were not to be had '. We eat what the German soil yields us. We will, through a timely explanation about the current supplies from time to time, advise the German housewife as to what foods are available and necessary, so that it won't be necessary for them all to stand in queues outside the shops.

I repeat—use as nutritious foodstuffs, as far as possible, those things that can be produced at home, because then the scarcity problem is alleviated. These scarcities occur in certain seasons, and they cannot easily be overcome. For instance, things like eggs, milk, butter and cheese are products which we cannot influence a great deal. There are certain times when chicken lay eggs plentifully and others when they lay only few. There are times when the cows give their milk plentifully, and in some seasons their milk does not flow so richly. My dear compatriots, so far human wisdom has not been successful in shaping the ways of nature differently to what is intended. Nobody has yet had the luck to make a hen lay an egg if she did not want to.

This tightening up of supplies and so-called scarcity of food has its peculiarities. There is, to our greatest sorrow, still a certain type of compatriot among us who has in fact, always wanted to go out and buy what is not there. When they hear of a so-called scarcity of eggs, although they never eat eggs, they rush out and buy them. They are the sort of people who, if one was to tell them in the middle of winter that straw hats were scarce, would instantly rush to the shops and buy up a dozen straw ' lids ', just to hoard.

The most important thing to us is that the broad masses of our people shall have sufficient food in order to work with all their strength. For that I will take the responsibility —that I will safeguard. Here, too, I am reminded of the words of our Leader, spoken in Nuremberg : " It is not so important to have to do without fat and eggs—that is bearable—but that we have done away with German unemployment, that we have made human beings once more out of these millions of people who were in misery, idleness and who were thoroughly demoralised—that is something great ". Who does not voluntarily deny himself a pound of butter for that is not worthy to be a German.

Scarcity obtains in the realm of raw material. Of course, again, it is because we have no colonies. But I can't sit down and browse over that. We do not possess them, and that is that. Therefore we must exert all our thoughts and resources to produce raw materials with the help of the inventiveness of our scientists and technicians. Here will lie the main task which I and my responsible men have to fulfil. Great work remains to be done in every field of endeavour. Here I would express my thanks to those who have already done great things, particularly the Economics Minister and the President of the Reichsbank, Schacht, and

Keppler, who up till now has been the deputy commissioner deputed by the Leader.[1]

Great achievements have been reached by both men, providing solid foundations to build upon. But it now becomes a matter of importance for us to change over from the experimental stage into the practice and production of what our researches have proved. We must show facts and deeds, with all our energies. During the next few months new factories will spring up, in which we will make our own rubber and cellulose, from which we will make our own weaving materials for clothing. We would renounce all this if only the nations abroad would realise that they can't tie us, and that we won't be shut off.

We could, God knows, create fruitful work, and it would surely be much more simple for us to trade in a world of sense and reason on an economic basis and to exchange goods and services, than to have to stand alone by ourselves in such a mad world.

We are now going to create petrol and mineral oils from German coal. I can tell you a secret. To-day we have already achieved the production of a good scented soap from our own coal. I could say much more about all those things which German genius, the German spirit of invention and the German energy and sense of discovery have brought about. He who to-day sticks to his work, receives a damned great respect for all that which has already been achieved.

We will also open up our own iron and other metal resources. The great point is, after all, always to master the matter. When known alloys become impossible through lack of raw materials, we will make new alloys, which will be just as good. In the case of light metals, such as aluminium, there are no end of things at our disposal. Coal, wood and German ore will in future be the basis for the factories engaged in the national production of raw materials and working materials.

[1] Wilhelm Keppler was a man of great experience in the management of food supplies and municipal control, before even the Nazi regime. Prior to the inauguration of the Four-Year Plan he had already been commissioner of food prices—virtually food controller, a position which will become more important in Germany as time passes. It is interesting to note that Keppler flew to Vienna a few days before the *Anschluss*, and his organizing ability proved of great value in bridging over many difficulties.

A tremendous programme ! Great buildings, mighty factories shall spring up in order to show to the world that Germany has not capitulated. Germany insists on its own right to live and will form its own destiny. So another economic boom will set in. But, remember, everyone of you who takes part in it—not for the individual, not for a few— but for the whole German nation. That can only come about when all help ; that can only be pulled through when every single one breaks with the old ideas, when at last this old terrible shyness for the new things is overcome. It need not always be foreign materials (for clothes). The German cloth will be just as decent. Be proud of your own product. Be proud of what the German brain and brawn have created. That ennobles you—not this everlasting running after foreign countries !

To be strong in yourself—to stand strong in your own nation, that must be our watchword, and therefore I call to you all once more for the output of all your energies.

To industry I would like to say one thing : It has a great, a very great responsibility. The individual factory owner and the great industrialist must not always wait for the state to make suggestions or for the state to order. They must, and shall, find by themselves ways and means, and shall not shy at some extra exertion and strain in order to help us in this work.

Now, my dear factory owner ! You always speak of the free initiative of industry, now you have the free initiative ! Use it ! When I say that the whole people must help with the work, that all must come and help and exert themselves, one thing must be understood. If I am to fulfil the plan in four years, if I am to do away with need and scarcity in four years, then something must happen—it does not come about by itself. We must work for it, and this working for it demands first of all the preparation of requisite factories. These are buildings and for these we need workmen, bricks and other building materials. That implies that in the future we shall have to ponder over which buildings in the German Reich are most important. The most essential are first of all those buildings necessary for our re-armament, the factories and buildings of the Four Year Plan and the houses for the settlement of our German workers. After that the rest will come. We will therefore go about this in a proper order, complying with the emergency of the thing.

Without the united and enthusiastic support of our German workmen the whole scheme, from its inception, would be impossible. That just shows how different the woes of the different nations are. We have to think where we can get sufficient workers from, and the others have to worry to find work for their labour. But I believe that our worry is the more beautiful one.

The question of to-day is, ' how can I get the necessary workmen ? ' The German workman must realise that he can help the plan of the Leader only when he works, works and works again, when there is no disunity and no quarrel in the various works, and when the work goes on from morning until night, until the work is finished. Therefore, everyone has to comprehend the need for peace in industry. In the factory itself, joy and the gladness of work must rule. All liars and denouncers must get out—they have no place in Germany !

In order to complete our work, we cannot, at the moment, increase the wage standard. It is impossible. As confirmation of that I will read you the words of the Leader : " It would have been possible for leadership in state and industry to increase wages by 20, by 40, by even 50 per cent, but raising wages without increasing production is self-cheating, which the German nation has experienced once before. By national socialist economic conceptions, it would be madness to increase wages and at the same time to shorten working hours. That means cutting production, for the whole wages of the nation are distributed over the whole production which can be consumed. When the whole income rises by 15 per cent, but the total production falls by 15 per cent, any increase in the wages of the individual will not only be without result, but will be just opposite, because the drop in production will lead to a complete devaluation of the money, and there would be the same dance, which we had gone through once before, to our own pain." It is therefore clear why we must explain to our workers why this is necessary. Just as much as it is the duty of the trustees, who have been put in industry by the state, to arbitrate upon and to equalise wage questions, and to be responsible for peace in the factories and in industry, so the German Work Front (Arbeitsfront)[1] has to throw itself enthusiastically, with all its mighty organisation, into the service of this plan, not only to educate the workmen in our conceptions, but to direct them again and again to the great aims, and to make clear to them, over and over again, what the Leader expects from them and to convince them that it depends on them, if Germany shall be reconstructed.

For the rest I can only say this : " He who is still communist to-day, after all the proof in Germany of re-construction, and after all the terrible ruin wrought in Spain, he can't even excuse himself by ignorance, he is just bad, he wants to be bad, he wants to destroy, and he does not want to know of building up ". When we demand fixed wages, we also pre-suppose the existence of fixed prices and their remaining fixed. Here too we will put ourselves out with all the enthusiasm we can muster. A price controller has been placed in office by the Leader, an old national socialist fighter, and I am going to give him directions for the necessary line of action. He will get from me the necessary authority to prevent, under all circumstances, any further increase in commodity prices and, where it is necessary, to compulsorily reduce prices which to us may seem too high. To foresee the development of conditions before they have started to develop is a good plan. The signs of coming difficulties have to be recognised at the right moment, and once the difficulty itself is realised, it can be overcome. The price controller will be furnished with such authority as he may need to combat the pests that abound in his field of operations—a pest, which for any nation in a position like ours, must prove fatal in the end—a pest which must be pulled out root and stem : This damned hoarding ! He

---

[1] *Arbeitsfront.* It is a common mistake in England to translate this into, and to consider it to be, workers' front. It has been assumed, wrongly, by most writers that this is a Nazified milk and water edition of the old social democrat trade union movement. Actually, for example, if one in England took the various trade unions and the various employers' federations and merged them into one whole, with a representative governing committee drawn from both types of organizations, one would have a fair parallel. Even the small shopkeeper carries on his door *Mitglied der Arbeitsfront* (Member of the work front.)

who hoards, commits a sin, violates the nation. He who stores away more than he can use, takes away from the others and is no compatriot. The same goes for those who drive up prices, for they are greater criminals against the people still. They think only of their own ego—their own belly is their god—and not of the German nation, of which they should think. It will be the task of the price controller to exercise constant vigilance, to control all prices, and to ascertain if prices are justified, or if they are made for egotistical purposes and spring from a lust for gain. If he finds this latter to be the case, then he will intervene ruthlessly. I can only say, that I will repress with draconian methods, be they so strict as to be thought barbaric, all attempts to use Germany's need for their own purpose. That I promise the German nation.

Speculators also come within this category. They too shall know that it will not be so easy for them in the future as it has been up till now. In this class also come those who hold their goods back from the open market, waiting for high prices and festival prices to come—who tuck away their stocks and thus create a sudden scarcity. If I should find that one may buy a certain type of goods to-day with ease, and that to-morrow a higher price is quoted for it, and then the supply has disappeared, I will have those goods dug out.

We will not only take the goods away, but these parasites will lose their means of existence also. No one shall wonder ! He who is ready to commit robbery of German possessions, to steal German goods, him we will dispossess and hand over his assets to the nation.

The task must come to success, because we will it and because we are national socialists, having the strength to bring our desires to fruition. Therefore criticism is no use. Criticism is not going to stop us, and also does not interest any one of us. If one of you wants to curse, do so with all your heart—it does not matter, we have also cursed and yet done our work. If one of you curse because some of the orders are not to your liking—well and good—but they have to be carried out. That is certain. We must attack the things with a fresh and healthy optimism ; for only optimism gives a fresh and joyous strength to work, which we need in order to shape things. We believe in our people. We know that it will be great, and we know that it has a great future and, because of that, we know that we have to go this way.

And with that I am coming to a most important point. To-day I take over the direction of this plan. That means, that we are to-day standing at a certain point, zero, the lowest point. To-day the need is greatest. It is a narrow pass through which we have to go. In six months' time the position will be improved a little, for by that time a number of measures which we shall have taken will by then already be successful. Within the year we shall be a few steps higher, and so we will go steadily onward.

The deciding factor is, after all, that I can, and am allowed to show you a clear aim. It is not like it was in the time of the ' system ', when you were asked to make one sacrifice after another ; when you had to bleed and had to pay tax after tax, when you had to give more and more money to a barrel without a bottom. One never saw another ray of hope than that most questionable ' silver stripe '[1] which, in passing, was shining for but a few. Compared with this, to-day we see clear aims. There it lies—there is the stake—we must get through and win it. That is clear. Therefore I must not make any empty promises, but must show you a positive objective, for which we have to strive—and then ? What is six months in which you will have a little less meat, what is six months in which it will be difficult to buy this or that piece of goods ? All that is not the end of the world, it is a ridiculously small thing in comparison with the great things to which we are going. It will be my duty, and the duty of my colleagues, to see that we do not resign ourselves to the fact that to-day there is a needy position in Germany.

As Germany has not got certain raw materials and food-stuffs in sufficient measure, perhaps we ought to be tempted to say : " Because Germany has not enough we must think

---

[1] Equivalent to silver lining, and in this case is a reference to a saying so often repeated by politicians of the Weimar Republic : ' *Ich sehe einen Silber-streifen am Horizont* ' (I see a silver stripe on the horizon).

of happy ideas to distribute the little it has ". No ! I don't waste time with that thought. No ! We will exert ourselves in a great effort, we will think and work, worry and work and work again and find out how we can get those things for the German people that are missing to-day. That is our job !—to which we will give all our energy and strength of decision. Therefore all should work with us. For our nation shall not be more worsely situated than any other nation on the earth. In order to get the missing things, which will have to be done complying with certain measures of time, we will have to take some passing shortage into the bargain. Now I will call once more to all. Follow my orders and measures. It is necessary that they are followed by all ; most of all it is necessary that they are followed with a happy heart, and that every single one shall have the feeling that he is helping the Leader, and helping Germany. Everyone must tell himself again and again : " It depends on me ! " When everyone takes that to heart, then we will get through. Then that will be the proof, the most wonderful and glorious proof of our national unity, which we can then give to the whole world. Do not believe that we give orders and issue measures in order to torture you or boss you about ; that we could not do.

When something has to happen, then it must happen for the good of all. When an individual is anywhere oppressed, then he must realise that it benefits someone somewhere else, and he must think that, in the end, from somewhere it will come back for his own good again ; that he must understand. It is not so great a sacrifice to give up some comfort in order to arrive at the freedom of the nation. The stronger we are armed, the more securely we stand and the less likelihood there is of being attacked.

The Leader, and we all here, the leaders—we demand nothing of you that we do not do hourly and what we are not ready to do ourselves. Too much fat—to many fat bellies ! I myself have eaten less butter and have lost twenty pounds.

We want to create a strong independent nation ! So I call out to you and to all the millions who are listening on the wireless in this hour, for work and help. Particularly do I direct myself to all inventors, to men of science, for their collaboration. ' Think hard, make experiments, work in your laboratories, give us new ideas, new inventions and new possibilities, and you will have done great things for Germany.'

I appeal to all industrialists and business men : " Think not to your profit, think of a strong, independent, national economy in Germany and throw in all that you have as your share—your great experience, your ability, your knowledge, energy and initiative ".

To the German workmen : " On you, on you most of all, depends the success of the work ; prove that class exists no longer, prove that you are Germany's most faithful sons ".

I appeal to the farmers of Germany : " You farmers have the life of the nation in your hands, your responsibility is greatest, the feeding of the nation. Secure us food, secure us bread. Germany has done a lot for you farmers during the past few years ; be thankful now and do everything for Germany."

With special fervour I address myself to the National Socialist Workers Party and all its organisations : " Your Reich is at stake. It is our state which you have conquered and which you have created. From now on I expect you to put your all at stake, as in the old fighting times. The leaders of the party—the old guard, standing at the head of the leaders of the districts (*Gauleiter*). Carry the people with you—march—and success will come to the work."

The national socialist movement proves that nothing is impossible, and that it will never capitulate.

I call upon the whole nation : " Forward in full strength ! Thank the Leader that he has created a new Reich, a new people and a new nation ! "

The Leader has given me a difficult office. I did not push myself into it. I have enough work to do and, quite apart from this, economy is not my territory. But I am ready to do my utmost, not as an expert—I say that quite openly— not as a great economist or still greater factory owner— but with a limitless will, with a flourishing belief in the greatness of my people and with an enthusiastic heart, from which alone great things can be done. I do not come as an expert. The Leader sends me purely and simply as a national socialist. As a national socialist fighter, as his deputy, as the deputy of the national socialists I stand here and will finish the work.

Nothing in the world can break down if the will remains. As long as the will remains unbreakable, all else is unbreakable, except that which the will seeks to break. Behind me stand the men of the state, the leaders of the party, the old fighters, the provincial leaders and the bearers of our movement ; not disunited and breaking down under the strain of the internal strife, as the press abroad tries to make out, but united and with a firm will for the deed.

And with that realise one thing : We do not work for ourselves, but for the happiness and security of those who come after us, for the peace and happiness of our children. They shall have a better time. The trust in the Leader— and perhaps that is the most deciding—the loyalty to the Leader and the good faith among each other, is our greatest capital. The money of the whole world cannot weigh against this and it is, too, the best and the most secure currency, on which Germany lives to-day.

The Leader does not ask the impossible of you. What he demands can be done, for he himself has always done things. What he has promised he has always kept. When one of you thinks that he, particularly, has to work very hard, and that he, especially, has to suffer and carry many worries, and he becomes weak, then let him cast his eyes to the Leader, and let him see how this man works and what sort of life he lives. Our Leader works for us. Think of his worries, think of the nights when he carries the destiny of the whole nation on his shoulders. Think of the terrible weight of some of his decisions. Think of his gigantic responsibility to the future of the nation. This man carries a terrific burden for you. Be ready to bear just a little burden for him.

What has he made for us out of that Germany which we found on taking over power ? He has led us upward out of deepest misery ! His trust in the nation has helped to overcome all difficulties in singular fashion ! It is a great time in which we are living. Be proud that you are alive to see it. Away with all these small matters—away with all egotism. A great time demands a great nation. Prove that you are the great nation. Be worthy of our Leader, Adolf Hitler !

Once again I tell you : Think, every one of you, what you can do for the success of this work, and let that work be our thanks ; the sign of our trust in the Leader and the badge of our belief in him. He has led the German people out of despair and unbelief, back to faith again, and through this has made us unbelievably strong. We believe in the great mission of the German nation. We believe that, under the Leader, there will grow up a Reich of strength, a nation of honour and a people of freedom. Those are our watchwords in this hour.

Therefore, in this hour in which we start our work, we pray with ardent faith to the Almighty : Almighty God, bless the Leader, bless his people and bless his work !

RESPONSIBLE LEADERSHIP IN TRADE AND IN-
DUSTRY. An article in *Der Vierjahresplan*, February,
1937.[1]

THE day of the national awakening this year was also
a day for thinking back and looking back over what
has been achieved in the first four years of national
socialist government. Back to what the Leader in 1933 laid
down as some of his great tasks—the removal of unemployment, saving the German farmer from ruin and recovering
for Germany the right of self-determination in the matter of
self-defence, accompanied by the building of the new German army. But the 30th January[2] was more than that; it
was the day of fulfilment, the fulfilment of the struggle for
German equality in the world. In his great speech to the
Reichstag the Leader has solemnly, and before the whole
world, denounced the (German) signatures which were set
to the Treaty of Versailles.

With this act he removed for ever the war-guilt lie, and
from this step the following may be drawn as logical
conclusions. The just right of Germany to colonies, the
reinstatement of unrestricted control of the Reich over the
Reichsbank and the German Railways. Germany has now
its full equality in the world and, in every regard, it has
won it back.

If the Reichstag meeting of the 30th January stood thus
in the sign of the successful conclusion of the first period of
national socialist state leadership in Germany, it also pointed
to the very important tasks awaiting us.

[1] The official journal of the office of the Four Year Plan.
[2] 30th January, known as the day of national awakening, has been set
aside in German life as a public holiday and ranks somewhat like the British
Empire Day. It celebrates the date of the Nazi accession to power and the
formation of the Third Reich.
[*Translated and reproduced in English with acknowledgment to :* Der Vierjahresplan.]

With great clarity, which cannot be misunderstood, the Leader has again given expression to the will of Germany to participate in the pacification of Europe and the world. He pointed back to his earlier constructive proposals and once again to the political task of all cultured nations ' to fight the world danger of bolshevism '. Only strong nations can participate in this task of world political and historical importance.

It is therefore not Chauvinism, but the expression of the will to live of the German nation, when the Leader has declared in the Reichstag our intention to carry on with the Four Year Plan ; for the Four Year Plan will lead us to this national strength and independence which is necessary for Germany's self-assertion.

Therefore, during the coming years, the Four Year Plan will govern the whole of Germany's social and economic life. Its success depends upon the close collaboration of its highest officials, and their absolute will to safeguard the freedom and life of the nation. It is this will which gives us this high right ; and this right, in some cases of necessity, will rise superior to individual laws, ·where it becomes possible no longer to do justice to the living necessity of the nation. But above all this stands the great aim of the people, as expressed by the Leader thus : " The real life of our people, as it has now taken shape in the form of the (Nazi) state, to seal it through a constitution for ever and eternally, and so to lift it up as an eternal fundamental law for all Germans."

Economy, and with it the practical carrying through of the Four Year Plan, must to-day direct itself by the uniform will of the highest Leadership, as well as by the highest standard, in order to exert and to use all our present working energies, and in order to fully cultivate the soil in our possession and to secure it for all time. " With this ", said the Leader, " it is firstly a problem of organisation." For us, economy is not just causatic mechanics, which follows its own laws. To-day the hypothesis of the liberal theory of German economics is less true than ever, and we, with our strong and uniform leadership in economics, are going to found our own organisations in all territories of economic life, which will fulfil their functions expertly and purposefully.

For instance, we are, therefore, in a position at all times to keep prices stable. With us there are no such things as ' price rising tendencies ', which are not justified and can be averted, except in special cases. The same goes for those ' preferences ' of supply in raw materials one comes across in single production fields. The highest economic leadership, through its organisations, will take steps to prohibit the growth of these unhealthy ' tendencies ' over our plan as conceived by us.

We do not recognise the sanctity of some of these so-called economic laws. It must be pointed out that trade and industry are servants of the people, while capital also has a rôle to play as the servant of economy.

Naturally, the economic experts and economic leaders will always, from their own standpoint, point out the need for raw materials as economic necessities and their expert judgment will always be the foundation on which the statesmen will base their final decisions. But beyond this, for his decision on measures, the statesman has also to take into consideration the foreign political, domestic political and psychological problems as factors, the knowledge of which, as a whole, is not as a rule generally known to the economists. In order to awaken the understanding of the whole nation and of every economist to his problems, the statesman will again and again appeal to the whole economic and political workers for a correct attitude to economy—to the factory owners as well as to the workmen.

But, as statesmen, they must always reckon with the fact that there are always errors which rule humanity and that errors will always occur.

The statesman can never entirely rely upon the good behaviour and the good wishes of the individual, but must reckon with both types of humanity—with well-intended help and with egotistical obstruction—and must direct his organisation accordingly. When to-day every single member of the nation is appealed to for untiring help in the Four Year Plan, responsibility falls equally upon the leading men in trade and industry, to do all in their power to enlist all available help, to bring it to the right effect and to remove misunderstanding wherever possible, which could injure the nation's welfare.

That is the duty and the responsibility inherent and implied in their office of leader. Next to the highest leadership (ministers), with their firm resolution to do everything for securing the life and freedom of the nation, they will be the guarantors of the real national unity, which sets all at stake in order to fulfil the Four Year Plan.

SPEECH AT A CONFERENCE IN BERLIN, GERMAN MUNICIPAL DAY, 8th April, 1937, in which the participation of the municipalities in the Four Year Plan is discussed.

M Y lord mayors and mayors ! Dear party members. I especially greet this opportunity of speaking to you on the Four Year Plan and of the share which the municipalities are going to take in it. The German municipal association and the municipalities which have been re-organised through it, have already stood their test during the past few years and are now able to tackle greater tasks. It is the aim of the German municipal association to create strong municipalities in a strong state. Perhaps this has not been quite achieved in some districts, but I am sure that the new decrees, which are about to come into law, and which will lay down the new constitution of the municipal association and set out orders governing the administration of the municipalities, will be finished in the very near future and will rectify this discrepancy.

To-day, gentlemen, I do not intend to talk to you about specific municipal problems, but I wish to explain to you how I think the municipalities can do their share in the Four Year Plan, which the Leader has given to me to put through and which, for the time being, is taking up all my working time.

The Four Year Plan, looked at from the political angle, is a powerful exertion of the strength of the whole of the German people for the security of its freedom and independence. This will be done by broadening the too narrow life (of the people), and through all economic, technical and spiritual things sharing the responsibility, this will be brought about quickly. This cannot come about without friction, because it means fresh needs encroaching on an economy

which is already busy. Through the existence of such difficulties, this position does not differ from the position in
which other governments before us have been.

But we national socialists are attacking the position in a
new manner. In earlier times the problem of production
was left to the so-called free play of economic forces, and
the state limited itself to just sitting in judgment on the
results, hoping that self-healing processes would set in.

In thus leaving industrial problems, in so far as they
affected the nation, to industry itself, the state itself put its
foot into any possible self-healing tendencies that might
have come about, and destroyed economy. This procedure
is sterile and does not appeal to us national socialists. We
are accustomed to grabbing difficulties out by the roots
and to remove causes, instead of trying to cure symptoms
near the surface.

In our Four Year Plan the increasing of agricultural and
industrial production takes first place, and the state will
press this forward by every means ; not in such a fashion
that the state itself is in charge, but in such a manner as
will assure to the state absolute leadership and control where
necessary, without waiting for economic laws to take effect
by themselves. The state does not limit itself to just adminis-
tering economic problems where industry does not itself
put the matter in order, but it will pursue a leading policy
according to plan throughout the whole Reich.

In this work the municipalities have both a share and a
duty. They must, for instance, in the matter of expenses,
exercise great care, because, through increasing demands
for raw materials, this would embarrass the Four Year Plan
and increase its difficulties in regard to supply.

The Leader, in his far-seeing policy, has undertaken to
enlarge four cities in Germany, through public utility
building in great style and on a tremendous scale, thus
making them the centre of the world. You all know them.
Berlin, the Capital of the Reich ; Munich, the Capital of
the movement ; Nuremberg, the city of the Reich's Party
Day, and Hamburg, the city of our foreign connections.
This task is filled with special meaning. Naturally, it will
be put through.

It is not necessary, though, for every other town to embark upon gigantic building programmes also, for between Berlin and ' Kyritz by the Knatter ' there is a great difference.[1]

Here the municipalities will have to play their part and decide the urgency or otherwise of new work. To-day it is of greater importance that they shall help through the development of supply organisations than through the building of town halls or even gymnasiums, necessary as these may be in normal times, and as necessary as their building will be after a certain stage in the Four Year Plan.

As a forcible necessity for fostering united national economy through the municipalities, I further see the need for an effort to prevent increase in local taxation. I have the happy impression that already, during the past few years, the municipalities have achieved the position of placing their finances on a sounder basis, and I notice that they have got rid of many of their debts, incurred during the time of the ' system '. New expenses, which would lead to an increase in taxation, must be avoided, as the whole financial resources of the nation must be placed at the disposal of the Four Year Plan.

On the other hand, it serves the purpose of the Four Year Plan when the municipalities, on the orders of the Minister of the Interior, put themselves out to decrease the indirect taxation contained in the supply tariff.[2]

This is particularly applicable to the rural districts, where the battle for produce is being fought, and it is hoped that cheap supplies of energies will be made available to make life easier for the overburdened housewife, and to lessen irritation and friction which has been created by the scarcity of farm workers. In the towns, too, it is desirable that the factory workers' household will benefit through a reduction in tariffs, and thus taking off a part of their burden.

Next to these general matters come special measures,

---

[1] This is a make-belief town, like Carlyle's *Weissnichtwo*. In Germany one always refers to ' *Kyritz an der Knatter* ' when one wishes to describe the smallness of a place.

[2] Referring to a nation-wide reduction in charges for electric power and current.

in which the municipalities have particularly to be of service to the Four Year Plan. When even the greatest undertakings of the Four Year Plan are financed by other means, so the municipal credit institutions, such as the savings banks, through their credit policy, must help the smaller undertakings under all circumstances. I am thinking particularly of the granting of medium term credits to agriculture, without which our demands for intensive cultivation cannot be done justice. I know that this particular matter has met with many difficulties up till now. The arrangements for a new ordering of this section of our national economy are about to take shape, and as soon as the new decree has been published, I expect from the heads of all the municipalities, as being also the directors of the communal savings banks, that they place the services of their institutions at the disposal of the task to the utmost.

Of course, great care must be taken to protect the savings of the little man deposited in these banks, and to see that his pennies are properly administered and safely invested. Otherwise than this natural precaution, the granting of credit, must, from the national economic point of view, be handled in wider measure than up till now, so that the credit-worthy person is strengthened and encouraged in his initiative.

Furthermore, I am of the opinion that the municipalities have great problems to solve in the sphere of dwellings policy. More important than the building of palatial administration palaces at the moment, is the need for cheaper dwelling-houses, the building of which disturbs us less, as for these buildings as a whole, practically unlimited supplies of materials are available, which are produced from our own earth. Here, though, we must take care that labour is not diverted to these, when it should be used on buildings of greater national importance. It is important to start this settlement work, however, since it was proposed by the Leader, and which, after the completion of the Four Year Plan, must be hastened to its conclusion. I hold that it is highly important for this scheme to be attacked in all seriousness, and that only the more ambitious side shall be left over for the time being.

When we came to examine our economic position we found that still large quantities of raw material disappear as waste, either from custom, laziness or neglect. It is really astounding to read of the many still useful materials which go to make up the refuse of a great city. We can no longer afford, gentlemen, to allow these valuable materials to be withheld from circulation in economy, and therefore the municipalities will have to put in some hard thinking as to how best they can utilise this material.

Another kind of city refuse is collected by the Nutrition Help Organisation (Ernährungshilfswerk) of the German people.[1] I have given orders to the National Socialist People's Welfare Organisation (Nationalsocialistische Volkswohlfart) to take these matters up especially, because the N.S.V. has given proof that it is in close contact with the German housewife,[2] on whose understanding much depends.

It has been reported to me that in seventy large cities and towns this organisation stands and works well, but that in other places the present difficulties could not yet be removed. I am clear in my mind about this one fact—this work cannot proceed on only a scheme. A short while ago, your president, Dr. Weidemann, put a plan before me, not to feed them (the pigs) from the freshly collected refuse, but to dry it in a municipal institution and to distribute it from there to the pig-fattening farms in the neighbourhood.[3]

[1] This was mentioned in an earlier speech, calling for all kitchen remains and scraps to be collected and sent to the cattle fattening centres.

[2] The N.S.V. collects every month the money saved on the *Eintopf Sonntag* —the one Sunday in each month, when every family, regardless of station of life, eats only a mixed vegetable dish, the actual cash outlay saved thereon being given to the Winter Help Fund, which is now administered by the N.S.V. This organization also collects the *Pfundspende* (similar to our pound day in aid of hospitals and the like), the pound of cereals, sugar, flour, etc. given each month by every household for the aged, who are very poor and/or who have lost their pension rights, through years of unemployment and consequent lack of contributions to the unemployment fund. This welfare is a cross between the English Public Assistance and the old Parish Relief. There is no need to add that in common with all other German public work this scheme is highly organized.

[3] This pig fattening is not an innovation of the Third Reich. There have always been special areas devoted to producing over-weight pigs for slaughtering. These farms are known as *Schweinemästereien*. In the courtyards of the large blocks of flats and dwellings in German towns, separate communal refuse bins are placed, into which is deposited the food refuse, as distinct from other household refuse. This is collected and taken to the nearest pig breeding centre. It may be of interest to note that some ten or so years ago, a public

Whether this or any other method is adopted, does not interest me in the least. The decision on this must come from the municipalities themselves, according to their own particular conditions and problems. But I do not wish that any community excludes itself from this work. If it is possible to get enough additional food for a million pigs, then it is a great success, the work for which, God knows, is really justified !

The country municipalities and their organisation, which have always directed their attention to the advancement of agriculture, will have in many other cases opportunity further to promote the measures of the Reich government and the Reich Nutrition Department in this battle of production.

On the other hand, I will not tolerate any municipality trying to evade work which has been carried out by them up till now, in order that they can be further managed and financed by the Reich. A short while ago, the Reich Minister for Nutrition was forced to announce in the Reich budget, a sum of money for acquiring orchards, caused by the fact that the municipality itself, because of some difference it had over street planning, refused to care further for the important orchards, as it had done previously. With my agreement, the Reich Finance Minister has refused to pass this sum of money in the budget, because it is perfectly impossible to make payments like these out of Reich finances. It is the duty of the municipalities to care for all such matters as these.

I cannot exhaust the possibilities of the share of the municipalities in the Four Year Plan now, and with the few examples I have given you, I will finish for the time being. It will not always be possible to work without the participa-

---

company was floated on the London Stock Exchange to produce animal food-stuffs from just such waste matter, collected on contract from Restaurants and Hotels. Another side of this refuse collecting problem in Germany has its humorous aspects. Children in the schools are asked to bring all such refuse as can be conveniently turned to account, either for animal fats or for their utilization in scrap metal factories, and according to their response to the appeal, they are given good conduct marks in their term report books. School-rooms sometimes take on the appearance of a rag and bone merchants' yard, when the children have been particularly zealous in their collection, and the refuse collection van rather behind hand in taking the material away.

tion of the municipalities, but that need not frighten the thrifty clerks of the Exchequer, for it is far from me to demand exaggerated things from you. But, I am of the opinion, that our great objective, at all times, demands a careful examination, and even one or the other administrative measures can be put in the background for a time, in order not to hamper the plan, and until we stand at a successful conclusion.

If the municipalities take their fair share in the work of the Four Year Plan, then they fill the measure of their task, which has been given them in municipal orders, namely, to help the state in achieving its object. You have at your disposal those organisations, more than any other section of the state machinery, which will keep you in closest contact with the people. Therefore, it is your task, in closest collaboration with the party, to win over the populace to the aims of the Four Year Plan and to put them to work on it. The leaders of the municipalities who hear the wishes and complaints of the compatriots first of all, experience very intimately many of the state's unpopular measures. But you have the duty to correct these things yourselves, as far as it lies in your power and to make known, just through this assistance, your help in the work of the state. That will not be a rare necessity, for I am clear in my mind about this, that difficulties cannot be avoided during the operation of the Four Year Plan.

We all know,—it has happened already,—that in the food-stuff market, tension has come in several places, and it may be that similar instances will occur again, during the next few months. In case this should happen, I ask you to think of the connections between all these things and not just to think, when perhaps tension arises in your own town : ' Ah ! We have to set heaven and hell in motion in order to obtain rations from Berlin '. Rather will it be the task of the responsible official in the municipality to make clear to the public the why and wherefore, and to assist us by proper leadership in the field of consumption accordingly. I can assure you this much. If I can't prevent a tension over eggs and butter or perhaps over meat or a certain type of sausage,—I can fully guarantee the daily bread,—

measures have already been taken which render superfluous all fear of that.

It can further happen, that because it has used up its stock of raw materials one or the other factories may have to go on short time, or that, to our greatest sorrow, the existing working on short time in the textile industry may have to continue for a while longer. This does not mean that it has become a matter of treating one town worse than another, but the whole situation is the outcome of our general position, which at the moment causes it to be of greater importance that we should import iron ore instead of textile raw materials.

We will shortly be in a position to ease the situation, when the cellulose programme can be further operated, and the short working hours can be better regulated.

Within this framework also belongs the assistance which the municipalities can render in the difficult work of the Reich Commissioner of Price Control. By continual observation, personal attention and through far-sighted planning, the leaders of the municipalities will be upholding social peace and their assistance will prove really valuable to my organisation.

Here is afforded the German municipalities a great field of work. As at the time of the creation of local self-government,[1] now also, the municipalities have to come once more to the front to work for the great aims of the nation. After the clinkers of the past have been removed, I am convinced that the municipalities will stand the test, just as well as they did 130 years ago. The more aptitude for responsibility the municipalities show for participation in the high aims of the state, the more they make propaganda for the idea of local self-government, which finds its most tangible expression in just your own organisation of the German Municipal Day.

---

[1] A reference to Freiherr vom Stein's reform of Prussia, from below upwards ; district councils and provincial diets were set up to establish municipal self-government. Stein laid the foundation of a modern state, the fruit of English influences being seen particularly in the super-structure, with the result that subjects became citizens.

SECURING FOOD UNDER THE FOUR YEAR PLAN.
An article in *Der Vierjahresplan*, April, 1937.

ON 23rd of March I introduced certain measures whose purpose will be, through a large increase in agricultural production, to secure the nutrition of the German people, as far as possible from the German soil. The uniform agreement with which these orders have been received, not only from the country folk, but from German industry and people, accompanied by the new and stronger readiness to assist shown by agriculture and industry, makes us realise that we have taken the right road.

The securing of the people's food is, next to the security of the defence forces, the greatest presumption for peace, for the new forming of the economic social and cultural life of the nation, and last, but not least, for the formation of new international relationships. We therefore greet with pleasure the understanding and respect which is growing up in foreign countries for the ruthless conclusiveness with which we in Germany attack things, in order to create the presumption for the absolute social peace inside the country, and to create peace in the world.

The farmer has had his place in the national union pointed out to him ; through different measures, he is now allowed to work his land in peace and productivity. Organised measures have also made it possible for him to walk in step with other occupations, in the fight for the existence of the German people. The Reich Nutrition Organisation now stands firmly and through its subsidiary associations, it has penetrated into every village, taking the place of the one-time agricultural associations. It now becomes important for it to utilise its newly found strength in all its collective energies on the new task.

[*Translated and reproduced in English with acknowledgment to :* Der Vierjahres-plan.]

That which perhaps could have hampered the full expansion of production has been disposed of during the past few weeks. From now on I expect the country people, from the smallholder to the largest estate owner, to take up our aims and to assist, in spite of all difficulties, to bring our programme to a successful conclusion.

Private economic doubts must not interfere with national economic success. Agriculture must pay heed to the call for more intensive production, in the realisation that this enables them to pay a part of their debt to the Leader, which they owe him for securing their means of livelihood. The scientific and technical instructions for bringing about far-reaching improvements and increased production are given. Well-managed establishments are rich in experience, and I demand from all who have the honour to farm German land, that they use all their experiences and work accordingly.

I also demand that the farmer takes every opportunity to improve the living conditions of his workers ; for I am aware of the neglect that has obtained in this respect. The farm-worker, too, must acquire a spirited feeling of the dignity of his work, so that he can use the joy he has in his work for the important life task of the German people.

In securing the nutrition of the populace, we have naturally not solved all our problems, but the most important question is to secure the daily bread. Beyond this, we have further problems, such as housing and clothing, and that we have not lost sight of these, is proved by the fact that in the scheme of the Four Year Plan we have attacked the problems of new methods of production, places of production, and by our new dwelling and land settlement measures.

The statesman cannot afford to isolate himself from any of these problems, nor can he tackle one without considering the others. In turning to one problem, be it the army, nutrition, or other things, he always touches the whole structure and connections of economics. The increase of manure and fertiliser supplies, for instance, through the all-round reduction in prices for the purpose of intensifying agricultural production, can neither be looked upon as a one-sided present to agriculture, nor as an unselfish sacrifice of industry. In the same way, also, these things become of interest to both farmer and industrialist and they are also not without importance to the workman, because through them all he will be ensured bread at the same price—and on the same wages. And so it is in many spheres of economics. In all plans for, and orders given in, economy, the statesman must always foresee the effect on the whole, and particularly on the lot of the workman. For social peace, which is the basis on which, in accordance with the wishes of the Leader, all work on the Four Year Plan must proceed, cannot be achieved in parts and pieces. Everything, at all times, is a matter for the whole nation—for the workman as well as the clerk—for the industrialist just as much as for the others. It meets at the same time agriculture and industry, wages and prices, internal economy and export trade. Therefore, it is quite wrong always to look upon measures of state economic policy from one-sided interests, from the interest of occupation or profession.

We have not rescued the German farmer out of the misery into which he was pushed by the ' system ', simply for his own good, but for the welfare of the whole German people, whose life and freedom are only secured for eternity through a healthy agriculture. The new measures and assistance also do not mean assistance to agriculture ; they are more to be looked upon as safety devices for the nutrition of the people. After all, agriculture is so closely connected with all other branches of economics.

The healthy and permanent flourishing of a national economy depends decidedly upon the fact that its own agriculture covers the home consumption as far as possible. If agriculture fails to do this, then it loses its permenance and its existence cannot be secured. The intensification of agricultural production and the discovery of means to achieve this, are problems in which not only the farmer, but the whole economy and state leadership are highly interested. The necessary measures which protect agriculture and enables it to fulfil its work more easily, have been prescribed earlier. It now depends upon the German farmer to use the power and assistance which has been given him, to the best of his ability.

That he will take his share I have no doubt, and I am convinced of success for the future. I hope that they will bring to the Leader at the Harvest Festival of 1937, the report of further and greater advances along the road leading to the freedom of our food supplies.

UNITED WORK SECURES PEACE. Article in *Der Vierjahresplan*, May, 1937.

THE 1st May, the festival of the German people, the festival of work, has echoed away. It was a tremendous confession of all German people who work for unity in work and in political leadership. It was a solid declaration of the will of the German nation ; not at all a singular demonstration, but an experience which will live long after the day, and which will develop new energies in the nation and its leadership.

Ever and again the proud certainty fills us, that there is only one man who gives orders in Germany. His will is the highest law and we all obey him willingly, in the firm belief that it can only go this way and no other. And it does go !

All subordinate themselves in this voluntary decision. The Minister as well as the worker ; the works manager as well as the civil servant. In this alone lies the miracle of German reconstruction. Destiny has given us great problems to solve. Nothing falls into our lap as a present ; we must meet the obligations of our generation in a hard fight for life, and prove, through the deed, that we can stand as men in history. Great efforts and high achievements are necessary in order to fulfil all our so very urgent problems, particularly those of the Four Year Plan. The Leader left no doubt about neither the greatness of the work nor about its difficulties, and I have taken great care from the very beginning, that the political leadership which was given to me by Adolf Hitler, takes steps in the tremendous economic turnover, with that same harshness and determination, which has characterised the Leader's own line of action. It is clear to us that with the erection of new factories, with the introduction of new methods of production, in short,

[*Translated and reproduced in English with acknowledgment to :* Der Vierjahresplan.]

on the whole productive side of economics, not all has been done. We cannot do this in one stroke, and even if we have still so many valuable and useful inventions and technical things at our disposal, here and there, we cannot avoid the occurrence of scarcity of supplies. For we must not forget one thing ! In the overcoming of these difficulties, we are all alone. One accuses Germany that it has turned its back on world economy, but the fact remains that the whole system of world economy is built up in the wrong way from its foundations.[1] The move to strengthen and render independent, national economy, has taken on nearly universal vogue and has come up against those nations who always accuse us of narrow-minded exclusion tendencies. But, if there is a land that is not really interested in exclusion from purely natural causes, then it is Germany. Our trading endeavours, bearing in mind the living necessities and independence of our nation, are always focused upon the building-up of better and saner international economic relationships, and through that also, to assist with all our ability, the restoration of world trade. As much as we have been successful in some directions, so we have been greatly hampered in other ways through obstacles and misunderstanding which we find are always put in the path of this policy of sanity. We therefore keep to the word of the Leader, that Germany, if it wants to live, has to keep all its economy like an orderly farmyard, according to plan and easily watched over. Our endeavours are not only trained to produce new and more things, but also to keep house with what we have got and to distribute it sanely and manage it wisely.

Impressionably and clearly, the Leader said on the 1st May : " This tremendous work, which will now grip our people deep down in themselves for four years, can only come to success by the united efforts of the German people."

---

[1] The national socialists, like many small political and monetary reform organizations in England, have seemingly hit upon a new structure for world trade. There are many who hold that precious metals need not be a basis for currency, and German economy during the past few years seems to be an illustration of this theory, so far unpractised elsewhere. Herr von Ribbentrop develops this theme in his *Vierjahresplan und Welthandel* (Four Year Plan and World trade), which is now issued as a supplementary handbook by the German Institute for Research in Foreign Politics.

The jubilation which echoed long after these words were spoken, was a powerful cry of a united declaration of will on the part of all working compatriots—to work still more firmly and unselfishly than up till now. That is the happy factor of the national socialist outlook,—that material things are not the prime considerations giving the spur to greater achievements. I know how the just rights, and the most necessary and useful things, have to be fulfilled first of all, and that to the greatest achievements must be given the well-earned reward. In national socialism, apart from the form the prize or the reward takes, there is only one basis, and that is the basis of achievement. That is : Deciding alone are the national economic achievements of the whole. It is the duty of the state and of its economic leadership, to see to it that these achievements are rising, and that through fair and sane wages and prices, the whole economic benefit of the increasing national achievements will be given to every individual according to his help. That is possible only when the foundation for the existence of the community itself is planted on firm grounds. All the important and necessary questions, the worries of the individual over his earnings and the struggle for existence, are dependent on the united work of our nation. It is the community of fate, the steel chain of which binds us together and which does not allow us to forget the old words. ' One for all and all for one.'

Fate has not placed us in a favourable position ; but we will prove that we can master the future. It is not quite so easy as some might think in the enthusiasm of first successes. We are sober and remain matter of fact, and strengthen our endeavours which only serve one aim, to make Germany free and independent in economy also.

The Four Year Plan is the clear and tangible reality of the united work of the German people. I know that the success of this work is bringing sorrow to the statesmen of other nations. That is unjustly so. Germany must be strong and must therefore be independent in economy. For in the end, it is always the weakling among the nations which brings trouble and conflict. We say nothing against other statesmen mobilising the strength of their own people in order to be better equipped for the fight for existence. Every nation has the right to do what it thinks fit to secure the existence of its people, and we national socialists would be the last to deny such right to anyone. But does such a will hinder the co-operation between the nations ? The Leader has said it clearly, and so often, that Germany is now, as always, ready to participate in a collaboration with other nations and to help other nations in the regulation of their economic interests.

It is natural that the interests of the nations—in politics as in economy—do not find agreement on all points. In the great and deciding questions of world economic affairs, the responsible men should come to an agreement—for with that they would only be doing their statesmanly duty—to contribute to a lasting and a well-founded satisfaction in the world.

It must not be, and cannot be, of no importance in the world, when dissatisfied and disintegrating powers gain the upper hand and make use of economic difficulties for their own purpose, particularly, not those nations who feel above all the sorrows of the others, through the richness of their own possessions ; in the end, no one will escape without having taken harm from the great social upheavals, which will have to take on chaotic forms, if realisation and reason be not victorious in the end.

From the very beginning, it has been the endeavour of the national socialist government to further the peace of Europe and to stabilise it. But with the greater pressure Germany pursues this great aim, the more it must see to it, that first of all its own national life, its own national independence, is strengthened in order to secure social peace. For this high aim, the Leader strives and exerts his whole strength, day and night. To help him in this is my order and my unshakable will. I will set all out to reach the goal and to create the necessary economic and social presumptions in Germany, and I am certain that the whole nation—in front all, the chosen bearers of responsibility—will help with all their power.

That is the path laid down for us national socialists. We go along it, and fulfil at the same time the mission we have in Europe and in the whole world.

ITALY AND GERMANY. An article in the Milan Journal *Gerachia*, April, 1938. On the occasion of a visit by the German Führer to the Italian Duce.

ADOLF HITLER is Germany ! The whole of Germany accompanies its beloved Leader with its thoughts on his tour through the beautiful Italian lands. And when, the day after to-morrow, the Leader and Reich chancellor of the Great-German Reich will stretch out the hand of friendship towards the illustrious Duce of the powerful rising Italian Empire at the Ostia station of the Eternal City, there will ring in the feeling that Adolf Hitler brings to the House of Savoy, to the Italian people and its chosen government chief, the hearts of 75 million German people. Then the world will get to know of the joy of all the Germans, who live beyond the German frontiers, especially those who have found a home in Italy.

Can the comradeship of two men, which has grown out of the respect for each other and the same high ideals, find better and more explanatory expression, than in the friendship of the two great nations which they lead ? Truly, the friendship of Italy and Germany is not founded on treaties which were created out of long-drawn-out parliamentarian conferences or democratic majority decisions. This friendship is no paper document of past epochs, but it is a lively reality, a comradeship which has been created by the leaders of two nations, and which has been consolidated and hardened in the storm of the times. Out of true manly comradeship grew a truly proven friendship of nations.

Unforgotten are the days when in the autumn of last year the Duce stayed in Germany ; unforgotten in Germany is the wonderful speech which the Marshal of the Empire, the first Fascist of his country, made at the Mayfield in the

[*Translated and reproduced in English with acknowledgment to :* Gerachia.]

Olympia Stadium in Berlin. Tremendous rejoicing was around the Duce, when in open, manly words he, the authorised spokesman of his nation, gave his assurance that Italy would never forget the upright and friendly attitude of the German people towards Italy during the fight in Abyssinia. Half a year later, a few weeks ago, it fell to us Germans to thank the Italian people for their understanding of our national interests in the return of Austria to the Reich, a thanks which our Leader in his historic telegram to the Duce, expressed as the avowal of a whole nation.[1] So we have, in the most deciding days of the early history of our nation's friendship, kept to this friendship, which Benito Mussolini and Adolf Hitler have cemented. This tie of friendship will remain. Following the will of two men who lead Italy and Germany, it shall possess eternal durability.

Fascism and national socialism stand faithfully together, not only because on the outside they have lots of things in common. The root of this union lies much deeper. In the defence against bolshevistic decay, against hatred and jealousy, against the arrogance of rank and politic of interests, after the storm of two glorious revolutions, they have grown out of the same ground, they have grown out of the feeling of the people for the homeland. Led by men— who have been chosen by destiny to be the saviours of their nations—led by men who have the same determination for people and fatherland, who have the courage of decision, the wisdom of statesmanly thinking and acting, and the unimpaired authority of their personalities in common, in both nations there awoke once more creative strength which spirits, foreign to the nation, had covered up.

Both nations have built up their economy anew, based on national ideas and have expanded it. North, as well as South of the Brenner, stand work and achievement, stand the creating working human beings with ability, as the centre pin of all economic plans. Here, as there, care is taken that the individual, with his righteous ambitions for success, is directed into the necessities of the great political unity of the nation. Therefore, Germany and Italy were

[1] 'Mussolini ! I shall never forget this of you. Hitler.'

able to loosen themselves from the sudden changes of opportunity and the speculation manœuvres of the world. Courageously and decisively, they took their destiny into their own hands. Both nations exchange in peaceful economic traffic their goods, and use with iron industriousness and unerring firmness the valuables of their soil for the welfare of their countries. Both nations, through the untiring application of science and technique, enlarged and intensified their agricultural space and production, have produced new raw materials, and have opened up additional production sources, thereby strengthening the economic and defensive resources of the nation.

The German-Italian economic relationship, which, after the Anschluss of Austria with the Reich, has opened up for both countries still far greater possibilities, is a warning example that international trade between two strong countries with highly developed economy and strict, national political leadership, flourishes best.

So the unshakable and firmly standing Rome-Berlin axis is a proof that national interests need not be oppositions, but that on the contrary, friendly work and understanding are together the surest guarantor of world peace.

ADDRESS TO THE DEUTSCHE ARBEITSFRONT,[1] at the Reich Party Day, Nuremberg, 10th September, 1938, calling for a concentration of all effort and all strength.

MY dear compatriots of both sexes ! Party comrades ! First, as last year, I am privileged to-day to bring you the greetings of our Leader, especially to the comrades of the Work Front from the Ostmark,[2] who are to-day taking part in this congress for the first time. The creative people of the Ostmark have, up till now, clenched their fists against a system of suppression, which so falsely tried to pose as German on the outside, but which ruthlessly suppressed everything that felt truly German and that behaved in a German way. Now, you creative ones from the Ostmark, your fists shall be clenched once more, but this time around a spade, the axe and at the turner's bench, in a work for the people and the Leader.

As belonging to the Ostmark, you are now fitted into our great German people's unity, into the German Work Front.

The ghost of unemployment has also disappeared from the Ostmark. Powerful, the arms are stretched out and everywhere work is stirring. Full of hope, the one-time dull and saddened eyes direct their glance into the future ! The fight which you have led was not in vain. To-day, your trust is justified. The Ostmark is happy ! The Ostmark is back again in the Reich.

We, in the old Reich, have so often forgotten that here, too, the curse of unemployment once ruled. We forget too easily those terrible times, when we had to run up and down stairs in order to beg for work, and when need and misery were daily companions of the people.

Too easily we forget, that in the time before taking over

[1] German Work Front.
[2] Austria is now known as the Ostmark—a province of Gross-Deutschland.

power, there was everywhere present in the German people a terrible need for work, a need for work which to-day finds its opposite in the need for workers. I believe, my compatriots, when you creative people just think it over carefully, how times were once, when no one of you could hope for work, and how we stand now, when after five years we only know one problem, how to find really enough workmen for an overwhelming mass of work and for great and tremendous effort—you will say with me—where is there anything like this in the whole world? Where is there another nation of 75 million people which has not enough workers to master the work available, which is urgent, and which our movement has provided for us?

I believe,—the Leader has rightly mentioned it in his proclamation,—it to be a really singular thing when to-day the foreign countries throw up in our faces that we have this difficulty,—this need for workers. The countries around us have a surplus of workers, but they suffer from a lack of work, which we have had to experience once before in all its terrible measures. Those years which part us from the burden of unemployment, have been used in Germany for rebuilding on a scale such as has never before been known in history. We can proudly speak of this reconstruction and of its achievements, for every one of us has had his part in it. No one can credit the success of it to his own account. No! The whole nation, throughout its length and breadth, has contributed its part in full measure. All of us have drawn our benefits from this rebuilding, but we all had to work to get it.

When, at the time, we attacked the work, there were many who would only grudgingly find their way to it. And abroad they said : " Oh ! that can't last long. They may perhaps be good politicians—otherwise they would not have been successful in winning the people over to them,—but, first and foremost, they are only good drummers, speakers and quite fair propagandists. But they must founder on one thing—on economy—for about that they have not the least notion. In this territory they are fantasts. The fact alone that they speak of solving the problem of unemployment in a few years,—they mentioned four years—a problem which has kept the best brains of our time busy and to which they have found no solution—is proof of that. How can these dilettantes, who have never tackled economy in their lives—how can they know anything about it ? "

I grant the gentlemen of the past one thing. Of course, if they were talking of the corrupt economy which they were controlling, then about this we don't know a thing. That is true. They so juggled things for us and tried to impress upon us that economics was a high science. Under the brush-wood of stock exchange schedules, dividends, tariffs, royal-ties, interests and calculations, was only hidden a collective striving for self-gain. They then called that the ' higher form of economy '.

Against this conception of liberalism and economics we set our conception of national socialism and that is : In the centre of economy stand the people and the nation, not the individual and his profit ; work and economy are exclusively only there for the whole people.

Now, my dear party comrades, it was not possible to save economy by any sort of calculation and higher science ; it could only be rescued by a decided will—by the will for the deed. But how is that possible ? To bring German economy into any sort of order at all, the leadership had to have, first and foremost, the faith of the workers, the loyalty of the German workman. For only with the aid of the German worker could economy be built up again. Only through the faith of him who created and worked. In his belief in the leadership, in the belief in his own fist and in the achievement of his daily work, alone lay the strength which led to a recuperation.

On the other hand, we had also to strive hard to secure from the employer the necessary understanding of our new times. This was especially so in the case of the young owners. We had to loosen them from their old-fashioned ideas and had to put them back in among the people. We had to let them know that no economy could flourish in the quarrel between owners and men.

Where there are great things to be created, only unity will guarantee success. Only the merging of all interests can fulfil a deed. So also in economy.

Faith of the worker and understanding on the part of the owner, then, were the suppositions. So there was formed in every works, a mirrored picture of a whole people changing over. Just as we forged the people's union as a whole, so here was formed, in a particular way, the works and factory community ; and when history comes to be written about the work of the German Work Front, then it will have to be recorded that in spite of all hindrances the creation of the community between factory owner and factory worker, was the greatest achievement of the Work Front.

It was also necessary to take up the fight along the whole line against incitement and instigation. I really need not remind you of the fact that all German workers' movements were so terribly incited ; no wonder—for years they were subject to the teachings of marxism and communism. Truly, it was difficult for the Party comrade Ley[1] and his men to instil the proper leadership in the Work Front ; for we could not look to those old wages schedule bigwigs, who had led the workers before. Here, more than anywhere else, we had to have men as leaders who were ' dyed in the wool ' national socialists. For only in the sign of national socialism could the German worker be won back once more, for his people and his Reich.

Here there started the practical work of the party and of the state, for the rebuilding of economy. Certainly it was a difficult road, but this road was followed, thanks to the determination of the leadership. It was also accompanied by the silent longing from the opposition, for a quick breakdown, but after they could no longer hope for this, after their treachery was smashed up, after the unity of the people could no longer be disrupted, there still remained for them the hope of economic breakdown. And as the stupid ones are slow in the uptake, they still nurse this hope to-day.

Certainly, when one takes the basis of economics, and their laws as they were valued by liberalism and compare them

---

[1] Dr. Robert Ley, leader of the German Work Front and leader of the Strength Through Joy movement. Visited London in the early part of 1939, as a German delegate to the International Fitness Congress. Dr. Ley and his organizations have probably done more to bring the lesser European states, including the Balkans, into the German orbit, than all the intrigues of the special diplomats with roving commissions.

with things of to-day, there is no connection whatever to be found. What we are doing looks like chaos. But, had these gentlemen thought a little, and considered that behind Germany economy stands the will, the belief and the strength of the Leader, and that this economy is now controlled by the party, then they would long ago have seen the light and realised that economy stands firmer to-day than ever before.

But when, just as an outside matter, they try to compare the economy of the neighbouring states, especially the states of the great democracies,—who after all, have taken a lease on all earthly wisdom,—with ours, then of course both sides do not equal out. According to their opinions all are phantoms, leading to a breakdown, for on the one hand they see a people—one hears and wonders—which, apart from employing all available labour, already has to obtain workers from neighbouring nations to satisfy its needs, and on the other hand, nations in which the tremendous number of the unemployed grows daily.

How can one try to bring these two things into harmony ? They say that in Germany we are arming powerfully, but they forget that they have started to arm at a tremendous rate, too. This cannot alone be the cause ; there must, after all, be other powers at work and other spurs for this tremendous change. Whilst out there (across the frontiers) unemployment grows, the crisis increases. We always read, that not only the crisis grows but also that prices rise ; the wages grow and following this, the prices increase again. Here I must really say that we in Germany once exercised this wonderful wisdom of economy. When Germany was still governed by the ' Scheide '—' Ross '—and other men,[1] then we came to know it. I would remind you of the fact that all these one-time stars have extraordinarily quickly found their way into countries abroad. Perhaps they have found there advisory posts in economic life, so that the same can be repeated there that bloomed for us once here.

We also see the ' dearly beloved ' strike pop up abroad every moment. That too we know ! We know it only too

---

[1] Reference of contempt to the preceding social democrat ministers, implying that they are so unimportant as to have their very names forgotten. It is like referring to Mr. Whatshisname.

well. Every strike needs naturally to a ' rise in production ',
every strike makes economy naturally ' more sound '.
No ! My dear compatriots, we have brought order and
herein lies the deeper law of our success. We have called
halt to the mix-up of individual interests. There is only one
interest—the German nation and its future—to that we bow !
Certainly we had great worries and tremendous difficulties, which towered up before us and which had to be overcome. I have never said that I am an economic genius.
I have only stated that I would set all my will, my strength,
and my best, to the task of creating order, where disorder
prevailed.

Here economy is no exception, for order is a uniform
conception which we have brought to the task in every
territory of our work. To-day, as I mentioned at the beginning of my speech, we stand before the great difficulty. How
are we to solve the great problem of workers ? To regulate
achievement and available workers is our greatest difficulty
to-day. It is the kernel of the greatest question of the
Four Year Plan.

The securing of the Reich defences has made it necessary
for me to pass a decree that I had no wish to issue. When it
was a question, my working compatriots, of securing the
Reich,—when it became important to build up in the West
a barrier which cannot be bridged, then I did not ponder
further ; I brought into being the ' duty work '[1]—and the
workers have followed me joyfully and willingly. Hundreds
of thousands of men have been taken away from the factories.
Why ? Because they had to be put to work which is necessary
for political reasons of state. I would like quickly to accentuate one thing here and now, in order to prevent any doubt
arising.

The putting in of duty work must be only undertaken for
really important work necessary for the security of the
Reich. The decision as to what constitutes important work
I have kept in my own hands, in every case. Should I find

---

[1] *Pflichtarbeit.* Work of national importance such as constructional work
on the Siegfried Line, the fortifications in East Prussia and Silesia, arterial
roads, canals, coast defence works, aerodromes and armament factories construction. This duty work is considered as important as the conscript military
service.

that labour for a task can be found in the usual way, then I will never give my consent to duty workmen being employed.

There must be no doubt that this decree is purely a special measure for certain national purposes,—for undertakings on which the fate of the nation depends. For the rest, all labour requirements must be covered in the usual way.

I would like to take this opportunity to take my stand against the incitement, which is creeping in from abroad, which wrongly suggests that forced labour is being slowly instituted in Germany. They do not understand how to bring force and duty under one hat. They forget that the German workman to-day has the categorical imperative of duty as the needle for direction within himself, and that he, too, is ready to do his duty. And the highest duty is the security of the Reich—about that we do not argue with anyone in the world.

I know exactly that one cannot get far with force. I know quite well that force deadens the joy and that would only deliver us over to mediocre achievements. I also know for what I appeal when I call up the German workman for the duty of securing the safety of the state. I would have wished the foreign journalists to have seen the trains which went from all parts of the Reich, to the West, filled with the so-called 'forced Labourers'. They were no forced labourers, they went jubilating, for they knew that they were to secure the frontier of the Reich. Thank God, with us Germans, the stepping in for the security of the nation counts, be it with the axe, the spade, with the sword or with the gun—it still remains the highest and most worthy duty of the German man.

I believe that at the moment we are in too high spirits, brought about by the surroundings in which we are, to want to go into such small matters.

Certainly there will always be certain difficulties brought about by the change, so that one or the other has to wait while his barracks are being built. That the one or the other will have to go without his dumplings or his meat, or that the third is missing his usual vegetables,—these are matters that can be solved in passing.

The most important is, what has to be created here ! Here, it was so wonderful that the demonstration of the strength of will, and the determination of hundreds of thousands who were ready to work, and joyfully so, made one ask oneself, over and over again : ' What can there be impossible to such a nation ? ' I would like to know of another nation which could manage to find at its disposal in a few days or weeks, an army of hundreds of thousands of workers, to collect them in one place and to carry out work there, the extent of which I hope the others need never convince themselves.

For the rest we can openly say—Germany has become a land of work. When we are short of labour, my dear compatriots, I cannot say : " There is not enough labour, ergo we cannot do the work." But I have to think hard,—what can be done in addition. And you know yourselves that when a great task presents itself to me and I cannot complete it owing to lack of workers, then I must overcome my difficulties by expecting higher achievements and must get more work out of the individual. Here, in this case, quality has to replace quantity. From this cause alone, it becomes necessary for our eyes to be directed towards the skilled worker and the rising generation.

It is necessary to educate not only the coming generation of skilled workers, but also the highly specialised people like engineers, chemists and other professions, who are at the Technical Colleges and the Universities. The German Universities to-day must exert all their power in order to do justice to their task in these times. We are far advanced in scientific research and in the education of the coming generation ; but the Universities must understand that to-day, the times of the sentimental Old Heidelberg romanticism are past, and that the law of the hour is called work !

The German has to think with the times and I would like to direct an appeal to German youth : Think, before choosing an occupation, which occupation the German fatherland needs most to-day, for it is always the highest fulfilment of an occupation, when it is carried out as the highest service to one's people !

The high tension of work is naturally influencing working

hours. It really is necessary, that for the time being ten and more hours a day have to be worked, and, I can assure you working people, that not only you do so. At one time, a cosy dozing was habitual in the ministries and government offices, and when, even if in the middle of writing a word, the clock struck six, the pen was laid aside. To-day all that is past. You can still see the light burning at midnight in the windows of the heart of the Reich. Still at midnight, the leadership of the Reich creates and works, in order to create for the people the basis of its security. To-day, the officials are in permanent service, and therefore, every single one has to do the same, no matter where destiny has placed him.

But, I promise you, you working ones, that I will never tolerate that overwork and overstrain is turned to personal profit. There, where overwork has happened, it has been done for the glory of the Reich.

The countries abroad find it easy to make their jocular remarks about us here. Many European states allow millions of mixed coloured men to work for them in their overseas possessions. The whip over the slave still rules there. There, well-being is not propped up alone from the resources of the motherland. Tremendous colonies, too, stand at their disposal. But the German people must get the last out of their thickly populated soil, and must, with all power and all devotion, create all from the German soil.

If we had kept the colonies, then you gentlemen would have no need to strain yourselves in thinking if the German people has to do forced labour. We know that we can only live from the work of our own hands. We can use nothing but what we have ourselves produced.

Tremendous gaps in the Weimar system can only be closed slowly. In spite of this, I would say that here we have done the impossible. We, that is, our generation, we have felt our special responsibility and we will not go around this responsibility in a cowardly way and we will not leave to our children what we ourselves could do. We are ready and must be ready, to set up all means of assistance for economy, both of organisation and of technique, in order that the foundation of our lives will be secured. Wages for work and life's maintenance are here closely connected. In the world of ideas of national socialism, my compatriots, a heavy demand on working endeavour pre-supposes also a fitting social policy. Social progress must always be guaranteed. Only when I am ready to give my utmost in social services, can I too demand of you your utmost willingness to work and your readiness to do your duty. In this connection I would remind you of my decree regarding holidays with pay and of the successful endeavours of the German Work Front in this regard. Following upon my decree, which has thrown greater responsibilities upon the trustees of the Reich, I have made it the duty of the factory managers to report every alteration in the work schedules of the factories. I also would like to emphasise that this decree must never be misused in order to bring about social retrogression. I have ordered the Reich trustees of Labour, not only to look after the wages question but also to give their attention to conditions of work, and if necessary to step in where the line of state policy is being overstepped. While we cannot go ' the whole hog ' in social betterment, at the same time we do not want to hold back artificially the tremendous advancement of our social life which has been taking place during the last few years.

Under all circumstances one thing must be understood. The present scarcity of skilled labour must not lead to a position where the factory managers are enticing workers from each other, through promising them higher wages or offering other extraordinary conditions. Among other things, this is what the decree is intended to prevent.[1]

My compatriots, you know yourselves, if I for one moment

---

[1] This decree provides, *inter alia*, that when one worker seeks fresh employment he (or she) has to prove to the new potential employer his actual last wages. The new employer has a right to communicate with the old employer to ascertain the real weekly or monthly salary or wages paid to the new employee by him at the time he was working there. For instance, if the maximum scale of payment in a certain occupation is fifty marks a week, the employer is not allowed to pay more, however much he may think his new employee is worth it for the business. The operation of this decree was reported fully in *The Times* quite recently and it appeared, from the instances given, that it imposed a bar to progress of the worker, particularly of the black-coat. For some time past, however, in Germany, it has been impossible for a factory worker to voluntarily leave his employment to seek other employment elsewhere ; therefore, this decree is more applicable to the office-worker, shop-assistant, and the junior grades of the professions.

tolerated the existence of such re-engagements or like breaches of contract, then in a very short time we would have in the distribution of labour a chaos without equal, and the completion of all our great economic and political state programmes would be highly endangered. Exaggerated conditions can in the end do more harm than good, and therefore I cannot tolerate them, but you can see for yourself that the standard of living has risen this year in all territories. Perhaps here and there is something that one could wish to be better—one must always wish—but so many things have happened and success shows everywhere. Apart from doing away with unemployment, we see rising turnover in all industries,—in transport, catering, theatres and cinemas, in watering-places and spas. How small compared to this are the individual questions which crop up here and there, but which in passing by cause a little annoyance. Quite possibly someone comes home and says : " Instead of half a pound of butter I only got a quarter ". It may happen that an ox is sold instead of a pig and the other way round. The one who wants pork must be satisfied with beef, and the other who wants beef must put up with pork—these are only matters of little importance. Let him get up who wants to declare : " I cannot get enough to eat in the Third Reich ! " I would like to speak to him. I myself am happy, anyway, because I can tell you that I know that the German people to-day live much better than they did five years ago, and much better than in the times of the shameful system.

I would like to go a bit deeper into the question of national nutrition, and particularly, because about this there are always, again and again, the greatest lies being spread about in the countries abroad. About this rules the greatest ignorance and to-day I will give my public views on the matter.

They say abroad that the question of our food supply is the weakest link in the Reich. Just remember the years of the blockade. One remembers the people starving to death ; one remembers that through the cowardly cutting off of supplies, they did not only hit the German men, but the German women and children also. One knows, that once that was the weakest point of the Reich. The remembrance of this blockade and the consequences of such blockade are brought up here and there in their papers, when they want to read the German nation a lecture, or when they want to threaten it. Then the hint creeps in : " The German people shall always remember that it is not self-supporting ; we are the great powers and we are able to cut off supplies from abroad." And other such stories.

I can assure these gentlemen of one thing, not only they remember the blockade, we too remember the blockade. And if we had not remembered it, then in this case particularly, I thank these gentlemen that through their repeatedly rubbing it in, they have reminded us of it.

Just now, in all the general political tension, one hears again and again about the food supply weakness of the Reich. I assure you of one thing ; when I was at the time called by the Leader, first to control and co-ordinate raw materials and foreign exchange, and then later for the Four Year Plan, I was very clear in my own mind that the first and most important matter was the nutrition of the people. I knew, come what may, that it had to be so secure, that if this Reich was surrounded by nothing but enemies, and that if a war lasted 30 years, everyone would still have enough to eat. To this purpose all my work was directed and I found it easier, for already our party comrade Darré,[1] had from the first hour of taking office, the identical thought. So we met with the same ideals.

To-day I can speak about it, and it makes me especially happy—that you must understand—when I can do it just at a moment when the sky is once again dark and cloudy. The Leader in his proclamation, and party comrade Darré in his reports, have already fully pointed this out.

I will to-day publicly give account to you, not—that I would accentuate—to create restiveness, for there is no cause for that. Apart from that you all know one thing about me. I always keep my promises. I may say to-day, too, hard things, awkward things, and heavy ones, if it has to be, for I have experienced during the world war, and in

[1] Walter Darré, Minister for Agriculture and Food. He is also known as the Peasant Leader.

later years, how terrible it is when a leader leaves the people in uncertainty and doubt, and then overnight dashes them from the heights into the depths. I am convinced that the German people at that time would not have failed—would not have lent their ear to the enticers—if the leadership had turned from the very beginning to the people, and had explained to them the difficulties of the times, and had appealed to it to keep together, instead of lulling it into a sense of security, and then to dash it into the depths. Then it would have been different. Never, my compatriots, shall you be lied to, never deceived, never lulled into false security. The German people is strong and demands to take its part in the nation's difficulties. Certainly we leaders will do everything. All our work is meant for your good, but when the times come that are difficult, then the people too will have to take their part and bear their burdens. Eye to eye in all difficulties, eye to eye in all danger,—thus one will master all difficulties. One need only know a thing to tackle it.

The more happy I am naturally, when to-day I can report good things. It was pointed out in the proclamation of the Leader, that the sense and purpose of the Four Year Plan lies, in the end alone, in the fact that we must make all arrangements which add to the security of the Reich to the utmost, and which will make the Reich independent in everything ; for only he who is independent need never give up his honour. We Germans know : There is nothing more terrible for a nation than to have to give up its honour. Our honour we will never, never give up again. And so that it shall be secured all this work is being done. It shall not be possible any more, first to starve a people out, then to make it rebellious through lies, and bring it in the end to ruin. These times have passed ; the experience has given us too good a lesson.

My dear compatriots, next to the work which has now been started in the Reich, next to the battle for nutrition by the party comrade Darré and next to the good harvest, I have been doing my best to collect stores, stores for all departments where they were necessary. Apart from this, increased production of all important produce was tackled and it had been brought to a high pitch. Raw materials were produced by us ourselves or substitutes found, but foremost our food has been secured. How was it possible to effect an increase here? A number of measures and decrees which I had made,—they are known to you—but particularly in nutrition, were difficult for the farmer at first. For instance, he could not feed bread cereals to the cattle any more, because he had to put it aside securely as the highest possession of the nation. I had to put some difficulties upon you and you had to have worse bread. Other little matters were added to these.

But you see, to-day, for all that, we have a store. The harvest is good. The dear God has come to our help, and now you see, that to the figures which you got to know yesterday from the department of Party comrade Darré, is added the store which I have collected within the frame-work of the Four Year Plan and which I have bought. And when everywhere, my compatriots, I have taken serious measures against hoarding, so I myself have hoarded, of that you can be convinced.

The great harvest of this year has yielded us a sufficient supply for two years. The additional purchases, which we have already made, have given us a store for many years. I could almost say that it would be sufficient to meet unforeseen times. If we should now have a bad harvest, even for two or three years, then these stores will be good enough to make up the loss, but I hope to the Almighty that this year of excellent harvest will be the first of the seven fat ones. Of course, this collecting of stores has presented us with many more difficulties, but, as I said before, never in our lives will we be rid of difficulties. Always when we have reached something beautiful, there are the new difficulties. These difficulties present themselves to me and to you. For me, I have got difficulty in storing these supplies. You know that we have our granaries already filled up to the roof, but we will build more, in which we can store with safety this wonderful gold which we possess to-day in the form of corn. I will have to use all available store-rooms which are in private hands and I shall also be forced to fill the gymnasiums. The gymnastics can be done in the open air,

Also I will have to fill the dance-halls, then you can dance in the open air, my dear K.D.F. trippers (*Kraft durch Freude*). Dancing in the open air is great fun, too.

I have to report to you good news, my dear compatriots, for I can now start to do away with a number of decrees which I installed some time ago in order to make possible the collection of this tremendous store.

Firstly : From the 1st October the addition of Maize to the breakfast roll will be done away with, and you will all once again have the beautiful white rolls, as before. I have specially ordered this with one eye on our Austrian sweet tooth.

Secondly : It is once more permissible to sell fresh bread.[1]

Thirdly : The fine milling of corn for rye bread is no longer compulsory, and once again you can eat our good old bread, and through this, more fodder will become available for agriculture in the form of bran.

Fourthly : In spite of the better quality of the bread, under no circumstances must even the minimum increase in price occur. And fifthly : If I was able just now to give a bonbon to the people in the Ostmark, then I will do the same for my Bavarian fellow countrymen—there will be a considerable increase in beer production.

I believe, my compatriots, that you really cannot demand more from me for the present. We have not only directed our attention to corn and bread cereals, but also to fat and meat.

To the stores which party comrade Darré has collected, must be added the further stores which have been bought by the Four Year Plan departments. When we spoke yesterday of the fact that we have fat stores for seven and a half months, then I must explain to you what that means. It does not mean that our total stock will last only seven and a half months, but it means that we have supplies in hand sufficient to last us for that time, over and above the fat which we ourselves produce in the Reich. This also means that our reserves of stock allow, with the additional fat produced from time to time, a manipulation over years

---

[1] For several years before this date it was forbidden for a baker to sell newly-baked bread.

of bad times. That is what I wanted to tell you so that there should be no misunderstanding. Now the potatoes : During last year we had a record harvest in potatoes and this year's yield will not be lower. We even have stores left over from last year's harvest, and we will have new stores soon, the storing of which will be rather difficult. Potatoes grow very well in our country. The daftest ones have always the best ones, because they have the biggest ones ; but that is always good for the whole, so we have to be just.[1]

Now the sugar : My compatriots, we have sugar in such quantities that already we can export.

Apart from this, we have laid in reserves of tinned stuff of all kinds, especially of tinned fish. Our fishing fleet has been fishing for the first time high up.[2] We are no longer the little nation that hangs behind. For the first time we have sent out our whaling fleet, and it has returned with tremendous results. So everything has been done that could be done, and I assure you that the storage accommodation which we have to-day is brim full. The German people need not fear anything. In spite of this, I must warn you what the Leader has said : Go on being thrifty.

I have not collected those stores so that they can be wasted, but in order that they may secure, in times of need, the daily bread of the German nation. This good stock shall not perhaps lead the land worker to think that now he could go away from the land to the factories, because ostensibly, they get there higher wages. No ! Now, more than ever stay on the land and work. One harvest must be better than the other, then we will be unconquerable and no one can overcome us.

Hand in hand with the storing administration in the department of nutrition, there naturally went one of the same type in the department of industrial economy. Here too reserves have been collected, in the first place, naturally, materials which we cannot substitute and the scarcity of which in times of a blockade would prove very awkward.

---

[1] There is a popular saying in Germany : ' The daftest farmer has the biggest potatoes.'
[2] Deep sea fishing.

We have plentiful stores of these things. Above all this, of course, we have collected ample reserves of all those things that are important in all departments of warfare.

But far beyond the store administration and the actual storage itself, we have tackled great production schemes. Many new production works, hundreds, yes, thousands of factories, have grown up under the ægis of the Four Year Plan, in which iron and other metals, copper, rubber, oil and petrol, cloth and so on are stored. To-day, we have no more empty barrels, which we could fill with petrol or benzol, because all are filled. We have forced up our production and extended the production works themselves, and generally have collected supplies which will make us secure for a long time. Here the Four Year Plan starts to show. Only two years have passed and factory after factory was built. The first factories are to-day already working at the peak of production. Ship after ship is being launched; one factory starts work after another and so production rises. Germany does not get weaker with every year, but becomes stronger as time passes. Its potentiality grows, be it in peace be it in war.

I give you this assurance. No one will be able to hinder us. Everything necessary to the life of the nation is being done day and night and it never ceases.

So a gigantic building up has taken place. I need only remind you of the Hermann Göring Works in Salzgitter and Linz. They are the greatest works in the world. In the whole world there is not one works which in any way approaches the extent and greatness of this works.

Everywhere, German ground is being opened up. Everywhere where iron, copper, lead, zinc, or tin is to be found, even in its smallest amount, it is opened up. Where there is petrol, the ground is drilled and everywhere it is corked off. I need only to turn, and there streams out this valuable possession of petrol ready for use.

We have not slept; That the world shall know. We have worked as never before, and at no time, a nation has worked. In fuel, cellulose and textiles we own the greatest and the largest number of factories in the world. But in spite of this, compatriots, once again the warning, remain thrifty! One must think it over. Think after all that all these valuable possessions have been created only through untiring industriousness, and always with an eye on the security of our people and our nation. Therefore, in the future, not the smallest particle of food or scrap must be wasted. The people who throw away the silver paper from a bar of chocolate are doing wrong. I also need the old corks, and when you open a mineral-water bottle, don't forget to give up the stopper. I am the greatest rag and bone merchant. I take everything and need everything. I have been laughed at for that. People said these were childish methods and did I think that I could regulate economy in this manner. They may go on laughing, for success speaks for itself, and it belongs to us. To top all this is the gigantic re-armament industry, which is always being built up and expanding. We possess factories turning out aeroplanes and motors in great number, which have a tremendous capacity. We are getting sufficient delivery of guns and machine-guns ; ships are being launched from the dockyards according to plan. Here too in re-armament everything has been done that could be done.

Yes ! In this respect we are especially lucky too. We started first and are therefore a few lengths ahead of the others.

I come now to a chapter, which I must confess, interests me least of all. In spite of this it is yet important. The stock exchange and finance. The development of the course of exchange has often given rich cause abroad to proclaim the ruin of German finance, carrying with it the ruin of re-armament, and all else. Naturally in this, as in most things, the wish alone was father to the thought. In a liberal economy the falling off in the course of exchange can be naturally of extraordinary importance. One need only to look at the different black Thursdays and Fridays which have occurred in America. In the national socialist economy, this sort of thing does not really mean anything. The stock exchange in our country no longer exercises a ruling position. That is past. It has one important function ; It serves for the turnover of securities and as an instrument for issuing capital and loans.

The value of assets, though, lies not only in the documents themselves, they are only paper, but in the amount of work which lies behind them. Shares, for instance, represent only the value of the factories and works and the work and achievement of the people in them, from the youngest apprentice to the managing director. They possess this value in black and white, nothing else. Under normal conditions represented by factories working full time, a large order book, smooth turnover and healthy administration, the value of the shares in themselves can hardly change. All this is more sharply shown in the Reich loans. Behind the Reich loans stand the tremendous work of the whole German people, the assets of the Reich and the guarantee of the Third Reich. I believe, the gentlemen have already felt the meaning of the guarantee of the Reich.

Naturally, differences in the course of exchange can happen. As I told you before, I am no expert on this subject. But when certain gentlemen start to push out shares and carry out other manœuvres, then something breaks artificially and unwanted. Sometimes arranged and sometimes not arranged—then something breaks off. But that is just a little teasing game, which the gentlemen on the stock exchange play between themselves, without it having any effect on the factory or the men who are employed there. How and what the shareholders are manipulating, need not interest you, my dear compatriots. When one thinks that he can dish the other (*übers Ohr hauen*) or make manœuvres or not, that does not interest the German national economy in the least.

When to-day somebody has stuffed himself up with assets and needs money for expansion, then he pushes the shares out,—I believe that is the expert expression. When he pushes off too many of his assets on to new ' paper ', then the others say to themselves : " Oh, boy, is there something fishy ? " (*Au Backe ist da etwas faul ?*) ; " he pushes off so many that now I won't pay a lot for these shares, but less——" and that is how exchange differences come about. But what does that interest German economy ?

It can of course be different, when really forced sales are

taking place, especially of loans. As long as they play blind-man's-buff with their exchanges and their shares, that's all right ; but when people get big orders from the Reich and have earned a lot through the Reich, which they would otherwise would not have earned, and when they want to invest their ' dough ' somewhere, then the least they can do is to invest this money which they have earned through the Reich in Reich loans. After all they can't sit on it, and they can't eat it either.

When there are all at once rumours that there will be war, or that there won't be war, or when they think that here or there things may alter, then some people go and say : " That is fishy, we have had this once before with the war loans ", and then they sell their Reich loans. That means then that these people are, after all, ready to take the good things that come from the Reich, but they do not have one spark of trust in the Reich and do not want to risk anything. But, worse still, appears the character of these gentlemen when they start to hoard goods or bank currency. I will have my special watchful eye here, and to-day, thank God, there are so many people watching in Germany that no harm shall come to our holy Reich, and so one will get to know about these things earlier or later.

No one can pull out of the destiny of the German com-munity. When the gentlemen are ready to enjoy the good things, then they shall also stand by the Reich when this Reich thinks that it is threatened. No one can pull out of their duty to the people and the Reich—no workman, no farmer, no managing director and no apprentice, and not even the shareholder or the hoarder of cash money. No one shall think that he can get out by some secret way and thus go around destiny. This thesis we have also experienced before. How often was it said in the early days of the breakdown that it did not concern the German workman and that here only the great heads, chimney barons,[1] were hit. But actually the German workman was hit first of all by the breakdown. I believe that even the most ignorant person should see that now. We are the property of the people's union and of the destiny of the union in good times, as in

[1] Industrial barons.

bad. We cannot turn away from it and no one who is decent wants to turn away.

Concentration of all strength—that is now the deciding question and a deciding problem. I said already, at the beginning, that it is highly important to find now the necessary working strength in order to solve the problems. When, here and there, I can't bring about a full solution of the task, because I have not enough workers for all the work and schemes, then I must look to a concentration of all strength and I must form a centre of gravity to which I can lead this concentration. So, my compatriots, when now we pull through this concentration in such a wonderful and instructive manner and place the centre of gravity in the Western forts, where it was possible to build up a wonderful work in a few weeks with hundreds and thousands of men, then it is also necessary that we shall always have to concentrate our strength there, where our most important work lies.

That is no chicanery. Believe me, I would be happy when every one of you enjoyed the best of times. But when I am forced now to demand that a workman shall leave his usual place of work—perhaps even his family, for a few weeks, in order to earn in another place, then I know that I demand something difficult from him. But he knows why that has to happen and that he will be rewarded for it—and if not he, then his children. Be assured. We leaders will at all hours remember never to demand anything which we would not be ready to do at any time ourselves.

My dear compatriots ! Difficult and tremendous things lie behind us. When we comprehend these tremendous happenings in all their great realities, then we have not only the right, but also the duty, to look with trusting eyes into the future. For a people which stands behind such leadership and has achieved such great things, has not only achieved great things in five years in order to do nothing for the next five years. May I therefore ask you, my creating friends, wherever you may come from—you ordinary members of the Work Front—you as national socialists, to be the bearers of this great trust for the future.

You have to bear this trust with your eyes to the front, following the Leader blindly, wherever he may lead us.

I must say that there are too many timid ones among us. It appears to me that people who think an awful lot, especially who read a lot, and who think themselves more clever than any one else, are the most timid ones. Perhaps it is because they think about too many possibilities and work them all out. The simple man trusts the Leader and that is right. There is no need for him to be timid.

I will not deny for one moment that heavy clouds have drawn up across the sky. A tremendous political tension is running through the pulse of Europe and the world. A small portion of the European people chicanes about a minority which has been entrusted to them, and has thus become the hearth of all the unrest in Europe. The pity is that they cannot see the hearth of the unrest itself, but that they continue to seek all around the periphery, seeking to recognise the tension instead of finding its starting-point. We know what is happening there, we know how unbearable it is that this little splinter of a nation down there—which is poor in culture—no one knows where they have come from—should suppress and pester a cultured nation all the time. But we know that it is not these ridiculous dwarfs in Prague. Behind it all stands Moscow ; behind it stands the eternal Jewish bolshevist caricature grimace. From there promises were made, which of course will never be kept. From there come the rumours, the lies and the calumnies. The instigation and incitement makes the whole world rebellious, and the democratic countries fall for it. How could it be different ? So the world once more echoes from war and war cries.

When the world of the democracies is echoing with war cries, then the democracies have quickly found the culprits. The culprits are always just the strong states of order, Germany and Italy. It is always said then that we are the starters of any unrest. Just those two nations who are ready and who have proved—in opposition to the others—that they are able to secure peace in their own countries.

In addition to which, both nations, who compared to the vague anonymous responsibility of parliament, own two men of the highest responsibility. That is different from the anonymous conception of majority and parliament, which can never take the responsibility and which never wishes to do so. These states, who in the inside of their nation have brought discipline and order, peace and happiness, have not done so in order to light suddenly the torch of war to the outside world, and to let loose the furies of war. Who talks the most of peace, is not so important as he who does the most for peace. That alone is important.

It would not suit England badly either if, before they talk in this land so much about peace and the threat to peace in Europe, they would first of all make peace with their old Jew state down there.[1] But for the time being we only read that down there there is murder and killing daily. When it has quietened down there, it starts somewhere else. To give us exhortations for peacefulness is considerably easy ; to keep peace themselves seems to be considerably more difficult. These instigations against Germany and Italy we are used to by now. We would really miss it if it was left out for once.

We stand here in perfect leisurely quiet and wait for the things, however they may come.

We have done, compatriots, what we could do in order to guarantee the honour and security of Germany. We have tried to find foreign political friends once more, there, where conceptions of the same ideals bind us. We have found them and in spite of all attempts to part us and in spite of all who do not wish to realise it, the axis and the friendship of Italy and Germany are firmer than ever before. With Japan in the Far East, both nations form to-day in Europe the only great bulwark against the world pest of bolshevism, and, with that, against world dissolution. We have done everything in order to consolidate the guarantee for honour and security.

A reserve economy as I have described just now, the building up of new raw materials for industry and the opening up of all valuables in the ground, secures Germany against any blockade, whether it be by so-called peaceful

---

[1] *In seinem alten Judenstaat da unten.* It was actually said like this. It refers of course to Palestine.

means or by warlike means. The building up of a powerful armament industry secures the fighting strength of our great army—fed by the wealth of 75 million people—secures the building up and the supply of the fleet, which is new, and the most up to date and which is steadily growing, and also the air fleet, of which I can say without exaggeration, and without conceit, that it is technically the most modern, the most prepared and, in numbers, the strongest in the world.

The air fleet, just as the army and the navy, is filled with great courage and confidence of victory.

Never in its history has Germany been so strong, so firm, so united. A zone of forts which has been built, based on the most up-to-date experiences, and with singular effort, secures the Reich in the west against all attack. Here, no might in the world can break through into German land.

A party, accustomed to fight and filled by the highest forms of idealism, has united the people into a wonderful community, which cannot be broken up by any lies or instigation. The workman and farmer has built its foundation out of granite.

So we stand, the nation Great-Germany (*Gross-Deutschland*), firm and united. No lies shall make us err, no flattery deceive us, no threat shall ever make us weak. I know that even now, again and again, threats are used against Germany, my dear compatriots. To this ridiculous attempt to make us nervous I would like to answer for the whole German people, particularly for the national socialist fighters, with the words of the War Minister, Field-Marshal Roon, and assure them of one thing : We have always been shooters, but never shitters. (*Wir sind allezeit Schiesser gewesen, niemals aber Scheisser.*)

We do not want to harm anybody, but we also do not want to suffer that harm is done to our German brothers. No one in the world, I believe, no nation wishes more fervently for peace than we, because we have had to miss peace for so long.

Do not forget, nations : Versailles has taken peace out of the world. And to-day you wretched creators of Versailles stand in front of your miserable work, not knowing which way to turn. The states of order brought peace back into the world—Germany and Italy. These two nations want to build for the world, a new and a just peace. It must now be proved if there rules in the world reason or hatred. We stand in the knowledge of our strength, ready at all times to step in for reason. But should hatred be victorious over the nations, then we are resolved with highest courage and resolution to follow the order of our Leader, wherever he may call us.

We know that the Leader, in all those years in which he was a Leader to us, has always, and in everything, done the right thing. We also know that nothing makes us so strong as the blind trust in him, whose powerful faith can do more than move mountains. His powerful faith in Germany has led our people out of deepest night and need, out of misery and despair, up to the shining light, and has lifted Germany up to a great power.

In all these years, the Almighty has blessed him and the people again and again. In the Leader He has sent to us the saviour. Unerringly the Leader went on his way and, unerringly, we followed him. The way was steep, but glorious its goal : Our Great Germany.

But in these days and hours, when from outside, again and again, attempts are made to bring about, here and there, pusillanimity in the German people, to awaken doubt in its leadership in the German folk, to flatter and cajole the German people, and to threaten, I can only say one thing to you and to the whole nation : German people ! Carry the steel certainty within you ; as long as people and Leader are one, Germany will be unconquerable. The Lord sent us the Leader, not that we should sink, but that Germany should be resurrected.

THE END